CW00919380

Loos 1915

The Unwanted Battle

LOOS 1915

THE UNWANTED BATTLE

by

Gordon Corrigan

SPELLMOUNT

British Library Cataloguing in Publication Data:
A catalogue record for this book is available
from the British Library

ISBN 1-86227-239-5

First published in the UK in 2006 by
Spellmount Limited
The Mill, Brimscombe Port
Stroud, Gloucestershire
GL5 2QG

Tel: 01453 883300
Fax: 01453 883233
E-mail: enquiries@spellmount.com
Website: www.spellmount.com

1 3 5 7 9 8 6 4 2

Printed in Great Britain by
Oaklands Book Services
Stonehouse, Gloucestershire GL10 3RQ

Contents

List of Maps

Introduction

At 1100 hours on Wednesday 20 October 2004, the body of Lance Corporal J Y Brown, a native of Glasgow, was buried with all the pomp and ceremony that the British Army bestows on its men who are killed in action. A bearer party of six Scottish soldiers of the same rank as the dead man slow marched to the graveside with the flag-draped coffin on their shoulders. The firing party presented arms. The coffin was lowered into the grave while a piper played the traditional funeral dirge *Flowers of the Forest*. The firing party fired three rounds over the grave, a bugler sounded last post, and earth was shovelled into the grave while the dead man's relatives looked on. A fairly normal procedure at any time – and it is a rare year indeed when a British soldier is not killed in action somewhere in the world – and something that has been repeated a hundred or so times in the last two years as soldiers killed in Iraq are laid to rest by their comrades.

The difference is that Lance Corporal Young wasn't killed by Iraqi terrorists, nor by Sierra Leone guerrillas, nor by Serbian gangsters, nor even by our old friends the IRA; rather he met his end at the hands of the German army nearly ninety years ago. Young was one of ninety-nine officers and men of the 6th Battalion the Cameron Highlanders killed at the Battle of Loos on 26 September 1915. The area was fought over again and again, it was shelled by both sides and many of the hastily dug trenches and shelters simply collapsed. Young's body, like that of many others, was never found, until in 2004 roadworks near the industrial town of Loos on the Franco–Belgian border, turned up the remains of a British soldier. He was identified by an engraved pen in his jacket pocket, and eighty-nine years later the British Army reclaimed its own.

In all the welter of books, films and television programmes dealing with the First World War, which seem to spring almost daily from pen and studio, little attention is devoted to the events of 1915. Students of the war, whether serious academics and military historians or interested amateurs, move swiftly from the great dramas of 1914, with its build up of opposing forces and the seemingly inexorable drift to war, to the 1916 offensives of Verdun and the Somme. For the British observer the last hurrah of the old army – the retreat from Mons, the battles of the Aisne, the race to the sea and the First Battle of Ypres – usually leads straight to the blooding of Britain's first citizen army in 1916. The year 1915 is seen somehow as a brief interval between the high water mark of the Old Contemptibles in 1914, and the new tide of the Pals' battalions in 1916.

And yet, in truth 1915 was a year of great significance for the war, and for the British way of waging it. It was the year in which Italy joined the war on the Allied side, and Bulgaria on that of the Central Powers; when the Allies began overtures to Greece (not acceded to until 1917); the year in which British Empire forces invaded German South West Africa; the year when the Turks butchered a million Armenians and a German student planted a bomb in the US Senate and shot and wounded the banker William Pierpont Morgan. It was the year when Asquith's British Liberal government gave way to a coalition of Liberals and Conservatives; when Lloyd George was appointed to the Cabinet and Churchill sacked from it; when Sir Horace Smith-Dorrien was relieved of command of the Second British Army for stating opinions which were sound militarily but unacceptable politically, and when the man who sacked him, Field Marshal Sir John French, was himself removed from command of the British Expeditionary Force. In the East the Czar hastened his downfall by sacking his professional commander-in-chief in 1915 and assuming command of the Russian army himself.

British social innovations in 1915 included the acceptance of a largely female work force in factories at home, and a decision to introduce adult male conscription for the armed services, something that had not been done since the Napoleonic wars and even then only for home service in the Militia. In that year too the British began to intern enemy aliens resident in the UK, although at least they were not subjected to casual stoning, unlike daschunds going about whatever passes for normal business in the sausage-dog world.

At sea, 1915 saw the first use of unrestricted submarine warfare; the sinking of the German battlecruiser *Blücher* by the Royal Navy; the first serious bombardment of British ports since the Hundred Years' War; and the official announcement of a British naval blockade of Germany, leading to protests from the only neutral that mattered, the United States. In the Black Sea, British submarines carried out a masterly campaign against Turkish shipping; while in the Atlantic the *Lusitania* was sunk without warning – not the first ship to suffer thus, but the one that attracted the most publicity.

In the air, it was 1915 that saw the first use of long-range bombing by aircraft, the first air raids on the United Kingdom home base, and the first Zeppelin to be shot down (or rather bombed down) by a pilot of the Royal Naval Air Service.

On land, the British fought the battles of Neuve Chapelle, Second Ypres, Aubers Ridge, Festubert and Loos, none of which seemed to achieve a great deal, and on land and sea fought the Gallipoli campaign, which by the end of the year was manifestly seen to have failed. The Territorial Force was now coming on stream, and the year saw the first deployment of units of the New Armies.

Technology, always given a boost by war, did not mark time. It was in 1915 that the experimental tracked vehicle with which the British were tinkering was named the tank. Fighter aircraft made their first appearance, the Germans acquiring a brief superiority by the introduction of the Dutch Anton Fokker's interrupter gear, which allowed machine guns to be fired forward through the propeller. Poison gas and the flame thrower were used for the first time on the Western Front; artillery procedures were refined by improved methods of artillery spotting using aircraft; Wilfred Stokes produced the first effective and easily man-portable trench mortar; and all sides began to replace the service dress cap, kepi and pickelhaube with the steel helmet.

More than anything else, perhaps, 1915 was the year when the British began to realise that the Asquithian method of waging war overseas, while maintaining business as usual at home, was no longer appropriate in an age of total war.

This book is about one of the battles of 1915, but one that was significant for the British Army as a whole. It was Basil Liddell-Hart who called Loos the unwanted battle, and while the reputation of Liddell-Hart as an historian has suffered since his death and the removal of his quite extraordinary – and often baleful – influence on the interpretation of military history, in that description he was surely right. Loos was an unwanted battle and it was never going to advance solely British aims. It was fought purely and simply because the French wanted it fought, and the French were very much the senior partner in this coalition war. Britain was and is accustomed to fighting on land as part of a coalition. A nation that relies on a tiny professional army which is only expanded to continental proportions in time of war, and which has long eschewed conscription in peacetime, has little option but to be part of an alliance if it wishes to take part in land operations of any scale. Britain did wish to take part, for there were very good British reasons why she should – perhaps the most obvious being that the only purpose Germany could possibly have for the blue water navy that she was building was to challenge the British. If Britain did not join this war by supporting the French then Germany would win, and a subsequent war against Britain alone would be inevitable – and would not be a war from which Britain would necessarily emerge victorious.

The British, despite portraying themselves as essentially amateurs who muddle through, in fact often prefer to be formal in much of what they do, and to be governed by rules – even if they often disobey them. The British

Army is no different, and this equally applies to the names given to battles, names that often bear little relationship to where the fighting actually took place. The most obvious example of a misnamed battle is, of course, that fought between the British and their allies on the one hand, and the French on the other in Belgium on 18 June 1815. That battle, perhaps the only one in modern British history to be known by every schoolboy, was fought on the ridge of Mont St Jean, opposite another ridge on which was a farm with the name of La Belle Alliance. The Prussians, co-victors with the British, wanted to call the affair the battle of La Belle Alliance, for perfectly good and obvious reasons; the French, if they admit to it at all, call it the Battle of Mont St Jean, again for good and logical reasons. To the British, however, and to the world, it is the Battle of Waterloo, after a village four miles away from the fighting and which played no part in the battle.

The victorious Duke of Wellington considered that his countrymen could not possibly pronounce names in a dubious foreign tongue, and so that was that. Things have become more formalised since the Great Duke's day, and we now have a Battles Nomenclature Committee, a body that sits as and when required and whose remit it is to decide what is a battle (as opposed to an action, a skirmish, an affair), when it started and when it finished, and what it should be called. Officially, to the British, Loos is that battle fought between 25 September and 8 October 1915, over a frontage of six miles between the La Bassée Canal and Lens, using the British First (of two) Army, of six divisions with three in reserve. Loos (or Loss to French speakers) is actually at the very bottom of the British sector, but was presumably considered easier to pronounce than Hulluch (in the centre of the battlefield) or Heute Deule (the eventual objective). Quite why the Battles Nomenclature Committee decided that the battle ended on 8 October is a mystery, to which even the Official History admits ignorance, for the fighting undertaken by the British on 8 October was but a prelude to that continued on 13 October, going on until 17 October. As far as this book is concerned, therefore, Loos began on 25 September and ended on 4 November, the date upon which the Commander First Army informed the Commander-in-Chief of the BEF that he could do no more.

To the French, however, Loos was but a minor part of the Second Battle of Champagne and the Third Battle of Artois, over frontages of fifteen miles and seven miles respectively, using three armies. In purely military terms the result of the French efforts would not have been affected at all by what the British did or did not do at Loos; but politically it was thought to be important for Britain to be seen to be playing her part. That the ground over which the British would have to operate was unsuitable mattered little to the French planners, for in any large-scale offensive (and Champagne and Artois were very large-scale indeed) there will always be some part of the frontage which is not ideal: it was just bad luck that the British happened to be holding that part. It was, however, a battle in which the obvious disadvantages faced by the British (and these were not just difficulties of terrain) might be compensated for by the use of gas, the first use of a weapon by the British who, as the war developed, would use it more often and to greater effect than the Germans, but without attracting the opprobrium of being the first to employ it. It was a battle which contributed in very great part to the dismissal of the Commander-in-Chief, and which exacerbated the already festering sores of the 'shells scandal'. It was a battle in which three of the British major generals commanding divisions were killed in action, proving that whatever else they were doing they were not sitting in comfortable châteaux far behind the lines; and in which Rudyard Kipling lost his son, provoking argument as to his whereabouts that continues to the present day. It was a battle in which the New Armies were exposed as being hopelessly untrained and unready for high intensity warfare, and in which the Guards once again proved that they are anything but chocolate soldiers.

Loos cost the British Army around 16,000 deaths, for what seemed to be very small gains. Perhaps the sadness of Loos is in the fact that it very nearly did succeed, as Philip Warner has pointed out. If it had, then Joffre's stated aim of forcing a major rupture of the German lines that would have led to a negotiated peace in 1915 might have been achieved. Whether a negotiated peace in 1915 would have put paid to German ambitions is, of course, another matter. In any event, all in all, Loos is a battle well worth closer examination.

Wars and battles continue to fascinate, as a glance into the window of any bookshop shows. There is hardly a day when one of the mainstream terrestrial television channels does not show a documentary about, or a fictional representation of, conflict, whether it is a factual account of battles, weapons or tactics, or an attempt to bring ancient battles to life by a mix of computer graphics and imagination. Perhaps as war becomes an ever more distant experience for the bulk of the population, so its vicarious attraction increases, and there is no shortage of university students signing up for war studies modules. It is rare, in Britain at least, for a week to go by without the publication of at least one major work devoted to the history of war and warfare.

In broad terms there are two extremes in the writing of military history. First there is the soldier who has lived through a campaign or battle and wants to tell about it. His version of events has the great advantage of being penned by a primary source, and the great disadvantage of being too close to events to properly place them in context. What he produces is a rollicking good read and has value as anecdotal evidence, but may lack academic rigour. The pure academic, closeted in his garret, relies entirely on documents and will be painstakingly accurate, but he will understand nothing of what motivates the fighting man of whom he writes, nor of how an army does its business, and his description and explanation of events will be the poorer for that. It is perhaps unfortunate that members of the latter category still have some influence over the writing of British military history. They are firmly of the view that soldiers should not attempt to write history – an odd standpoint when soldiers have no great objection to academics writing about war, despite most of them never having seen a shot fired in anger (nor a shot fired, come to that).

It is of course possible to be an authority on motor cars without being able to drive, and to have a good eye for a horse without being able to ride, but you have to work at it.

Fortunately the purely academic old guard (names deleted to protect the guilty) are now being shuffled off into obscurity, to be replaced by scholars who, while they may never have undergone military service themselves, have followed the example of Sir John Keegan and Correlli Barnett and have taken the trouble to find out how soldiers think, how they react and how that extraordinary organism, an army, operates. In the centre of the two extremes of military historical writing are those who combine scholarly credibility with military understanding: John Bourne, Gary Sheffield and Mark Connelly spring to mind as prime examples of the young entry.

I make no secret of what I am: a soldier with an all-consuming passion for the practice and history of the profession of arms. I was a regular soldier from the age of 17 ¾ until leaving the service at 55 ½. Inevitably the way in which I think, act and write is indelibly coloured by my training, and my experience. Of course I do not claim to be the intellectual equal of some of my academic acquaintances, nor have I been able to devote the time to the study of history, military or otherwise, that they have. What I do claim is that military service gives an insight into how armies operate, and into how soldiers think, feel and act, an insight that is denied, through no fault of his own, to the pure academic. Having lived, slept, eaten and existed in a trench allows some empathy with the men who manned the firing line in 1915; having marched for twenty miles and more carrying a weapon and sixty pounds (more in jungle) gives a fairly clear idea of what it must have been like for the reserve divisions hurrying up to take part in the fight. It may be claimed that re-enactment allows the academic or the non military person to relive the experiences of men in war, but however realistic the scenario the organisers may strive to create, dressing up and playing at soldiers for a day or two can never replicate the fear, the stress, the pressures and the responsibilities of those who really have taken the shilling and are subject to military law at worst and a loss of career prospects at best if they get it wrong.

It is not only the writers of military history who are changing, but perforce the way in which military history is written. From the end of the Second World War until 1959 Britain, for the first time in her history, filled the ranks of her armed services in peace by universal adult male conscription. National Service lasted for two years and had an impact on every family in the land. It was a very good thing for society, and a very bad thing for the army, but it was the only way in which armed forces of the size then needed could be maintained. Even with the ending of conscription, and for many years after that, there was some inherent military understanding in the population: men had done their National Service, women had seen their husbands, brothers and sons do it, and those too young to have served heard the tales of those who had. Writers of military history could take for granted that their readership understood the necessity for discipline and order, even if they may have tried to evade it at the time; that it accepted the existence of an hierarchical system; that it understood communal living and physical and mental stress, and that it knew the difference between a lance corporal and a brigadier. Today this is no longer the case. Britain has reverted to the military system that she is most comfortable with, and which best suits her traditions of waging war: small, professional, all-volunteer forces kept well out of the public eye. Military historians can no longer assume any knowledge or understanding of matters military amongst their readers, and, if they are to get any sort of message across, they must not only tell their readers what happened, but why it happened, how it happened and in what context it happened. They must explain, or they fail to convince.

The population in 1915 had as little understanding of military imperatives as does today's, but while in many ways everyday life may not have been all that different a century ago, attitudes certainly were. England before the Great War was a man's world, where almost the only form of employment open to working class women was domestic service, where a woman aspiring to a university education was a rarity, and where, apart from the suffragette movement and a few liberal males, most people saw nothing very wrong with that. Anti-immigrant feeling there certainly was, but whereas today it is based mainly on skin colour (despite many blacks and Asians having been born in this country, many the second generation to be so), then it was directed against Russians and Jews. Racism as we know it today hardly existed away from the ports, for Britain was overwhelmingly a white, Christian country. No one in the years running up to the war would have seriously thought that the rights of the individual could override those of the state; nor that someone must be found culpable for every accident; nor that anyone could possibly have their life valued at a sum far, far greater than anything they could possibly ever earn. While it may sound trite to say so, people did, by and large, know their place in 1915; most would have considered it perfectly natural that those who had education should direct the affairs of those who had not; and while the class system was a constantly evolving structure, Britain was still a country where birth and breeding mattered, and where Jack was very rarely as good as his master. It is important to understand this today when people ask – as they often do – why British soldiers in the Great War went uncomplainingly over the top when the chances of survival were miniscule. The answer is twofold: firstly the chances of survival were quite reasonable; even on the so-called bloodiest day of British military history – the first day of the Somme offensive in 1916 – eighty percent of those who attacked survived the day. Secondly, the British Army, for all its difficulties, was well led and well looked after. Unlike the French, Russian and German armies there were no large-scale collapses of morale or breakdowns of discipline in British units. The average British soldier was stolid, dogged and determined, but he was not stupid, and had the soldiers not believed in what they were doing they would not have done it, and no amount of firing squads could have made them.

In the preparation of this book I must pay tribute to the unfailing help and courtesy of the staffs of the Imperial War Museum, the National Archives at Kew, the British Library and the Prince Consort's Library Aldershot. Historians are incredibly fortunate in the United Kingdom; I know of no other country where the most obscure piece of paper is produced for inspection from the national archives within twenty minutes, and without a penny being asked in payment. Jamie Wilson and his team at Spellmount, including David Grant the editor and Martin Brown the cartographer, have been invaluably helpful (and extraordinarily understanding about deadlines), and my wife is still, I am delighted to say, my wife, despite her having had to survive yet another session of author's tantrums. To all of you: much thanks.

J G H Corrigan
Eastry
2006

CHAPTER I

Theirs Not to Reason Why

At five o'clock in the morning of 25 September 1915, General Sir Douglas Haig, commanding First Army of the British Expeditionary Force, stood in the open air outside his headquarters at Hinges in northern France. One of his staff officers was ordered to light a cigarette. The smoke curled up in the air and then drifted gently to the north-east. The general and the assembled staff watched in silence. 'Carry on,' said the general quietly, and turned to climb up his wooden observation tower. The Battle of Loos had begun.

Loos achieved little in strategic terms; a few thousand yards of ground here, a German redoubt or two destroyed there. It occupied the attention of 150,000 British and 20,000 Indian and Gurkha soldiers for a fortnight and cost the lives of nearly 16,000 of them. It caused a major shift in the higher direction of the war with the Chief of the Imperial General Staff and the Commander-in-Chief of the BEF being replaced, and a diminution in the powers of the hitherto unassailable Secretary of State for War, Lord Kitchener. Withal, the battle was considered vital to the well being of Anglo–French relations, and there were very good diplomatic reasons for fighting it, even if those reasons would not have been readily apparent to the soldiers obliged to carry out the orders of their political masters.

By the time of the Battle of Loos the war was just over a year old. In August of the previous year France had mobilised sixty-nine infantry divisions on the Western Front, while Britain had provided just four. The British Expeditionary Force might not have been a very big army by European standards, but it was the only army Britain had, or at least the only one immediately available for Continental adventures. Britain was a naval power; it was sea power that, ever since Trafalgar, had allowed a small offshore island to control the greatest empire the world had ever seen. The British Army was a missile fired by the Navy, an imperial gendarmerie, a preserver of order in Ireland, and a stiffening for the only other army of any consequence that Britian had – that of India – and while there had been an Expeditionary Force since 1908 there were many possible theatres in which it might have to fight.

Small though it was, the British force that deployed to France and Belgium in the early days of August 1914 was formidable in quality. Man for man it was superior in training, in leadership and, save for some exceptions such as grenades and trench mortars, in equipment to French ally and German enemy. It was the only army that was composed of volunteer professional soldiers, with their units brought up to strength by reservists who had themselves been full-time professionals. It was the only army that wore a uniform designed for combat rather than for parade, and the only army whose cavalry was trained and equipped as mounted infantry. As important as any of these was the fact that, unlike most French and German soldiers of 1914, the majority of the men of the BEF had actually experienced active service. In the twenty years leading up to the outbreak of war British soldiers had fought Boers and Zulus, Chinese and Tibetans, Pathans and Abyssinians. They had tramped across Ashanti, Sierra Leone and Bechuanaland, and climbed the heights of Chitral, Malakand, Tirah and Sikkim. British soldiers had been shot at, admittedly in colonial campaigns against third class enemies who were no match for Germans in numbers, training or firepower; but a ball from a ten rupee jezail kills as surely as that from a modern Mauser. The British soldier had the confidence of knowing that, to use a phrase much loved by his modern equivalent, he could hack it, and the belief that he was part of the best regiment in the best army in the world.

It is an unfortunate fact of life that a good little 'un will find it very difficult to defeat a not so good but very much larger big 'un. The BEF went to France in the first week of August. It advanced into Belgium and met the Germans at Mons. It executed a fighting withdrawal all the way back to the Marne, then advanced to the Aisne, switched to the left of the French army and fought the first Battle of Ypres. By the end of the year 1914, after nineteen weeks of fighting, the BEF had lost 1,471 officers and 23,492 Other Ranks dead. This was not very many compared to French, Russian or German deaths, but for the British it was significant, and a tiny army could not possibly sustain that rate of attrition. Nor, of course, would it have to. Lord Kitchener had made it clear from the outset that the war would not be over by Christmas, and that he would need a lot of men. Specifically, in 1914 Kitchener thought that the war would last three years and that he would need a million men. While in the event the war lasted four and a quarter years and the British Army needed eight and a half million men, even Kitchener's relatively modest initial estimates horrified some of his cabinet colleagues, although they had, perforce, to accept them.

The first source of reinforcement for the BEF was, of course, the Army Reserve, but the bulk of this, consisting of men who had served their time with the colours and then had a liability for recall in time of war, had already been absorbed to bring units up to strength from their peacetime establishment to that required for war. The next obvious source was the Territorial Force, but that had never been intended to reinforce the army abroad, rather its role had been seen as Home Defence, in order to release regular army units for service abroad. Territorial units could only serve abroad if all its members signed up for 'general service', and while the process of persuading men so to agree had begun before war was declared, in only five units – of which only three were infantry battalions – had all members signed up. The vast majority of Territorial soldiers would of course sign, although there were a few incorrigibles who steadfastly refused to do so, and spent the war safely at home, oblivious to the taunts of their comrades. Quite apart from the signing issue, in August 1914 most Territorial units were not fit for war. There was no doubting the Territorials' enthusiasm, but much of their equipment was obsolete or simply not present; training was rudimentary, and many units lacked specialists from machine gunners to cooks. It would take time for the Territorial Force to augment the BEF, but from mid-September Territorial units and their cavalry equivalent, the Yeomanry, began to arrive. By the end of 1914 there were six regiments of Yeoman cavalry, six field companies of Territorial engineers and twenty-three battalions of Territorial infantry on the Western Front. Many of the infantry battalions were not yet ready to go into the firing line, but they could carry out duties in the rear and be gradually introduced to front line duty. It was a start, but far more would be needed.

Neither the Regular Army nor the Territorial Force could produce the one million men sought by the Secretary of State for War. Apart from India, which provided two infantry divisions and a cavalry brigade in September 1914, the dominion armies were as yet far too small to be of any meaningful assistance. Swift expansion was needed, and Kitchener's solution was to raise a brand new regular army – the New Armies, or colloquially the Kitchener Armies – by voluntary enlistment for three years or the duration of the war, whichever came last.

In hindsight Kitchener might well have been better to have based the expansion of the army on the existing Territorial Force: this could have been quadrupled relatively quickly by having each Territorial battalion raise a new battalion from each of its four existing companies. Each new battalion would be painfully short of trained manpower, but there would be at least some experience spread across the rank structure, which was not the case with New Army units. As it was, Kitchener was suspicious of the Territorial Force, with its peculiar legal standing and under the control not of the War Office directly, but of county associations, and he preferred expansion to be controlled by himself and his staff alone.

The BEF now began its often-painful metamorphosis from an all-regular professional body to one diluted with Territorial Force units, followed by New Army men, followed in time by conscripts. By the end of the war, in 1918, whatever the name of the battalion or regiment, there was little if any practical difference between regular, Territorial Force or New Army units, the possible exception being the Guards who, in keeping with their traditional and honoured status as the monarch's personal troops, had no Territorial Force battalions and raised no New Army ones, remaining regular, in outlook at least, to the end. Besides this constant evolution in composition, and therefore in the outlook of its individual members, the BEF varied in competence too. Thoroughly capable in August 1914, the BEF probably reached its professional nadir on 1 July 1916, when an under trained and inexperienced body consisting very largely of men whose first experience of major offensive action this was, attacked strongly fortified defensive positions which had been eighteen months in the preparation. Having learned from the Somme, the BEF began to re-ascend the slopes of professional competence, until by 1918 it was the only army on the Western Front capable of inflicting military defeat on the German army.

1915, the year in which the events described in this book took place, was very much a year of change as far as the BEF was concerned. On initial deployment to France in August 1914 the original BEF included fifty-two infantry battalions, all of them regular. By late October 1914 the infantry component had more than doubled, to 106 British, fourteen Indian and six Gurkha infantry battalions, again all of them regular.[1] By May 1915, by which time the British had fought Neuve Chapelle and the Second Battle of Ypres, the infantry had almost doubled again, to 207 British, twelve Indian, thirteen Canadian and six Gurkha battalions, but for the first time almost half of the British battalions (ninety-three of them) were Territorial Force units, up from forty-eight in February.[2] While to begin with Territorial Force battalions were included in regular brigades (usually in the ratio of four regular and one Territorial Force battalions to each brigade), now there were four infantry divisions (out of sixteen) composed entirely of Territorial Force battalions (47, 49, 50 and 51 Divisions). Not only was nearly half the British infantry on the Western Front Territorial by May 1915, but the supposedly regular units had been greatly diluted. Of battalions that had been on the Western Front since Mons, by 1 May 1915 the 2nd Battalion King's Royal Rifle Corps (1 Division) had lost 432 men killed, 2nd Battalion Grenadier Guards (2 Division) 394, 2nd Battalion Royal Dublin Fusiliers (4 Division) 287, 2nd Battalion King's Own Yorkshire Light Infantry (5 Division) 507 and 1st Battalion Gordon Highlanders 341. These are typical figures for battalions that had arrived in France nine months before, and when the deaths are added to those wounded, taken prisoner and 'missing', it is clear that from a battalion establishment of 1,022 all ranks not much of that original expertise and experience was still about. Regular they remained in name, but their ranks were by now very largely composed of recruits and reservists.

It was not only the expertise at battalion and regimental level that was severely diluted by 1915, but staff experience as well. Staff officers were and are responsible for the management of war; it is their responsibility to facilitate the commander's wishes by ensuring that the soldier is trained, fed, clothed, equipped, supplied, accommodated and moved, so that he is in a position to engage the enemy. Staff officers do not just appear, nor can regimental officers be turned into staff officers overnight, but the huge and unprecedented increase in the size of the field army required a commensurate increase in the number of staff officers to organise and administer it. Trained staff officers were just not available, and while those who were found their workload vastly increased, and while arrangements were put in place to train new entrants to the staff, there was an inevitable decline in the quality of military management – the surprise is that it was not more marked than it was.

Munitions and equipment of all types were in short supply for most of 1915. Peacetime estimates as to likely ammunition expenditure were wildly inaccurate, and industry was in no position to instantly increase its output to what was needed. This was hardly surprising: nobody – on either side – had predicted that the war of movement for which everyone had trained and prepared would after a few months become siege warfare, where both sides would occupy progressively more comprehensive defensive systems which could only be breached by the use of prodigious quantities of ordnance. Both 1915 battles of Neuve Chapelle and Aubers Ridge had been 'closed down' (to use the phrase then current) because there was insufficient ammunition to continue.[3] The British Commander-in-Chief, Field Marshal Sir John French, felt so strongly about the failure to provide him with the quantity of munitions he considered he needed, that he used his friendship with a journalist, Charles Repington, to plant stories about it in the newspapers, and sent two of his staff to England to lobby politicians whom he thought would be sympathetic. The resulting 'Shells Scandal', combined with a general dissatisfaction with the leisurely way in which the government appeared to be prosecuting the war, and the resignation of the First Sea Lord, Admiral Fisher, in protest against the Gallipoli campaign, led to the downfall of the Liberal government and its replacement by a coalition – still at this stage with Asquith as Prime Minister – the appointment of Lloyd George to the newly created post of Minister of Munitions (he had been Chancellor of the Exchequer) and a diminution of Kitchener's powers as Minister for War. Despite this, it would take time for the new procedures to work through, and munitions would not be available in sufficient quantities for some time yet.

The western Allies had survived perhaps the most dangerous phase of the war – 1914 – whereby they had prevented the Germans from enveloping Paris and taking the Channel Ports. They were further fortunate in that German policy in 1915 was to stand on the defensive on the Western Front and look for a decision in the East. There they did force the Russians out of Poland and they defeated Serbia, although both Russia and the Serbian army remained in the war. The German concentration on the Eastern Front did however encourage Joffre, commanding the French army, to see the year as an opportunity to attack in the West, with the hope of breaking through and ending the war.

Despite what were by British standards very heavy casualties in the war so far, the French were constantly urging more. The British, in the opinion of their major ally, were not pulling their weight – and by French standards, they weren't. Determined that only ever more ferocious offensives could compensate for the German advantages of a larger and better equipped army, France had consistently gone on the offensive in this war, and with a population nearly seven million less than that of the United Kingdom, she had suffered 360,000 dead in 1914, compared to 27,000 dead Britons.[4] British protestations that the Royal Navy controlled the oceans to the advantage of all the Allies fell on deaf ears, as did pleas that an army of continental proportions could not be created overnight.

To the British Neuve Chapelle and Second Ypres were major battles, but compared to the French First Battle of Champagne they were mere skirmishes; Aubers Ridge and Festubert, fought by the British on 9 May and from 15 to 25 May 1915 respectively, were hardly more than scuffles compared to the Second Battle of Artois. At Aubers the British committed three infantry divisions; simultaneously the French Tenth Army was attacking with fourteen. The facts were that the French were fighting on their own territory and for the very survival of France. The British could always withdraw back to their island fortress, where their navy could protect them from any invasion. France needed Britain's purse and Britain's navy in this war, and for perfectly understandable reasons she wanted Britain to take on as much of the common burden as possible on land as well.

The British would have preferred to wait until the New Armies were ready, equipped and trained, and then to have mounted an offensive that could have had decisive results, but as the junior partner on land in a coalition war, this was just not going to be an acceptable option. Whether it liked it or not, the BEF would be under pressure from its own government and from its French allies to continue to conform to the original directive given to Field Marshal French in August 1914 which required him to make every effort '... to coincide most sympathetically with the plans and wishes of our Ally ...' French's difficulty was that the same directive also pointed out '...that the numerical strength of the British force and its contingent reinforcement is strictly limited, and with this consideration kept steadily in view it will be obvious that the greatest care must be exercised towards a minimum of losses and wastage.'[5]

The strategic thinking of Joffre and the French High Command, to which the British were privy, was relatively simple. A large portion of Belgium and northern France was held by the Germans. The front line had stabilised in late 1914 and was where it was because the Germans could not move any farther west, and the Allies could make no progress east. German-occupied territory was a huge triangle. The line ran from Newport on the Belgian coast roughly south for 120 miles (of which the BEF held thirty miles), when it turned east for another 130 miles before turning south-east to the Swiss border. It was in effect a huge salient with its nose between Noyon (held by the Germans) and Compiègne (held by the French). If enough men, materiel and ammunition could be amassed before the German reserves were brought back from the Eastern Front, then a huge pincer attack on both west facing and south facing sides of the salient would not only pinch out a huge area of enemy-occupied territory, it would also destroy most of the three German armies, 300,000 men in total, that held the front from La Bassée to Verdun.

The envisaged attack would not be a simple wearing down operation, rather the northern pincer would aim to cut the German communication routes which ran roughly north to south across the Douai plain between the Ardennes mountains and Artois. This northern thrust, from Artois going east, would be the task of the French Tenth Army, attacking on a relatively narrow frontage of about twelve miles, while from Champagne the French Fourth, Second and Third Armies would attack north over twenty miles of front. The original plan presupposed that the French would take Vimy Ridge, a German-held piece of vital ground between Lens and Arras which overlooked the Douai plain, before the northern thrust was launched.

It was an enormously ambitious plan, with the final objectives being the line Mons–Namur, fifty miles from the northern jump off line, and seventy from that in the south. It all depended upon having sufficient weight of artillery to create real breaches in the German lines, enough infantry to widen those breaches, and the cavalry and motor lorry borne infantry to exploit the breakthrough.

On 4 June General Joffre sent a copy of the French plan to the British General Headquarters (GHQ). There were two things that the British were asked to do to help. Firstly they were asked to take over twenty-two miles of the French sector of front astride the Somme river, in order to free up General Pétain's French Second Army to take part in the Champagne offensive, and secondly they were invited to attack on the flank of General d'Urbal's French Tenth Army, advancing east from Artois, it being left up to the British Commander-in-Chief which flank to attack on.[6] Field Marshal French agreed in principle, although in the event it was but fifteen miles north of the Somme, from Curlu to Hebuterne, that the British took over. On 19 June French explained to General Foch, commanding the French group of armies of the north, or GAN, that he intended to attack on the left of the French Tenth Army, over a frontage of seven miles, using two divisions reinforced by at least two others. There would be diversionary attacks north of the La Bassée canal and the whole operation would be entrusted to the British First Army, with the order of battle adjusted so that the best available British troops would take part.

As it was the First Army that would have to execute the British part in the overall plan, on 20 June the Commander First Army, General Sir Douglas Haig, was instructed to submit his detailed plan for the operation. Three days later his comments arrived at GHQ. Haig was not at all enamoured of the prospects. Having reconnoitred the proposed area of attack, he considered the German defensive positions to be very strong indeed. Not only that, but they overlooked the British line throughout its length, and the ground between the two sets of defences was open and devoid of cover. Any attempt to assemble the necessary troops would almost certainly be discovered by the Germans, and they could bombard forming up places, assembly areas and supply dumps. Only by a greatly increased supply of artillery – which could not be forthcoming – could the attack be contemplated, and even then it would involve fierce hand to hand fighting through the immensely strong German trenches and bunkers. Haig considered that if an attack had to be made – and in view of the shortage of artillery ammunition he considered that it should not be – then only subsidiary attacks should be carried out south of the canal, with the main attack being astride and to the north of it.

It is difficult to disagree with the Commander First Army's assessment. Even today the line then held by the Germans is obviously the dominating feature in the area, and even with the roads and buildings that were not present in 1915, to stand on the proposed British jump off line and look east towards German territory brings it home to even the most tactically unaware that Haig and his men were being asked a great deal. In view of what Sir John French said later, it is surprising that he had not come to the same conclusions as his subordinate. One presumes that French had actually looked at the ground, and as an experienced cavalry officer he would have had that instinctive feel for terrain that distinguishes the tactician from the mere pounder – and French, despite his corpulence, well-lived-in features and Blimp-like appearance, was not a fool. French had the option of selecting the left of the French (as he had done) or the right. While the right would have provided a better approach, assuming that Vimy ridge had been captured (as everyone did assume, albeit that it did not happen), the administrative difficulties of splitting the BEF either side of the French ruled that option out, and one cannot blame French for deciding on the left, northern, flank. One can, however, blame him for not properly thinking through the outline plan before its flaws were pointed out to him by Haig.

Haig's point in regard to artillery was especially valid. Despite the recent changes in arrangements for the procurement of munitions, it would be some time yet before industry could be cajoled or coerced into providing the amounts needed. Attempts were being made to increase the workforce in munitions factories, but these were coming up against the entrenched attitudes of trades unions, who objected to the employment of women and unskilled or semi skilled men, and were prepared to, and did, take industrial action in support of their views. As one officer on leave in England in May 1915 said in his diary:

> It seems monstrous that in the same desperate struggle, men volunteering as soldiers, undergoing great risks and hardships for about two shillings a day, should be liable to be shot for disobeying orders in the field, while munition workers, miners and other civilians, well paid, safe at home, and engaged in work vital to the needs of Army, should be at liberty to 'down tools' when they like without incurring any penalty.[7]

While Sir John French was telling General Foch that the BEF could assist in the major offensive of 1915, and General Haig was advising that they should not, a Franco–British conference was taking place at Boulogne. It was attended by the ministers of munitions of both governments and by representatives of the French and British armies. The purpose of the conference was to discuss the supply of munitions to both armies, but inevitably the scope of the conference widened to include not only the problems in regard to artillery and artillery ammunition, but general lessons from the war to date.

On 1 June 1915 ammunition actually held in France for the standard British field gun, the eighteen pounder, was but 413 rounds per gun, and for the six-inch howitzer, seventy-three rounds per gun. It was estimated that German and Austrian industry was turning out 250,000 artillery rounds of all types each day, while the French produced 100,000 and the British a mere 22,000 rounds. Contracts had been placed by the British in America for large amounts of artillery shells, but most had not yet been received. Things would improve, but it would be some time before they did.

Another difficulty was that neither the British eighteen pounder, nor the French seventy-five millimetre, the famous *soixante quinze*, was much good at breaking up concrete bunkers, collapsing deep dugouts or cutting through barbed wire.[8] Partly the problem was that shrapnel was bad at cutting wire, only high explosive could do that, and even if enough high explosive ammunition was available – which it was not – a graze fuse was needed to ensure that the shell exploded once it hit the wire, rather than when it hit the ground. That piece of technology would not be available until 1917. Eighteen pounders and seventy-fives were very good in the immediate defence of allied trench lines, in that shrapnel shells were exceedingly effective against attacking infantry in the open, but if a major offensive was intended – as it was – then what was wanted was heavy guns. Artillery experts agreed that for an army to take the offensive on the Western Front, and sustain it, then a minimum of one third of its guns should be heavy (defined as 5.9 inch or bigger). In June 1915 the French had around one heavy to every four field guns, or twenty per cent of their available artillery, and were aiming for fifty per cent, while the British lagged well behind with only around five per cent of their guns being heavies.

Views on what artillery could do and how much and of what type was needed was based on experience so far. There were other lessons too, and the British and the French identified them according to their own peculiar circumstances. So far all the British offensives of 1915, except for Neuve Chapelle, which could be considered a special case, had failed.[9] The reason they had failed, thought the British, was that not only were there insufficient guns and insufficient ammunition to support them, but the attacks were all delivered on a very narrow frontage, which could then be enfiladed along all or most of its length by German artillery. The reason they were all delivered along a narrow front was that there was not enough infantry to take on a greater distance, and this led inescapably to the British conclusion that much more infantry was needed before an offensive of any magnitude could be undertaken. The Empire contingents were now beginning to appear, and the raising of the New Armies was well under way. By the middle of the following year, 1916, the BEF would muster around fifty divisions, or about twice the number it had in mid-1915, and they would be ready to take the offensive. In the British view, therefore, there should be no major offensives on the Western Front this year.

It was all very well for the British to arrive at the conclusion that the Allies should go on to the defensive for the rest of 1915, only going over to the offensive in the spring of 1916 at the earliest. From the British perspective this conclusion was eminently sensible, but it failed to take into account the unacceptability in France of any government relaxing ceaseless efforts to expel the invader. That Sir John French now argued the conclusions arrived at by the British at Bolougne, while only a few weeks earlier he had agreed to Joffre's plan in principle, only weakened the British Commander-in-Chief's case.

Subsequent discussions between British and French planners led Sir John French to modify his stance somewhat. He would support the offensive, but now he was converted to the view of his subordinate, Haig. The British could mount an attack north of the La Bassée canal, or about ten miles to the north of the French Tenth Army. Joffre would have none of this and insisted that a British attack would 'find particularly favourable ground between Loos and La Bassée'.[10] Quite how Joffre had arrived at this idea is inexplicable. Had he actually examined the ground between Loos and La Bassée, he would have seen that from the British line the ground sloped gently upwards towards the German positions, ranging from 100 yards away in the north of the area, to 600 yards away farther south. There was virtually no cover between the two forward defence lines, and any attempt to advance from the British line could not possibly be concealed from the defending Germans. Worse, while the German front line was no more than fifty feet above the British trenches, the Germans were on a ridge, the reverse slope of which would not be visible to the attackers. This would not prevent German reverse positions being bombarded by British artillery, such as there was of it, but it would mean that the success or otherwise of artillery missions could only be confirmed by air reconnaissance, with a consequent delay in response times. Even if the British could penetrate the German first line, they would then find themselves having to fight through and around the factories and slag heaps with which this industrial and mining area was littered. Even if this could be overcome, there was yet another German complete defence system from two to four miles behind the present front line, and if any worthwhile progress was to be made, then this too would have to be broken through. All in all, an attack between La Bassée and Lens was not an inviting prospect.

The area north of the canal, over which French, converted by Haig, was now proposing to advance, was not much better for the attacker, but did at least offer some cover and was not overlooked to (quite) the extent as was the case to the south. From the British perspective, such an operation might capture the Aubers Ridge, always attractive as it would prevent the Germans overlooking a long stretch of the British line, and shift the British front from the wet, boggy Flanders plains to a piece of high ground that would not only be strategically useful, but would be a lot more comfortable to live on. Any attack north of the canal would, however, be separated from that of the French Tenth army, and could therefore be only a diversion. It might distract some German troops from what was happening south of the canal, but it could never be more than a peripheral operation. The French wanted a wholehearted British commitment, and who could blame them?

Before meeting the French army group commander, Foch, again to discuss the forthcoming offensive and what the British contribution to it might be, Sir John French consulted with Commander First British Army, Haig, and considered a number of alternatives. One possibility might be to thin out the British troops from the La Bassée sector, and use the six divisions that might be released to attack on the right of the French Tenth Army, in the Arras area, where the ground was more conducive to the advance, and German defences were considered to be less formidable. The trouble with this plan was that it would involve moving British troops away from the Channel ports – a major concern – and it would involve further fragmentation of the BEF. Planning was not proceeded with.

On 27 July another Allied conference between Sir John French and General Foch took place at Frévent. French reiterated the British view that an attack between the canal and Lens was pointless, and instead repeated the offer of a British attack north of the canal to capture Aubers Ridge, but with the addition of an attack on Messines ridge, south of the Ypres Salient. Again, from the British point of view this idea was eminently sensible: the German positions on Messines Ridge dominated the south of the salient, and made any Allied movement there very difficult. Any attempt to break out of the Salient would have to be preceded by the capture of Messines. Messines was, of course, captured in June 1917 as a preliminary to the Third Battle of Ypres, but it is difficult to see how the British could possibly have attacked Messines and Aubers Ridge simultaneously in 1915 with any hope of success. They were unable to take Aubers alone during the Neuve Chapelle battle in March 1915, or by a two-pronged attack in May. How could they possibly have hoped to take it and Messines (a larger and more dominating objective) but a few months later? One is left with the conclusion that French, having agreed to help out in principle, was casting about for anything that would avoid what he and his advisers now saw as a pointless slogging match that would achieve nothing.

Foch was not to be moved. The British proposals were interesting but irrelevant. Nothing less than a full-scale attack by the British on the immediate left of the French Tenth Army would do. Foch acknowledged that the industrial complex of Loos, Lieven and Lens, studded as it was with pitheads, factories and miners' cottages, would probably not fall to a direct assault; but it would, he insisted, fall when outflanked from north and south.

Writing to General Joffre, Foch's superior, on 29 July, Sir John French attempted to sway the French Commander-in-Chief. Sir John accepted that he had originally agreed to the French plan whereby the British Army would attack south of the La Bassée canal, but now that he had had time to study the ground and to reflect, he was strongly of the view that such an attack could achieve nothing, and that the British effort should be directed against Aubers and Messines instead. Joffre, like Foch, was not to be diverted from the original plan and said so in no uncertain terms. Sir John now appeared to give way gracefully, and on 10 August he wrote to Joffre saying that while his views were unchanged, he would no longer press the point and would cooperate by adhering to the agreed plan.

Sir John's interpretation of adherence to the agreed plan did not coincide with that of the French, however. The British would attack between the canal and Lens, but, proposed French, not with infantry. In his instructions of 7 August to General Haig, the British Commander-in-Chief had said: 'The attack of the First Army is to be made chiefly with artillery, and a large force of infantry is not to be launched to the attack of objectives which are so strongly held as to be liable to result in the sacrifice of many lives.'[11] Now to the French he explained that he intended to reinforce the First Army, particularly with artillery, and that he could thus neutralise the German artillery on that portion of the front, hold the German infantry in place, and wait until the German artillery in the Loos/Lieven/Lens area was rendered ineffective by being outflanked by the French advance to its south, before committing his British infantry. Joffre was not going to fall for that, and the matter now became a political issue to be resolved between the French Minister for War, Millebrand, and his British opposite number, Lord Kitchener.

Up to this point French must have been confident in the backing of his political master (and late military master too), Lord Kitchener. Kitchener was averse to battles that might attract large casualties. His whole military upbringing had been in a tiny army that had to be husbanded, and while the British Army was now expanding, and would continue to expand, the experienced component was small and valuable – it should not be risked. Additionally, Kitchener had made little secret of his view that Germany could only be defeated by an overwhelming Allied mass of men and ammunition. That overwhelming mass was not yet available, and so the time to mount a major offensive on the Western Front was not now, but in 1916 when the BEF would attain its greatest strength and the New Armies would be trained and equipped to take part.

Several things had happened to change Kitchener's opinion. Firstly, matters on the Eastern Front had taken a turn for the worse. One of the reasons for Joffre's optimism about an offensive on the Western Front in 1915 was the removal of German troops from there to the east, and now that removal was bearing fruit. On 2 May German and Austro–Hungarian troops launched an attack along a twenty-eight-mile front against Russian positions in Galicia – the Gorlice-Tarnow offensive. By 14 May the attack had penetrated eighty miles from the jump off line and by June the Russians were in full retreat. On 5 August Austro–German forces under Field Marshal August von Mackensen captured Warsaw, and were pressing on east. Kitchener believed it was essential to keep Russia in the war – one of the reasons for allowing himself to be persuaded to sanction the Dardanelles expedition – as a counterweight to German numerical superiority in military manpower, which could otherwise devote its undivided attention to the Western Front. As things were now going very badly for the Russians, an offensive in the west would have to be supported. What initially seemed to be an advantage for the Allies was the entry of Italy into the war against Austria–Hungary in May (she did not declare against Germany until August 1916), which might have been expected to draw off some Austro–Hungarian troops from the Russian Front, and provide much needed relief for Serbia. By August, however, Italian efforts to force the Austro–Hungarian defences along the Isonzo river had so far failed, with heavy casualties. Finally Gallipoli was not going well, and anything that diverted public attention from that campaign might help politically.

On 16 August Kitchener visited the Western Front. Although privately agreeing with French and Haig that the area over which the British were expected to attack was totally unsuitable, he had to avoid an open break with the French. He now agreed that the BEF would take part in the proposed offensive in accordance with the wishes of Joffre and the French High Command.

The scene was now set for a battle that no senior British officer wanted to fight, but which most realised was probably inevitable. As Lord Kitchener said: 'we must act with all energy and do our utmost to help France in their offensive, even though by doing so we may suffer very heavy losses.'[12] What mattered now was how to make the best of a bad situation.

Notes

1. The British total includes six battalions with the Indian Corps, where each brigade had three Indian or Gurkha battalions and one British battalion.
2. Six British regular battalions and seven Territorial Force battalions (including one Special Reserve battalion) were integral parts of the Indian Corps. The Canadian battalions were twelve in 1 Canadian Division, and Princess Patricia's Canadian Light Infantry, part of 27 Division.
3. Mainly insufficient artillery shells, but the expenditure of small arms ammunition could not be sustained either. At Neuve Chapelle the Indian Corps fired around three million rounds of .303 ammunition from rifles and machine guns.
4. Duroselle, J, *La Grande Guerre des Français*, Paris: Perrin, 1998.
5. Edmonds, J E, *Military Operations France and Belgium 1914*, Vol. I, London: Macmillan, 1926.
6. Pétain had done well as a corps commander in the Second Battle of Artois, and had recently been promoted to army commander.
7. Terraine, John, *General Jack's Diary*, London: Eyre & Spottiswoode, 1964.
8. To be fair, nobody had ever thought that it would have to, until circumstances began to alter cases.
9. A special case because the German wire was mostly on knife rests and not picketed to the ground, because Neuve Chapelle was an exposed salient, and because German reinforcements were slow in arriving. The Bois de Biez was not captured, and nor was Aubers Ridge.
10. Edmonds, op. cit., Vol. II, 1928.
11. Ibid.
12. Ibid.

CHAPTER II

The Plan

Now that the Allies on the Western Front were agreed – albeit that British agreement was reluctant – the plan could be given its fine-tuning. Overall there would still be two major thrusts, one from Artois going east and one from Champagne going north. The two thrusts would meet somewhere in the area of Namur, and would isolate the three German armies holding the Noyon Salient, who would then be mopped up in detail. The major change to the plan originally proposed was that it could no longer be assumed that Vimy Ridge would be in French hands. The French, despite prodigious efforts in May and June, had failed to capture it, and it was patently obvious that they would not be able to do so before the great offensive.

As Vimy would not now be in friendly hands prior to the attack (although the French would attempt to capture it during the offensive), the mass of men and equipment originally proposed could no longer be assembled around Artois, for that plain was overlooked by Vimy Ridge. Instead of the Artois pincer being the main thrust, it would now be subsidiary to that from Champagne, the latter being strengthened at the expense of the former. The Champagne attack would be entirely a French affair, carried out by thirty-four infantry divisions, supported by eight cavalry divisions and 850 heavy guns (in addition to the field artillery of each division).

The Artois attack would be the responsibility of the French Tenth Army and the British First Army. The French would have seventeen infantry divisions supported by 670 field guns and 420 heavies, with two cavalry divisions on stand-by to exploit any breakthrough, while British First Army would muster six divisions and another three in reserve, with five cavalry divisions ready to exploit, the whole supported by 114 heavy guns.[1] This attack would be subdivided, with the British initially attacking between the La Bassée Canal and the north of Loos, while the French would deal with the area from the south of Lieven to Arras. In recognition of the difficulty of a frontal attack on the industrial complex of Loos/Lieven/Lens, the French Territorial[2] division holding the 4,000 yards of front facing it

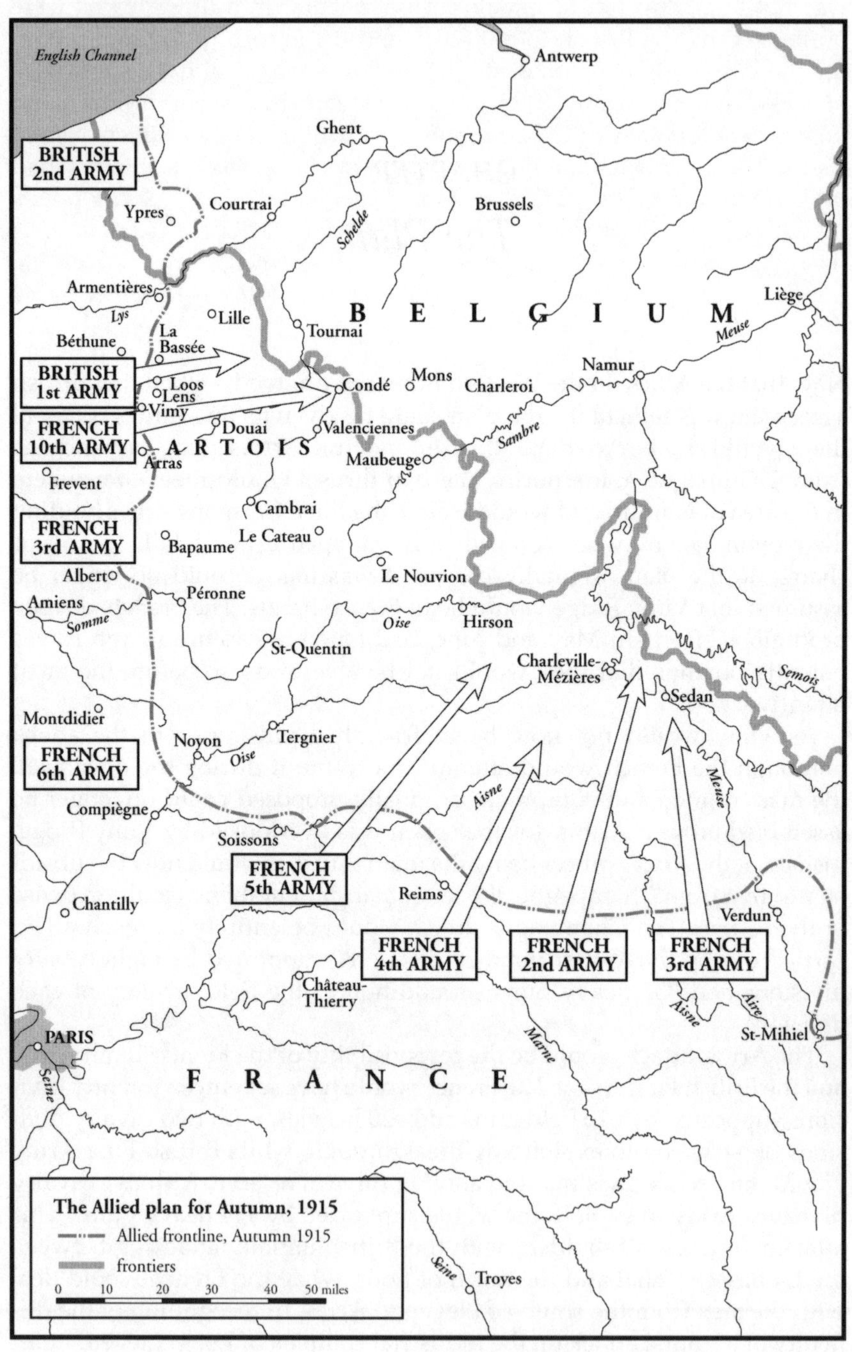
English Channel
Antwerp
Ghent
BRITISH 2nd ARMY
Ypres
Courtrai
Brussels
Schelde
Armentières
Lys
Lille
La Bassée
Béthune
Tournai
B E L G I U M
Liège
Meuse
BRITISH 1st ARMY
Loos
Lens
Vimy
Condé
Mons
Charleroi
Namur
FRENCH 10th ARMY
Douai
Valenciennes
Sambre
A R T O I S
Arras
Maubeuge
Frevent
Cambrai
FRENCH 3rd ARMY
Bapaume
Le Cateau
Le Nouvion
Albert
Amiens
Péronne
Somme
Oise
Hirson
St-Quentin
Charleville-Mézières
Semois
Sedan
Montdidier
Noyon
Tergnier
FRENCH 6th ARMY
Oise
Aisne
Meuse
Compiègne
Soissons
FRENCH 5th ARMY
Reims
Chantilly
Verdun
FRENCH 4th ARMY
FRENCH 2nd ARMY
FRENCH 3rd ARMY
Château-Thierry
Aisne
Aire
PARIS
Marne
St-Mihiel
Seine
F R A N C E
The Allied plan for Autumn, 1915
Allied frontline, Autumn 1915
frontiers
0 10 20 30 40 50 miles
Seine
Troyes

was not to assault but to remain in its trenches until those towns were outflanked by the British to the north and the French to the south. Both for the Artois offensive and in Champagne there would be subsidiary attacks designed to draw off enemy reserves and distract his artillery, and on both fronts there would be a preliminary artillery bombardment lasting four days, after which the infantry would assault. Once the infantry had broken through the two German defence lines and taken crossing points over the Haute Deule Canal three miles beyond the second German line, the cavalry would pour through and pursue the beaten enemy, preventing him from making a stand. The cavalry would be followed up by reserve infantry, some of it bus- and lorry-borne, and throughout General Joffre laid emphasis on dash and speed of movement. The success of the plan depended on two factors: there had to be sufficient artillery pieces and the ammunition for them to neutralise the German defence systems in the initial bombardment, and to support the infantry forward in their subsequent assault; and there must be enough infantry to carry the attack forward through both German defence lines.

The date of the attack, originally scheduled for late August, was postponed until 8 September, then to 15 and finally to 25 September. One of the reasons for postponement was that in deciding to attack a sector in Champagne which was devoid of villages (which could be stoutly defended by the Germans and which had proved very hard to capture) the planners had perforce to select an area without any roads, and a major road building programme had to be carried out before the troops and the stores they needed could be assembled.

By September the British artillery situation had improved from the sorry picture presented at the Bolougne conference in June. Then the BEF disposed of fourteen 9.2 inch howitzers, now there were twenty-two; 8 inch howitzers had increased from four to forty, and overall the heavy guns available to the BEF in France had increased from seventy-one to 147. Not all of these guns could be used for the forthcoming offensive, however. The Second Army held the Ypres Salient and would need some heavy guns there, and the portion of the line recently taken over by the British north of the Somme river could not be entirely denuded of heavy guns. While General Joffre did not presume to tell Field Marshal French how to use his British artillery, it was accepted by both Allies that during the preliminary bombardment heavy guns would endeavour to destroy German machine gun posts, fortified houses, redoubts[3] and artillery observation posts. The field guns would concentrate on cutting the German wire, it now being accepted that neither the French 75 nor the British 18 pounder was able to do much damage to concrete emplacements or deep dugouts.

After the initial bombardment the infantrymen would advance, either from their own permanent trench line or from a jump off line of temporary trenches, with the aim of getting into the enemy trenches, killing or incapacitating the occupants and capturing the trench. While the attacking infantry was crossing no-man's-land, their supporting artillery would fire on the defenders' trench as long as it could. As long as the artillery could fire on them, the defenders had to stay in their shelters or dugouts, or remain in the bottom of their trench, and could not fire on the attackers. There came a point, however, when the artillery supporting an attack had to lift, for if it did not then it would start to cause casualties amongst its own advancing troops. What this safety distance was depended on the ground, the type of gun and to what degree of exactitude the range to the target was known, but it was rarely less than 100 yards, and usually more. This meant that once the supporting artillery was forced to lift, the operation became a race. Could the attacking infantry get to the enemy trenches before the defenders emerged from their shelters, replaced their machine guns on their mounts and manned the firestep? The answer was that if the distance was short enough, and there were no obstacles in front of the trench being attacked, they probably could – but both sides sited obstacle belts of barbed wire in front of their trenches for the very purpose of preventing unwelcome visitors.

Wire obstacles came in various shapes and sizes but the most common were the standard entanglement and the metallic trellis. The entanglement, or what today is known as the low wire entanglement, was a criss-cross maze of bull wire, or, preferably, barbed wire, fastened to vertical pickets driven into the ground, the whole varying from two feet eight inches to four feet in height. The metallic trellis used barbed wire coils to create a rather higher (but more visible) obstacle, and there were all sorts of permutations including the Brun system, which in essence involved chucking barbed wire coils about any old how and generally used to create a rapid obstacle on the enemy side of a newly captured trench.[4] Whatever their type, all wire obstacles, or combinations of obstacles, had to be at least 100 feet in depth, that is more than the maximum distance that anyone could throw a grenade, and had to be covered by fire, for if they were not then an attacker could cut through them at leisure. Where possible wire obstacles were camouflaged – not difficult if the area in front of the trenches was grass or scrubland, but much more difficult after any covering had been burnt off or destroyed by shelling.

Clearly, before an attacker could have any chance of capturing a trench, he had to be able to get through or over the wire obstacles. He could, of course, creep up to it at night and cut through it, using the wire cutters issued, but this became an increasingly dangerous occupation. The obvious way to get through obstacles was to use the artillery to cut lanes through the wire before the infantry attacked. The problem was that it didn't always work. At the Battle of Neuve Chapelle, in March 1915, the Indian Corps artillery did cut through the German wire, allowing the infantry to capture and hold the village, but at that stage of the war the German wire obstacles around Neuve Chapelle mainly consisted of barbed wire coils attached to wooden knife rests, in some cases not fixed to the ground. The Indian shelling did not so much cut the wire, as blow it out of the way, but the belief persisted that the 18 pounder high explosive shell – or even shrapnel – would cut wire. In fact this was very much a hit or miss affair (literally) and it would not be until the introduction of a graze fuse that field artillery could guarantee to cut a lane through wire, and in any case by September 1915 the Germans (and the British and the French) were picketing their wire obstacles securely to the ground.

Assuming that the infantry did manage to get through the German defences, it was recognised that one of the problems might lie with the very large numbers of miners' cottages facing the northern, Artois, pincer. These buildings were cheaply built, two storeys high and usually made of brick. A high explosive shell from a field gun could demolish them easily. The snag was that they all had cellars, and once the brickwork collapsed, the cellar became an excellent defensive position which could only be penetrated by a shell from a heavy gun. This meant that if the advancing infantry were not to be held up by defenders fighting from the cellars of collapsed cottages, then the heavy guns would, at some stage, have to move forward in support. Field guns were relatively easy to move – after all they were designed to support the infantry – but the roles of the heavies rarely required them to move at other than a leisurely pace, and their forward movement was something that the artillery staffs would have to consider.

The second factor considered necessary for the success of the great offensive was an overwhelming superiority of infantry. Joffre and his staff thought that a superiority of five or six to one could be assembled both in Artois and in Champagne. On the Western Front overall, there were, in August 1915, 102 German divisions opposing 132 Allied divisions, far from a five to one superiority. Of the Allied divisions six were Belgian, and the Belgian government had made it very plain that they saw the role of the Belgian army as being the defence of the sliver of Belgium not under German occupation, and otherwise unavailable for anything more ambitious than limited local offensives. Additionally, of the twenty-eight British Empire divisions, six had arrived from England only in July 1915, and were still adjusting to life on the Western Front. A further six British divisions would arrive in August and September and one on the day the battle was due to open, 25 September, but again these divisions could not be considered the equal in experience of the German troops facing them.

While sections of the front could be thinned out to try to obtain local superiority, the fact is that when the battle opened on 25 September, two Allied armies (the French Tenth and the British First) would attack one German army (the Sixth), and in Champagne four French armies (the Second, Third, Fourth and Fifth) would attack three German (the Third,

Fifth and Seventh). While the Allies might achieve superiority in some specific sectors, overall they could not even achieve the three to one attacker to defender ratio generally recognised as a very rough rule of thumb, never mind the five or six to one for which Joffre hoped.

Once the Allies had agreed the overall plan, it was now for Sir John French to issue instructions to his subordinate commanders, and particularly to Sir Douglas Haig, whose army would fight the British share of the Artois pincer. The main British assault would be delivered between the La Bassée Canal and Grenay by two corps, or six divisions, of the First Army, whose other two corps would mount subsidiary attacks north of the canal. The Second Army would continue to hold the Ypres Salient, but would also mount diversionary operations and be ready to advance should the enemy retire on its front, which might happen if the Artois attack was successful in driving the Germans so far back that their positions round Ypres were liable to be outflanked. The newly formed Third Army, totalling nine divisions in three corps, which had taken over from the French north of the Somme, was instructed to assist the French attack with its artillery, and to be prepared to cooperate with the French should the Germans be driven back.

As this was the largest operation that the BEF had so far undertaken on the Western Front, the Commander-in-Chief, Sir John French, wished to have a strong general reserve under his own control. This was perfectly normal practice: a commander with no reserve cannot influence the battle, and at every level in military operations there was and is a reserve. At platoon level the platoon commander will have one section of ten men as his reserve; a brigade commander's reserve will be a battalion and so on up the chain. The purpose of a reserve is to deal with the unexpected, to reinforce success, to mount counter-attacks, to exploit gaps, to pursue a beaten enemy and as a last resort to prevent disaster. Sir John French was perfectly entitled to retain command of the reserve himself, and to decide when that command should be delegated. It might be expected to be delegated to the army commander fighting the battle, but it might be used elsewhere – if, for example, a subsidiary attack north of the canal turned into a real opportunity for a breakthrough. Nevertheless, it was the handling of the reserve that was to cause much acrimony later on, and which today is still a matter for debate amongst students of the Loos battle.

This reserve was to consist of four cavalry divisions, two British Cavalry and two Indian, and XI Corps, of three infantry divisions. The British cavalry was to take up position near Thérouanne, about twenty miles from the front, and their Indian opposite numbers would stand by at Doullens, twelve miles behind the Third Army front on the Somme. All the reserve infantry would be earmarked for action on the First Army front, and their assembly area was to be around Lillers, fourteen miles behind the jump off line. The positioning of the reserve was something a commander always had to think about. Too far away and by the time it got to where it was needed it might be too late; too near and it could get caught up in the initial fighting or in the artillery counterblast. Lillers is an eight-hour march from the front,[5] a long way for a reserve in this type of operation, but it had communications and billets where the troops could wait in comfort until needed, and they could always be brought closer to the front before Zero Hour. On the other hand if buses could be made available, and enough for an infantry brigade were positioned at Lillers, under command of the Cavalry Corps, then the time could be reduced to a couple of hours at most. All in all the selection of Lillers as the waiting area for the infantry reserve was not unreasonable.

The air would play an important part in the overall plan. Originally, official Britain had paid little attention to powered flight. The Wright brothers had shown that it was possible in 1903, but until an engine that did not overheat was invented it would be little more than a circus attraction. Eventually, in 1909, the French produced a rotary engine, and military aviation began. In 1910 the Chief of the Imperial General Staff, General Sir William (later Field Marshal Lord) Nicholson said flying was 'useless and expensive', and the First Sea Lord, Admiral of the Fleet Sir Arthur Wilson, announced that the aviation requirement for the Royal Navy amounted to just two aircraft. Even in France, despite the start that nation had made in the manufacture of aircraft and aircraft engines, the commandant of the army staff college, Brigadier General (later Marshal) Ferdinand Foch, said aviation was 'worthless'.

Fortunately, despite the expressed opinion of the CIGS and the First Sea Lord, there were others in Britain who saw the immense potential of aircraft. Many of these were young enthusiasts; some were men thwarted in their previous career paths and who saw a chance of advancement in the new arm, and two were those well-known (in the popular imagination) technophobes Lord Kitchener and Sir Douglas Haig. The Indian Army had adopted the aircraft with enthusiasm, as a means of observation and communication in a land where roads were few and where, in the mountains of the north, cavalry could move only with difficulty. It was in India, during his time as Inspector General of Cavalry, that Haig came to know and understand the value of the aeroplane. The navy too came to embrace the aircraft, largely as eyes over the horizon for the fleet and as a defence against the German Zeppelin. In 1912 the Royal Flying Corps was formed, with the Royal Naval Air Service formed the same year, albeit receiving official recognition only in 1914. In August 1914, five years after the very first cross channel flight, sixty British military machines flew from Dover to France on the outbreak of war. Lord Kitchener, shortly after taking up his post as Secretary of State for War, asked the Royal Flying Corps how many squadrons of aircraft they would need for the expanded BEF when the New Armies were ready. The aviation staff, in trepidation at recommending a huge expansion of this new and expensive arm, said they thought they would need fifty. The paper came back with 'Double it. K' written in the margin.

Even Sir John French changed his mind about aircraft. Having disbelieved RFC reports of advancing German forces before the Battle of Mons (in which he was encouraged by Major General Henry Wilson, then Sub Chief of the General Staff), and having had those reports prove only too accurate, by the end of the retreat to the Marne he was describing the RFC as being of 'incalculable value'.[6]

By September 1915 the total number of serviceable British aircraft on the Western Front was 160, in three wings totalling twelve squadrons. In just a year the British had almost trebled the size of their air arm and had introduced a new generation of machines. From being capable of reconnaissance, elementary air photography and artillery spotting in 1914, RFC and RNAS aircraft could now fight German aircraft for domination of the skies above the battlefield. They could produce accurate photographic montages of German positions, bomb targets way behind German lines, support the infantry by machine gunning targets on the ground and they could direct artillery by radio. It was the beginning of a technological leap forward that by 1918 would have been unimaginable four years before.

Of the three wings of aircraft available for the Loos battle, Number One Wing would devote its attention to working with the artillery of the First Army, while Numbers Two and Three would concentrate on bombing the railways in the Lille–Douai–Valenciennes triangle, with the aim of disrupting German supply lines and preventing them bringing up reinforcements. This bombing campaign would begin on 22 September, three days before the main attack. Additionally, all wings would provide reconnaissance aircraft to identify German strongpoints, locate gaps and keep track of the progress of the attacking infantry.

Having been given his instructions by the Commander-in-Chief of the BEF on 18 September, it was now for General Haig to work out how these instructions should be implemented by First Army. Haig had, of course, been aware for some time that the offensive was in the offing, but detailed planning so far had largely been within the parameters of Sir John French's preferred options: an attack north of the canal or, failing that, an attack by artillery only between the canal and Loos, with a possible advance once the French had succeeded in outflanking the Loos–Lieven–Lens complex. Not until late August did he receive orders to plan for a full-scale assault, an assault that was confirmed with only seven days to go. Now the First Army commander and his staff had to plan for a full-scale assault in only seven days' time. Fortunately this was not (quite) such a rush job as it might appear. Hitherto planning had assumed an artillery bombardment before the main attack and during it, and had foreseen the need to have six divisions on the ground. The only difference as far as planning was concerned was that now, instead of waiting for the French to soften up the Germans before the British moved, those six divisions would jump off as part of the main offensive.

Sir John French had assured General Joffre that the First Army would be reinforced and that the best of the BEF would be made available for the battle. On the face of it this was true. The British and Indian cavalry (in reserve except for one British cavalry division which was under command First Army) and the Guards Division (also in reserve) were up to the highest standards, and the units of the Meerut Division of the Indian Corps (which would mount a diversionary attack north of the canal), while they had taken very many casualties and had many recruits in their ranks, still retained a good stiffening of long service regulars including four battalions of Gurkhas. 8 Division of III Corps, which would also create a diversion north of the canal, was a regular division, as were three of the six divisions that would mount the main attack. Available to or acting in support of the First Army would be eleven divisions:

Diversionary attacks: Two regular divisions (8 and Meerut).
Main attack: Three regular (1, 2 and 7), one Territorial Force (47), two New Army (9 and 15) divisions.
GHQ Reserve: One regular (Guards) and two New Army (21 and 24) divisions.

A proportion of six regular divisions out of the eleven divisions that would be associated with the attack would seem to provide a good stiffening of professionalism and experience, but the composition of the infantry battalions of these divisions had changed since arriving on the Western Front. 1, 2 and 7 Divisions had been out since Mons, and we have already noted in Chapter One the casualty rate from the outbreak of war to 1 May 1915. Since 1 May, 2 Grenadier Guards (then 2 now Guards Division) had a further forty-nine men killed, 2 King's Royal Rifle Corps (1 Division) 120, 2 Royal Dublin Fusiliers (4 Division) 330 and 1 Gordon Highlanders (7 Division) 160. There really wasn't much regular about them now, except – and this is what mattered – regular officers called back from posts away from their regiments, a good leavening of regular senior non-commissioned officers, and a tradition of doing things in a professional way.

Again, on the face of it, the attacking British infantry outnumbered the German defenders. Allied intelligence estimated that there were thirteen German battalions, each with an established strength of 800, holding the sector to be attacked by the First Army. Six British divisions mustered seventy-two battalions, each with an established strength of 1,022, so even allowing for bayonet strengths being well below established strengths, 73,500 men would be attacking 10,400, or well above the five or six to one ratio that General Joffre hoped the Allies might achieve. It was not, of course, as straightforward as that.

General Haig could not simply hurl all his 40,000 or so effective infantry at the German firing line in one Napoleonic stroke. To begin with they would not fit into a frontage of 10,000 yards, of if they did they would be packed together so closely that they would present a target that even the most callow German recruit could not possibly miss. Secondly, if all the available infantry were thrown at the firing line in the first phase, there would be no fresh troops to carry on the battle through the succeeding lines of defences. The standard tactic in these situations was for a division to attack with two brigades forward and one in rear, each brigade with two battalions forward and two in rear, and each battalion to have two companies forward and two in rear, and each company having two platoons forward and two in rear. This would mean that a division would attack a thousand yards of enemy-held trench in a series of waves, each wave between fifty and 100 yards apart, with the first wave arriving at the objective with around 700 men. The attack would thus be made in great depth: if the first wave could make no progress then they would be swiftly reinforced, and there would be sufficient men following on to continue the advance through successive lines of objectives.

The ability of the leading and following waves of men to reach the defenders' trench on the other side of no-man's-land depended upon having enough artillery to destroy dugouts, bunkers, shelters and machine gun posts. General Haig and his staff considered that even with the promised augmentation of the First Army's own artillery with all the heavy guns that could be spared from other parts of the British-held front, there would still not be enough to guarantee that the opposing trenches would be so pounded as to allow the attacking infantry to cross no-man's-land without unacceptable casualties. There was really only enough artillery and associated ammunition to attack on a two-divisional front, or around 2,000 yards, not ten or eleven thousand, and even that predicated that most of the ammunition would actually work, which experience showed it would not. The officer commanding 35 Trench Mortar Battery, part of 35 Brigade in 12 Division of XI Corps, reported that at 1000 hours on 19 September 1915 his men fired six heavy and fifteen light mortar bombs at the German front line. Five of the heavy and six of the lights were blinds (that is they failed to go off at all) and another light went off 'air high' (that is it burst in mid-air, rather than on reaching the target). The remainder (less than half) 'appeared to be most effective'. On 22 September the same unit fired sixteen bombs at the Germans as part of the pre-attack bombardment, of which nine were blinds and one was air high.[7]

An attack on a narrow frontage was in any case out of the question. Not only did the French expect a full-scale attack over the entire sector, but nearly all previous British (and many French) offensives had foundered by being made over frontages so narrow that they could be enfiladed by German artillery to the flanks. How could this 'damned if you do and damned if you don't' conundrum be solved? One solution might be to advance along the whole front behind the protection of a smoke screen. Smoke does not provide any cover from fire, but it does provide cover from view and if the smoke screen was extended well beyond the flanks of the attack, the Germans would know an attack was coming in, but would be unable to see exactly where. It was but a short step from considering smoke to proposing an altogether nastier substitute for insufficient artillery – gas.

The first use of gas in war had been by the Germans. They may have fired gas shells at the British positions south of Ypres in the winter of 1914 (the evidence is sketchy and it seems to have had no effect) and they appear to have fired some form of gas on the Russian front in early 1915, but again it appears to have achieved little (possibly because of the very low ambient temperature). Abandoning shells in favour of cylinders, and replacing various types of tear gas with chlorine, the Germans tried again to the north of the Ypres Salient on 22 April 1915, at the opening of what would be known as the Second Battle of Ypres. On a fine spring afternoon, when the wind was blowing gently in the right direction, the Germans released 180 tons of chlorine which, turning from liquid to gas on release from the cylinders, drifted across no-man's-land and reached (mainly) the 45th Algerian Division of the French army.

The division had only recently arrived in Europe from North Africa and had been put into the trenches on the Ypres Salient because that was a quiet place for them to become accustomed to life on the Western Front. To their east was 1 Canadian Division, also placed there to acclimatise to European warfare. There had been rumours that gas might be used, but nothing substantive was known and the troops had neither been briefed nor issued with protective clothing and equipment. The Algerians broke and fled, and who can blame them? Fortunately for the Allies, the Germans were almost as surprised as they were: this was not an all out attempt to capture Ypres and press on towards the Channel Ports, but merely an experiment. The Germans did not have the reserves necessary to capitalise on the initial success of their new weapon, and while there were some anxious moments, a combination of French, British, Canadians, Indians and Gurkhas held the salient. The battle dragged on until late May, but although the Allies were not able to drive the Germans back to their original start point, they did stabilise the situation, and Ypres would not come under serious threat again until the spring of 1918.

The Allies complained long and hard about this latest manifestation of German beastliness, exaggerating the casualties caused by this first use of what the Allies announced indignantly was a banned weapon. While the Hague convention of 1907 did ban the use of artillery shells to deliver injurious gasses, it said nothing about cylinders, which did not stop the British claiming that the German action was certainly not cricket and a very bad show all round. Having said all that, the British and the French then began to examine how they too could use gas as an adjunct to their own activities.[8]

The decision to retaliate in kind was not an instant one. Opinion in the United Kingdom was divided, and there were those who sincerely believed that the British should not descend to the level of the Germans by using this noxious weapon. There was also some doubt as to whether the British chemical industry was actually capable of retaliation to any meaningful extent, and no doubt the eventual assurances that it was swayed the pragmatic view. Discussion went to Cabinet level, and in May 1915 approval was given for the British Army to use gas, and four Special Companies Royal Engineers were established to do so. The men were obtained by transfers from the infantry and by recruitment from civilian life of those with the required qualifications and given the intriguing rank of 'chemist corporal'.

On 22 August 1915 a demonstration of the 'chlorine wave' was laid on for General Haig and his corps and divisional commanders, who were duly impressed. It was on the very next day that Sir John French, having had his instructions from Lord Kitchener, informed Haig that any ideas of confining action to the north of the canal, with artillery only, or on a two-division front only were out: the First Army was to fall in with what the French wanted and mount a full-scale attack across the whole of the front south of the canal.

On 6 September Haig briefed his corps and divisional commanders, and explained that, whatever his previous views, he now accepted that provided sufficient gas could be made available – and he had been assured that it could be – then a six-division attack between the canal and Grenay was, after all, feasible. In his briefing Haig explained that as chlorine was heavier than air it would seep into cellars and underground bunkers where artillery could not penetrate, and would drive defenders out into the open. Trench raids had confirmed that German respirators were primitive, and while some machine gunners seemed to have been issued with breathing apparatus, it lasted only for thirty minutes or so.

Haig explained that the best way to exploit the use of gas would be to penetrate the German defences as far as possible in the opening attack. Not all wire would be cut, and not all strongpoints would be overcome, but enough would be cut, destroyed or neutralised to allow the infantry to break through on a wide scale, and with any luck both sets of defences might be taken in the first attack.

Haig's briefing on 6 September was followed by confirmatory orders issued on 19 September, or six days before the main attack was due to be made. The British army operated on the cascade principle: that is, the army commander issued orders telling his corps commanders what to do; they in turn gave orders to divisional commanders, who instructed brigade commanders, who gave orders to regimental or battalion commanders, which were then translated into orders for squadron and company commanders and troop and platoon commanders in turn. As the orders process progressed downwards, instructions became more detailed. This meant that from army commander to platoon commander there were seven sets of orders given out – to say nothing of orders for specialists ranging from cooks to machine gunners to quartermasters to signallers. This may seem unnecessarily complicated, but orders that attempted to tell everybody what they had to do would need a wheelbarrow just to carry one copy. Everyone in Number Four Platoon of A Company of 8th Battalion The Black Watch needed to know that Private McStrap was the platoon runner. They did not need to know the names of the platoon runners in the other 2,111 platoons taking part in the operation. Every man in 1st Battalion the King's Regiment had to know where the King's Regimental Aid Post was: they did not need to know where the RAPs of the other 132 battalions were. In general, at army, corps, division and brigade level orders were written, usually preceded by a verbal briefing. Battalion commanders would give oral orders, sometimes confirmed in writing if there was time; company and platoon orders would almost always be verbal. As most battalions had only one typewriter, this was probably just as well.

Army orders to corps explained that, assuming the weather allowed the use of gas on 25 September, the First Army would advance in the direction Henin–Lietard–Carvin. Each corps was then given its task. In the north I Corps was to attack between the La Bassée Canal and the Vermelles–Hulluch road, with the aim of capturing the crossings over the Haute Deule Canal between Bauvin and Pont-à-Vendin: in other words they were to advance across both German defence lines and on to the canal, to a distance of between 8,000 and 9,000 yards from their jump off line. Additionally the brigade of that corps north of the canal was to attack the German positions in the Givenchy and Canteloux area. The southern half of the attack was to be carried out by IV Corps, which was to attack between the Vermelles–Hulluch road and the Double Crassier (a huge double slag heap) and to seize the Haute Deule Canal crossing at Pont-a-Vendin and the Lens–Carvin road south of Annay, again an advance of over 9,000 yards. Both I and IV Corps would carry out the advance in three phases: phase one would be the carrying of the first German line, phase two the second, and phase three would see both corps along the Haute Deule Canal. The most northerly and the most southerly divisions of the main attack would provide flank defence once they had broken through the first line of German defences. North of the La Bassée Canal, the Indian Corps were to attack the Moulin de Pietre and then press on if they could, while III Corps, to the north of the Indians, was to attack Le Bridoux and link up with the Indian Corps on Aubers Ridge.

The artillery bombardment was to begin on 21 September, and the air campaign on the 23rd. On the day of the attack, gas and smoke would be turned on at Zero Hour[9] and at Zero plus ten minutes the diversionary attacks north of the La Bassée Canal would go in, while the main attack would be at Zero plus forty minutes. The time of Zero Hour would be given later, as it would obviously depend on the wind direction.

It might transpire that gas could not be used at all. As he considered that the artillery available was insufficient to support an attack by all six divisions, Sir Douglas Haig was adamant that if gas could not be used then the attack should be postponed until it could be. This was unacceptable to the French, who intended that 25 September should be the day of the offensive, come what may, and Haig was overruled by Sir John French, who did however permit a truncated plan to be implemented if gas could not be used, provided that it happened on 25 September. Thus a second set of Army orders explained that if, for whatever reason, gas could not be used at Zero Hour then only two divisions would attack in the first instance. In the north of the British sector 9 Division, the centre division of I Corps, would attack the Hohenzollern Redoubt, and in the south 15 Division, the centre division of IV Corps, would attack north of Loos. If the wind subsequently improved then gas would be used and the full attack launched, either later that same day, or on 26 or 27 September. If the wind still had not improved sufficiently to allow gas to be used by 27 September, then the attack would be cancelled altogether.

It was now for the two corps commanders to translate their corps objectives into tasks for their divisions. In the north of the sector was I Corps of three divisions, two regular (2 and 7) and one New Army (9 Division), the whole commanded by the 44-year-old Lieutenant General Hubert de la Poer Gough. Gough's origins were in the nearest the British Army has to an East Prussia, ascendancy Ireland. He was the son of a general who had won the Victoria Cross, an Old Etonian and originally a 16th Lancer. He was widely experienced and had seen active service in India and in the South African War, where he had commanded a mounted infantry battalion. Since then he had been an instructor at the Staff College before commanding his own regiment, after which he was promoted to brigadier general in 1911. He was lucky to survive his command of the 3rd Cavalry Brigade in the Curragh, when he allowed a large number of his officers to state that they would resign rather than be a party to the enforcement of Irish Home Rule on the Protestant north. That Home Rule should not be imposed by force was an opinion shared by many – perhaps most – of the officer corps, but British officers did not and do not descend to the political arena, and those officers who, despite their strongly held views, held to their duty resented the acclaim that accrued to Gough for not holding to his. Fortunately for Gough the war came just in time. A cavalry brigade commander at Mons, and a good one, he was promoted major general and given command of the 2nd Cavalry Division in September 1914, 7 Infantry Division in April 1915, and further elevation to lieutenant general and command of I Corps in July 1915. He was an energetic and forceful commander, younger than most of his peers in rank, and if he was perhaps inclined to be guided too much by impulse, he had plenty of moral and physical courage. If the Loos offensive did develop into a battle where objectives had to be captured in a rush, and then further advances made, Gough was the right man to oversee it.

Taking on the southern half of the front was IV Corps, of one regular (1) one Territorial Force (47) and one New Army (15) divisions, commanded by Lieutenant General Sir Henry Rawlinson, a 51-year-old infantryman, and, like Gough, the son of a general and an Old Etonian. Rawlinson too was highly experienced, having seen active service in the Sudan and the South African war, and he had been commandant of the Staff College before commanding successively a brigade and, from 1910, a division. He went to war in 1914 in command of 4 Division, and after a month was promoted to lieutenant general and placed in command of IV Corps.

In less than a year Gough had increased his span of command nine times, going from commanding a brigade of around 4,000 men to a corps with 60,000 all ranks, while Rawlinson had increased his threefold. This applied throughout the BEF: Sir John French commanded four divisions and the cavalry division in 1914, now he commanded twenty-eight infantry and five cavalry divisions, with more arriving by the day. Haig went from commanding two divisions in August 1914 to fourteen infantry and one cavalry divisions a year later. The General Officer Commanding 2 Division, Major General Horne, had been an artillery brigadier general until June 1915, GOC 7 Division, Major General Capper, had been promoted to that rank before the war, but only just (in May 1914), and GOC 9 Division, Major General Thesiger, had been but a colonel when the war started so promotion a month before the Loos battle increased his span of command twelve times in the space of a year.

It was the same story throughout the BEF, and all the way down: battalion commanders were now in charge of brigades; platoon commanders were running companies and sergeants were RSMs. It could not be otherwise in a nation that eschewed compulsory military service in peacetime and had a tiny professional army that had to be expanded hugely to meet the requirements of total war. Everybody was learning on the job, and the wonder is not that mistakes were made, at all levels, but that so few were made and that the system worked as well as it did.

The two corps sent out their operation orders the next day, 20 September. First Army had told I Corps to seize the crossings over the Haute Deule Canal between Bauvin and Pont-à-Vendin. Now the corps operation order divided that objective up into three divisional tasks. The northernmost of the corps' divisions, 2 Division, was to attack between the La Bassée

Canal and the Hohenzollern Redoubt with two of its brigades, 6 and 19, and form a defensive flank facing north-east, to prevent interference with the main attack from the north. North of the canal the third brigade of the division, 5 Brigade, would capture the Givenchy Salient.

In the British Army it is the history of the regiment that counts. Even today most private soldiers might know which brigade their unit is in, but would have little knowledge of and no interest in the division. Divisions in the British Army do not really have a history, however much divisional commanders would like there to be one, and while there is a written history for most British divisions in existence during the Great War, one feels that many were produced as a duty rather than as a labour of love. Soldiers could visualise their own battalion or regiment – which usually recruited its men from the same geographical area – in which, with very few exceptions, they would remain throughout their service; the division was far too big and amorphous to have a personality of its own and was often regarded and referred to by Tommy, Jock, Taffy or Pat as 'them'. There were of course exceptions. More than one division did manage to attract a loyalty of its own, either because of where it originated, or due to the personality of its commander, or from some peculiarity of its composition. The Guards Division, some of the Territorial Force divisions and the 16th (Irish) and 36th (Ulster) Divisions are examples. Despite the foregoing, there had been a 2 Division in the British Army for a very long time, indeed since Sir Arthur Wellesley had adopted the divisional organisation for the British army in Spain and Portugal in 1809. Prior to the outbreak of this war the division had been stationed in Aldershot as part of the original Expeditionary Force, and even after the casualties since August 1914, and the removal of 4th Guards Brigade to the Guards Division and its replacement by 19 Infantry Brigade, each of its brigades still had four battalions that were, in name at least, regular, with an extra five Territorial Force battalions spread between the brigades for training and acclimatisation.

In the centre of I Corps was 9 Division. Its task was to break through the German positions in front of it, link up with 2 Division at Haisnes, and drive on to the Heute Deule Canal where it would hold the crossings and also detach a flank guard to face north from Berclau. The official title of this division was the Ninth (Scottish) Division, and they were one of the first (numerically the first) to be raised from the flood of recruits who answered Kitchener's call to arms in the early days of the war. Many joined for patriotic motives, or from a sense of adventure, probably as many for the economic attractions of three square meals a day and a fair wage, but the standard of the early recruits was high, and many who were turned down in 1914 would have no trouble being accepted in the latter half of 1915 or the early part of 1916, before conscription put a stop to voluntary enlistment.

The New Armies raised no new regiments as such; all infantry units of 9 Division were new battalions of existing regular regiments. Initial induction of recruits was carried out at regimental depots in Scotland and units, once formed, then went to Salisbury Plain for training. As with all New Army units it was the training and development of officers that was most difficult. Of officer qualities there was no shortage, but of experience there was. Not only did those selected as platoon commanders and company seconds-in-command have to learn everything that their soldiers had to become proficient in, from shooting to drill to marching to digging, but then in what was laughingly known as spare time they had to study the requirements of being an officer. While the army did have tactical manuals, including the excellent Field Service Regulations, it did not have a manual that told young civilians how to behave as officers, how to look after their men and what behaviour and demeanour they should develop – the regular army did not need that to be written down because the newly joined second lieutenant would learn such matters from the senior subaltern. When the senior subaltern was as ignorant as everybody else it was not possible to learn on the job, and all sorts of unofficial manuals, sold in bookshops, proliferated. Eventually such information would be imparted in official publications, but in those early days battalions had to make do as best they could.

Eventually, everyone was clothed, taught how to shoot and how to dig, and hardened physically by drill, route marching and PT. Tactical training started at section level and progressed through platoon and company training until the whole battalion could operate as a team. Then it was time for formation training, at brigade and finally divisional level, and at long last, in May 1915, eight months after it had been raised, 9 Division was judged fit to go to war. Between 8 and 15 May the division moved to France, the first of the New Army divisions to reach there. On 28 June the division entered the trenches for the first time, near Festubert, and began the process of rotating units and subunits between firing, support and reserve lines and billets in rear.

There were no infantry attacks on the division during this period, but they were frequently shelled and mortared, without being able to do very much about it. The shell supply system was improving, but stockpiles for the coming offensive had to be built up. Between the division's firing and support lines was an abandoned trench known as the 'old German line', which had indeed at one time been occupied by the Germans. It was neglected and filthy, and not used by 9 Division except for the Prince of Wales (later King Edward VIII and later still Duke of Windsor) who was an inveterate collector of battlefield souvenirs. As an extra ADC to Sir John French he was not overworked and he frequently prowled the old German line to see what he could find. Although not used by 9 Division the Germans thought it was, and frequently shelled it. As this used up explosive that would otherwise be directed to where men of the division really were, small patrols of two or three soldiers were often sent into the old German line to light fires and then withdraw swiftly. By doing this – presumably when the Prince of Wales was not souvenir hunting – the British continued to encourage the Germans to shell the empty trench.

There were problems faced by 9 Division that would not affect their English comrades. Sgt McHardy, a member of the machine gun section of 8 Black Watch, was on duty in the firing line during an unexpectedly heavy shower of rain. Having managed to sit down in several large puddles, he found that his kilt was soaking wet. As things were quiet and no important personage was expected to visit that section of the line, Sgt McHardy took his kilt off and hung it up to dry on the back of the trench. A German shell overshot the trench, exploded just behind the parados, and blew the kilt off into no-man's-land. McHardy could do little but wait until dark, when he managed to slip over the parapet, crawl into no-man's-land, find his kilt and retrieve it. As Scots soldiers were and are forbidden to wear anything under the kilt, it cannot have been a comfortable excursion.

On 18 August the division was relieved in the trenches and moved to a training area near Busnes, where for the rest of the month they practised offensive tactics, before moving into the trenches east of Vermelles on 2 September, to prepare for the Loos attack. At this stage the exact date was not known, but all ranks were aware that it could not be far off.

The right hand, southernmost division of I Corps was 7 Division. Its task was to capture the trench systems of Hulluch, Cité St Elie and Haisnes, on the second German line, and then to press on and hold from the bend in the Heute Deule Canal south to the Loison–Harnes road. Like 2 Division, the seventh was a regular formation, but unlike 2 Division it had been raised and broken up over the previous century as the situation demanded, and for this war was resurrected in August 1914 at Lyndhurst in the New Forest, when it took under command regular units stationed at home that had not gone to France with the original BEF, and, from September, regular units returned from overseas having been replaced by local troops or by Territorial Force units from the United Kingdom.

Despite only coming into existence as a division in late August 1914, 7 Division had fewer problems than the four regular divisions that had gone to France on the outbreak of war, or the two that followed shortly after. These first six divisions had all been stationed in England and were at peacetime home establishment. On mobilisation they had been faced with absorbing up to thirty percent reservists to bring them up to war establishment. Although the reservists had all been regular soldiers, many were no longer up to the demanding physical standards of the 1914 army, and they needed time to get fit and shake down in their units – time that they could not have. The units coming to 7 Division from abroad, on the other hand, were already at overseas establishment and needed far fewer reservists, and even those units in the United Kingdom had received their reservists at the beginning of August and there had been plenty of time for them to readjust to army life and to be absorbed.[10]

The division was ordered to proceed on foreign service on 4 October 1914 and by 7 October was concentrated at Bruges. A projected move to Antwerp was, fortunately, cancelled and the division moved first to Ghent and then to Ypres. In the First Battle of Ypres (19 October–27 November 1914) the division, arriving with a strength of 18,000, lost 1,020 killed and 4,877 missing; at Neuve Chapelle (10–12 March 1915) 552 killed and 318 missing; at Aubers Ridge (9 May 1915) and Festubert (16–18 May 1915) 706 killed and 626 missing, and at Givenchy (15 June 1915) a combined total of 387 killed and missing, before the division was moved to the Loos sector. Some of the missing genuinely were lost, and would reappear, but most were either taken prisoner, and thus lost to their units, or killed and their bodies not found, or if found not identified. Added to those so badly wounded that they could not return to duty, the professional regular element was severely reduced by the time of the Battle of Loos. Further dilution took place in the first week of August 1915 when the two Guards battalions (1 Grenadier Guards and 2 Scots Guards) left to join the Guards Division, to be replaced by two New Army battalions straight out from England, the 8th and 9th Battalions the Devonshire Regiment.

First Army had ordered IV Corps to attack between the Vermelles–Hulluch Road and the Double Crassier. To its right was the Loos–Lens–Lieven complex, which would not be attacked until outflanked by IV Corps and the French Tenth Army to the south. The corps staff now issued instructions to the three divisions under its command.

The left hand, northernmost, division of the corps was 1 Division. This regular division had a provenance going back to the Peninsular War, but having been out since the declaration of war there were now a great many recruits in the ranks, and it had two Territorial Force and two New Army battalions as well as its ten so-called regular battalions. The tasks of the division were to take the German first line trenches from the south of Hulluch to Bois Hugo, then to push on to the German second line, and finally finishing on the Haute Deule Canal.

The corps' centre division, 15 Division, was a New Army division, the first of the K2 army, or the second augmentation, authorised by parliament in September 1914. Like the 9th, the 15th was a Scottish division, and once recruits had been attested the division assembled at Aldershot for training. Such were the problems faced by the textile industry that there were still no uniforms, and the division paraded in civilian clothes to be inspected by the King on 26 September 1914. On 22 January 1915 the division was inspected again, this time by Lord Kitchener accompanied by the French Minister for War, and even then only DP[11] rifles were available, and then only for the front rank. Horses arrived but there was no tack for them, and the artillery trained with logs of wood mounted on obsolete gun carriages. Things improved slightly when an enterprising artillery officer burgled the Ordnance Corps officers' mess and purloined one of their trophies: a brass nine pounder muzzle loader, last used at Waterloo. Weapons and equipment did arrive eventually, although it was not until June 1915 that modern gun sights arrived, and the division was considered fit for war and warned for overseas service in July 1915. On 17 July 1915 the division joined IV Corps. Loos would be its introduction to war.

The task give to 15 (Scottish) Division was to take the first line of German trenches, then to fight its way through Loos (once that town had been outflanked) and on to the German second line before closing up to the Heute Deule Canal. Between Loos and the second line was the heavily fortified German strongpoint of Hill 70, which would have to be taken before the canal could be approached. It was a lot to ask.

On the right of IV Corps was the only Territorial Force division to be involved in the first phase of the Loos offensive, 47 (London) Division. This division was formed in 1908 as part of Haldane's reforms which created the Territorial Force out of the old Volunteers, Militia and Yeoman Cavalry. It was originally the 2nd London Division, being renumbered after deployment to France as 47 (London) Division[12] so as to avoid confusion with 2 Division. Intended primarily for home defence, the Territorial Force was entirely voluntary and part time, with members carrying out military training at weekends, evenings and annual camp. Inevitably it was as much a social as a military organisation, and its units varied greatly in military efficiency, from moderate to reasonable given time to prepare. Its members ranged from those who were there for the beer to the keen as mustard but inexperienced. Given the lack of compulsory military service it was, however, the best reserve Britain was likely to be able to get. The Territorial Force attracted the genuinely patriotic who were prepared to defend the country in the event of war, but did not wish to make a career of it; and those who joined for the fun, or the annual bounty, or the companionship. Inevitably there were officers who wanted the social cachet of a rank but did not wish to do the work associated with it, balanced by those who took their duties seriously and strove to discharge them efficiently. The present day Territorial Army is little different.

The Territorial Force divisions were supposed to mirror their regular counterparts, but in reality much of their equipment was out of date, or simply not available. Basic items – individual uniforms and rifles – were generally present, but much that was vital for war but not necessarily needed in time of peace was not. 47 Division's transport companies and the ammunition columns (responsible for feeding the gun lines with shells) had men but no transport, and on mobilisation wagons and horses had to be requisitioned from civilian sources. Unfortunately the carts were not the right type and could not be pulled by teams of horses, leading to all round embarrassment when the divisional train was unable to get up the (not very steep albeit long) hill at Stanmore on its way to its war station at St Albans. All Territorial Force divisions, and the brigades in the divisions, had regular commanders and staff, and battalions had regular adjutants and a number of regular instructors. Overall the Territorial Force in 1914 was well under its established strength, but at least most of its divisions were concentrated in one place, as for many of them annual camp was going on when war was declared. In the case of 47 Division, most of its units were on Salisbury Plain on 4 August 1914.

Recalled to London to complete mobilisation procedures and to draw the necessary kit, the division moved to its war station around St Albans, where it began the serious business of preparing for war. All the infantry battalions of the division were battalions of the London Regiment, with their own particular sobriquet in brackets.[13] The 8th Battalion was known to all as the Post Office Rifles. Its Other Ranks were, almost without exception, employees of the postal service: porters, drivers, telegraphists, sorters and postmen. It would appear that the postal service of the time did not employ gentlemen, as none of the officers of the battalion were remotely connected with letterboxes. The commanding officer (Lord Liverpool) was unable to turn up for mobilisation as he was otherwise engaged as the Governor General of New Zealand, but his place was taken by a retired captain of the Irish Guards. The second-in-command was a civil engineer of the Egyptian Service (a little late in turning up, but he got there); there was one fellow of an Oxford college and another from Cambridge; four barristers (including one King's Counsel); three solicitors; the secretary of a bank, two members of the Home Civil Service and a sprinkling of youths straight out of university. One officer made his way to the reporting centre from Hong Kong (overland), one got there from Russian Siberia, and eight of them were Old Etonians. They might not know an awful lot about soldiering, but there can be no doubting that there was plenty of natural leadership there, and no one could say they were not keen to do their bit.

There were insufficient public buildings to house the rapidly expanding army, and 47 Division found its officers and men billeted in private houses if they were lucky, or in schools, barns or sheds if they were not. Initially local residents vied with each other for the privilege of 'having a soldier', but as more and more men arrived in the area the subaltern with his own bedroom soon found himself on the floor with three others.

In February 1915 the Great Jam Scandal broke. It was discovered that throughout the 47 divisional area, and that of its neighbouring 46 Division, civilians were enthusiastically munching jam, cheese and sugar, all obtainable from local shopkeepers and sold in tins and packets bearing the unmistakeable arrowhead logo of the War Office. Someone was flogging the rations! The AQMG of Third Army, the senior staff officer with responsibility for quartering, rations and stores, amongst other things, and a brigadier general, no less, began a formal inquiry. Rumours of instant arrests and courts martial flew about as it emerged that unit quartermasters, quartermaster sergeants and even, heaven forfend, regimental officers, were selling all manner of items issued by His Majesty for consumption solely by his troops. It transpired that even portions of the meat ration were being sold to local butchers and the prognosis looked bad indeed.

The findings of the inquiry were announced in March, just before the division moved to France, and exonerated everybody! Apparently the men of the division, and those of 46 Division too, had been complaining that there was no milk provided for their tea (true), that brown sugar was issued when they would prefer white (true), that far too much plum and apple jam was issued and the men were fed up with it (true), that cheese was issued which they disliked (true), and that so much meat was issued that there was always some left over (again, true, but only because the cooks were inexperienced). All that the officers had done, said the report of the inquiry, was to recognise the justice of the men's wants, sell the unwanted brown sugar, cheese and jam and the surplus meat and use the money to buy milk, white sugar, currants (for puddings) and other additions to the men's rations. A regular division would never have got away with it, but Territorial Force officers might just have been naive enough to try.

The division moved to France in mid-March 1915, initially to Bethune, where it began to prepare itself for trench warfare. Although far less experienced than regular soldiers, the Territorial Force generally attracted a more intelligent, and possibly more independently minded soldier. Some of the peculiarities of the regular army were not lost on them. In April 1915 a Corps Routine Order reminded readers that the provisions of King's Regulations regarding the shaving of the upper lip were being disregarded, and that in future offenders would be severely punished. The regulation said that all soldiers, of whatever rank, were required to have moustaches, but were forbidden to have beards. The flouting of the rules was not in that soldiers were suddenly growing beards, but that many were not growing moustaches, for the simple reason that they were too young to be able to do so. 47 Division soldiers remarked that this was an odd rule in an army where the King had a beard and the Prince of Wales was entirely clean-shaven. Shortly afterwards the pre-war regulation concerning compulsory moustaches was withdrawn.

From Bethune the division had its first taste of action at the battles of Festubert and Givenchy, before moving to the Loos sector in June 1915. Its tasks in the Loos offensive were to seize the German first line between the Bethune–Lens road and the Double Crassier, then to push on half way along the Crassier and finally to form a defensive flank facing south-east between Loos and St Laurent.

Once the divisions had received their orders from their respective corps, the divisional staff could break their objectives down into tasks for their brigades, and brigade staffs could issue orders to battalions. Meanwhile stores and ammunition were being stockpiled, targets were being registered and the Royal Flying Corps was doing its best to prevent German aircraft from seeing what was going on.

Notes

1. For the Order of Battle of the First Army at Loos, see Appendix I.
2. French Territorials were reservists in the upper age bracket. After completing their compulsory military service (of two years up to 1913 and three years thereafter) with the active army from the age of 20, all French males served on the army reserve until the age of 33 and from then to the age of 45 in separate Territorial Army units. In practice not all Frenchmen were conscripted, as there was insufficient funding for so large an army in peacetime. There was a serious shortage of experienced officers in all the Territorial formations.
3. A redoubt was a strongly fortified position, usually consisting of concrete bunkers with underground shelters, heavily wired and with machine guns sited to fire along likely avenues of approach. Sometimes they included trench mortars and often an artillery observation officer. If captured or destroyed – never easy – defences on either side tended to collapse.
4. *Trench fortifications 1914–18, A Reference Manual*, London and Nashville: Imperial War Museum and Battery Press, 1998.
5. An eight-hour march at best. Weather, the state of the roads and traffic jams could increase the time considerably.
6. Barker, Ralph, *The Royal Flying Corps in France*, Vol. I, *From Mons to the Somme*, London: Constable, 1994.
7. War Diary 35 TM Bty, National Archives WO/95 1853.
8. The British became the best practitioners of gas warfare, developing nastier gasses, better ways to deliver them, and better means of protection against them. From 1915 to 1918 the British launched roughly twice as many gas attacks as did the Germans, but were careful not to escalate first. Thus, the Germans attracted the opprobrium of being the first to use gas, while the British gained what military benefit there was (not much).
9. Zero Hour was the time an operation was scheduled to begin. This was later changed to H Hour, to conform to the French practice (H for *heure*), and H Hour it remains to this day.
10. For example the 2nd Battalion Scots Guards, originally in 7 Division, although in the Guards Division by Loos, had on joining 7 Division a ration strength of 1,122 all ranks, of whom 748 were reservists!
11. Drill Purpose, i.e. incapable of being fired.
12. Of the infantry divisions the Guards, 1–8 and 27–29 were regular; 9–26 and 30–41 were New Army; 42–69 were Territorial Force, 63 (RN) was a mixture of Royal Navy, Royal Marines and army units, and 71–75 were mixed. All told the British produced ninety divisions for all theatres (including the UK).
13. This would change, but only slightly. 1/4th Royal Welch Fusiliers became the divisional pioneer battalion when this addition to the establishment was authorised in 1915.

CHAPTER III

The Preliminaries

As preparations for the British offensive began in earnest, the battalion and company commanders coming up to the firing line to look over the ground across which they would have to attack must have found it a depressing sight indeed. Until the 1870s nobody had been very interested in the area, except for the occasional smuggler operating across the French border into Holland or Belgium. The soil was poor, there was little trade and the flat, chalky scrub was unlikely to attract visitors seeking the beauties of nature. Then, after the Franco–Prussian War, everything changed. An unusually rich seam of coal was discovered, and suddenly there was work for all, even if the landscape was made even less attractive than it had been before.

Before 1914 there were two mining companies operating in the area, one based in Bethune and one in Lens. With the coming of war, the Bethune company's mines were all save one in the British sector, and the Lens company's were under German control. By the terms of their concessions rival companies did not join their mines up underground, so there was no great risk of all-out subterranean war, but the British did take the precaution of sealing off any galleries running from mines on their side of no-man's-land to pitheads in German territory. Altogether along the British front for the attack, between Grenay and the La Bassée Canal, there were six fosse, or major pitheads, and a number of subsidiary shafts or puits. These pitheads were imposing structures, and took on great tactical significance. At each fosse there was a tall metal gantry tower, which contained the winding gear for the cage that took miners and their equipment down the shaft of the mine, and brought coal and miners up again. Beside each gantry was a crassier, or dump of spoil or slagheap, and a collection of mining administrative buildings. There were also a series of villages that had grown up solely to service the mines, with names indicating a grandeur that was certainly not there: Cité Jeanne d'Arc, Cité St Laurent, Cité St Elie and the like. Many of these *cités* were linked together by trenches and wire to form the second German defence line.

Both sides used the fosse as observation posts and for artillery spotting, and both sides did their best to make those of their adversaries untenable.

The Germans had the advantage as their Fosse 8, located just behind their first line of defences and 2,000 yards south of the La Bassée Canal, could look well beyond the British firing line and well into their back areas as far as Bethune. Similarly to the south the Germans made use of what the British called Tower Bridge, an imposing latticework of iron belonging to a fosse in Loos itself. This could look at least two miles beyond the British forward positions, and try as they did the British heavy artillery was unable to destroy it before the battle started.

The British too made use of the fosse winding towers and crassiers, but their principal one in the north, at Annequin, was a good 5,000 yards away from the German line, and the southern one, the crassier of Fosse 5, just behind the British firing line, was limited in what it could see by spurs in front of it. The fosse and the crassiers on both sides of no-man's-land were not only used for observing, they were fortified and defended as well, and would not be easy to approach or to fight through and round.

All along the Loos sector there were actually two German defensive systems, the second varying from 1,000 yards to 4,000 yards behind the first. Generally in this war a typical sector of British front would have consisted of three lines of trenches: the firing line, that nearest to the enemy; the support line, some way behind and intended to stop any enemy penetrating the firing line; and the reserve line, usually well back and there as a last ditch defence if the enemy penetrated the first two lines. The French and the Germans operated a similar system, but often without a reserve line, considering that their artillery could do the reserve line's tasks rather than having to commit infantry to it. As the French and Germans had considerably more artillery than the British this was not unsound reasoning. Whether or not there was a reserve line, the defensive layout adopted by both sides did provide for defence in depth, and it was very rare indeed for either side to achieve a complete breakthrough. Attacking troops might get through the firing line, but would then find themselves slowed up or stopped by the support line. Those who did succeed in getting through the support line – if any – would nearly always be insufficiently strong to break through the reserve line or its artillery equivalent. With the Germans at Loos having two complete and separate systems, once through the first firing line and support line the attackers would then have to take on another of the same, as well as having to deal with fortified positions situated between the two systems

Along the first German line, which the British would hit between two hundred and four hundred yards after leaving their own trenches, were a series of redoubts, or fortified positions, with names like Railway Redoubt, Hohenzollern Redoubt, The Pope's Nose, Loos Road Redoubt and Lens Road Redoubt. From north to south the principal obstacles to movement that the British would have to overcome were the mining village of Auchy, situated between the two German defence lines in 2 Division's sector, the

Hohenzollern Redoubt and Fosse 8 in front of 9 Division, Tower Bridge on the boundary between 15 Division and 47 Division, and the double crassier, two slag heaps side by side running west to east back from the German firing line and over 100 feet high. They would have to be dealt with by 47 Division. Only in the centre of the British attack, along the inter-corps boundary from Vermelles to Hulloch, where 7 and 1 Divisions would advance, did the ground look at all reasonable from the attackers' perspective, but even here the second defence line, 500 yards behind the first, contained a number of *cités* and strongpoints that would not be easy to deal with. So much would depend on what the artillery could do before the battle, and what the gas could do during it.

While the infantrymen and the gunners were looking at the ground, preparations for the use of gas were well in hand. From the first week in September gas cylinders began to arrive in the Loos sector, and by 19 September 5,500 cylinders containing a total of 150 tons of chlorine were in place. The movement of the cylinders, each weighing 120 pounds (and some 160 pounds), to divisional dumps was straightforward enough, but for the last mile or two they had to be manhandled up communications trenches at night, placed in position in specially dug recesses under the parapet of the firing line trench, and then covered in sandbags to protect them from German artillery fire. No fewer than 8,000 men were employed as fatigue parties for this task, three men to a cylinder, and specially made yokes and harnesses were issued to them. Some divisions gave the task to one battalion, training them specially for the task. In 47 Division each night, until all the gas was in place, men of the Civil Service Rifles, otherwise known as the 15th Battalion The London Regiment, wound their way up and down the communication trenches bearing their cylinders lashed to poles. Once in the firing line, the cylinders became the responsibility of the Specials Companies RE, who would look after them until Zero Hour and turn them on when required.

It was considered that forty minutes of gas was needed to support the attack on 25 September, because intelligence suggested that no German gas mask could give protection for more than thirty minutes. One cylinder covered twenty-five yards of front and was exhausted in two minutes. The planners concluded that there were insufficient cylinders to provide forty minutes of gas all along the front, and so the discharge would be intermittent, being substituted and augmented by smoke.[1]

Smoke was not something that the British Army (unlike the navy) had much experience of, and this was the first time it would be used in an operation of any magnitude. Methods of delivering smoke ranged from cylinders placed in no-man's-land and ignited by electrical detonators, smoke bombs that could be fired from the newly arrived Stokes Mortar, and smoke candles that could be lit and thrown, to Threfallite grenades (originally designed to burn off grass in front of trenches, which might give cover for an enemy raid, they contained phosphorus[2] which also produced smoke). Along parts of the front not earmarked for the offensive, battalions stockpiled bundles of wet straw. These would be lit and thrown over the parapet at Zero Hour, thus extending the smoke screen and, it was hoped, confusing the Germans as to the extent of the attack.

As in any operation involving the movement of large numbers of troops, much work fell to the Royal Engineers and to the logistics units. The engineers were responsible for preparing jump off lines forward of the British trenches where the distance across no-man's-land was considered too great to be assaulted with a reasonable chance of success. This was done by digging saps forward from the existing trenches, and then joining the heads of them up. The actual digging was done by the newly instituted pioneer battalions of divisions, and by working parties from the infantry battalions, with supervision and planning from the Royal Engineers. The existing trench in the 47 Division area of the attack, for example, curved back from the double crassier and was up to 700 yards from the German first line. The engineers planned a new trench which, instead of curving back, would join up both extremities with a straight trench much closer to the first objective. Every night a battalion of infantry would parade at the division's headquarters at Les Brebis, and march the two miles or so up to the front where they would spend the night digging with the engineers and the pioneer battalion. They started on 27 August, and by 17 September they had dug the whole of the new jump off line, communications trenches and assembly trenches, all revetted and with ladders in place, a total of two miles of trenches.

In some cases Russian Saps were dug, these being tunnels driven just below the ground, the roofs of which could be removed at the last minute by explosives or by men bursting up through them. Tunnelling companies of the Royal Engineers burrowed under the German lines and placed mines in position, ready to be exploded when the attack began. Trenches behind the firing line had to be bridged to allow cavalry and artillery to advance, and extra dugouts for medical units constructed. For each brigade one communication trench was dug for use by wounded only. It was wider than normal and had fewer corners, so that stretcher parties could move quickly along it, and ran back about 2,000 yards from the firing line to a dressing station. Dumps had to be built to hold a resupply of ammunition and water, and wire and digging implements for use on a captured objective had to be stockpiled. Routes for the cavalry had to be constructed and a seven-foot ladder was placed every five yards along the British firing line, to enable troops to emerge quickly once the attack began. Digging here was far easier than in the sodden ground of Flanders to the north, but the chalk of Loos was almost impossible to hide, and it was clear to the Germans that something was up. Despite this, preparations for the attack proceeded with little or no interference.

One of the great difficulties in this war, and not solved for another generation, was communication. When in defence commanders could communicate with superiors and subordinates by personal visits, telephone or runner. Once an advance started it became far more difficult for a commander to obtain up-to-date information and to influence the battle. Telephone lines were laid by advancing troops, but because they could not be dug in they were likely to be cut by shelling, and the most reliable means of delivering information, the runner, could get lost or shot. If Loos was to develop into a fast moving battle, as everyone hoped it would, it was important that commanders in rear, and who controlled the follow-on troops, understood what was happening at the front and knew where their own troops had got to. Infantry battalions were issued with lamps, flags and pigeons to supplement telephone and runner, and each division had a wireless set operated by four signallers. This latter was not easily portable, nor was it soldier proof, but it should ensure that what was known to divisional headquarters would be rapidly passed on to corps, army and BEF level.

The artillery bombardment started at 0700 hours on 21 September, with heavy guns and howitzers taking on the defences, and the field batteries concentrating on wire cutting. For the bombardment all artillery was taken under command of the respective corps headquarters, although divisional artillery would revert to its normal owner at Zero Hour. Each field battery (of four or six guns) was allocated 150 rounds per gun for each twenty-four-hour period, and was responsible for cutting 600 yards of front line wire. This seems a prodigious amount of explosive to be detonated in a very small area: it is not. The wire obstacles in front of the German trenches were a minimum of ten yards deep, and in some cases twenty. This meant that in the four days of the bombardment there would be, at best, 2,400 eighteen pounder shells landing on 10,000 square yards of wire, and even assuming every shell went off (and many were duds) this was not enough to guarantee passable lanes through the obstacle belt. There were problems in placing the field batteries so that they could fire on the wire. Sited under cover from direct observation – in a sunken road, on a reverse slope, in a dip in the ground – they could not always achieve the trajectory needed to hit targets immediately to their front, so some of the wire was taken on by guns firing from a flank. Normally this would not matter – a man is killed equally well whether the shell approaches from his front or his side – but in this case it meant that while batteries bombarding the wire at an angle would still create lanes, they would be longer and thus require a greater expenditure of shells. Another snag was that these lanes would not be visible from the front and would not be obvious to assaulting infantry.

In order to prevent the Germans from repairing by night breaches created during the day, shrapnel was fired at irregular intervals throughout the night at areas of cut wire, and battalion machine guns[3] fired at communication trenches and at gaps made by the artillery in the wire. The second German defence line had wire in front of it too, and as the field batteries could not reach that far into German territory it was agreed that the second wire belt would be dealt with by the heavies, with their longer range. There was, however, a problem in observing the results of shelling, particularly on the first two days of the bombardment when the dry weather led to great clouds of chalk dust obscuring the targets. This meant that the second wire belt was still intact for much of its length when the attack began.

It was hoped that the attack would make rapid progress, and in that event artillery would be needed to support the infantry as it moved out of range of the initial battery positions. Orders were therefore issued that during the last night of the bombardment – 24/25 September – two field batteries per division, or eight guns, were to be taken out of position and limbered up (attached to their horses) so that they could follow on immediately after the infantry.

The air bombing campaign began on 22 September, under the direction of 'Boom' Trenchard, then commander of the RFC in France. Prior to the official opening of the RFC's part in the Loos preliminaries, the fitters and the aircrew had been carrying on their normal tasks by day, while they fitted bomb racks to the aircraft by night. Given the size of the bombs capable of being carried by aircraft of the time and the relatively simple bombsight, the softening up missions flown by the RFC achieved more than many thought possible, even if they did not materially affect the outcome of the battle. Initially they destroyed railway bridges, sidings and stations, and on at least one occasion bombed a German troop train. That they did worry the Germans is evident by efforts to camouflage trains and by the siting of anti aircraft guns, rocket batteries and infantry-manned machine guns along railway lines, and particularly along cuttings, for the RFC had learned that a bomb dropped inside a cutting was more effective than one detonated in an open area.

It was at this time that the RFC first met the German Fokker E1, an aircraft that would give the Germans a temporary ascendancy in the air. On the outbreak of war aircraft were unarmed, except for the crews' personal weapons. Firing rifles and pistols, or throwing hand and rifle grenades, from a wood and string contraption moving at around eighty miles an hour was not the best way to obtain domination of the skies, and both sides began to fit machine guns to their aircraft. The British used the Lewis gun, a reliable weapon and lighter than the Vickers. Not only was it air cooled, but also the slipstream when in flight provided sufficient cooling of the barrel to allow the casing and fins of the ground version of the Lewis to be removed, thus saving even more weight. A difficulty was that the gun had to be mounted well above the pilot, so that it could fire without hitting the propeller. This made aiming a highly skilled affair, and meant that aircraft guns were really only effective at very close ranges. If some way could be found to fire the machine guns forward through the propeller disc, then aiming would be much easier – the pilot would only have to fly his aircraft straight at the target and then open fire as soon as he came within range.

The French devised a system whereby the guns fired forward, through the propeller disc, but they fitted angled deflector plates on the propeller blades, so that those (relatively few) bullets that did hit the propeller would ricochet off to one side, without damaging the propeller. A number of French machines were fitted with the new system and sent up to forward units for trials. Unfortunately not all the pilots trying out the new device were as security aware as they should have been, and one pilot, shot down over German territory, failed to burn his machine before he was taken prisoner. The Germans realised what they had found, and handed the wreck over to Anton Fokker, a Dutch aircraft designer working for Germany,[4] with instructions to manufacture something similar for machines flown by German airmen. Fokker took the principle – forward firing machine guns – and improved on it by resurrecting a pre-war idea and perfecting an interrupter gear, which prevented the guns from firing when a propeller blade passed in front of the muzzle. Combined with the speed and manoeuvrability of Fokker's new scout aircraft, the interrupter gear was to turn many young RFC pilots and observers into 'Fokker fodder' before a counter to it was found. Fortunately the Germans took some time to appreciate just what a major advance had been made, and the Fokker E1s were deployed in ones and twos rather than being concentrated into separate units which might have had a devastating effect on Allied aviation.

While the gunners and the sappers, the airmen and the suppliers were preparing for their part in the attack, the infantry too were training hard. Divisions found such areas as they could well behind the lines and rehearsed their battalions over taped out representations of the German trenches. On occasions units in the line were directed to lay on a feint attack. For these the artillery would stop firing and the infantry would wave bayonets, or even dummy men, above their trenches. The idea was that the Germans would think the attack was about to be launched, would man their fire trench and then be caught when the British artillery resumed firing. It rarely worked: indeed the Germans seem to have taken little interest in any of the preparations, contenting themselves with staying in their shelters and dugouts and engaging in desultory shelling of the British lines.

Apart from some of the regulars who had been at the Battle of Second Ypres, few of the soldiers who would take part in the attack had any experience of gas. Most regarded it with great suspicion, were nervous about carrying cylinders, and disliked the idea of them being positioned in the same trenches as they would assault from. In fact the British smoke helmet, the hypo helmet, was the most effective gas mask that there was on the Western Front. Introduced in July 1915 it consisted of a flannel hood with celluloid eyepieces, which covered the head and face completely, being tucked in to the neck of the tunic. The flannel was impregnated with hyposulphite and thus removed all chlorine from the air breathed in through the helmet. True it was uncomfortable and hot, the eyepieces could mist up and hearing and being heard was not easy, but provided that men kept it on, it offered complete protection. The trouble was that many of the soldiers simply did not believe in it, and so they had to be convinced and accustomed to wearing it. Trenches were dug in back areas and filled with chlorine, through which the soldiers filed wearing their smoke helmets. It helped, but there was not enough spare gas for there to be much available for training, and there was always the fear that German agents would see the training and realise that a gas attack was to be made. In hindsight, not enough familiarisation training in gas warfare was done. For the attack itself each man would have two smoke helmets: one rolled up on his head ready to be pulled down when needed, and one in his pack.

During the preliminary phase the soldiers who would take part in the attack were issued with all the extra impedimenta that they would have to take with them. In addition to his two smoke helmets, each man had to take 200 rounds of rifle ammunition, dry rations to sustain him during the day, an emergency 'iron' ration, a full water bottle, a field dressing, an entrenching tool and such personal kit as he might wish to carry. Selected individuals carried hand grenades (known as bombs), wire cutters, signalling equipment and telephone wire. In addition each man carried two sandbags and a proportion of those in the second and subsequent waves carried picks and shovels so that captured German defences could be turned to face the other way. Since Roman times (and no doubt before) infantry soldiers have always carried much the same weight of clothing and equipment – around sixty pounds but sometimes more. It was never sufficient merely to capture an objective: it had to be held and consolidated and used as a springboard for the next advance. All this required equipment, while at the same time the soldier had to be capable of sustaining himself and his weapon until resupply could reach him.

Preparation and planning for the great offensive took a heavy toll on the staff at the various levels. With the enormous and unprecedented expansion of the army since August 1914, the supply of pre-war graduates of the Staff College had long run out, and most staff officers, like their contemporaries in battalions and regiments, were learning on the job. Compared to today's army, there were very few staff officers to deal with all the work that came their way. A division, of around 18,000 men, had only fourteen officers to help the commander run the organisation. There were three staff branches, G (operations and training), A (personnel) and Q (logistics). As the whole purpose of an army is to carry out military operations, everything else is in support of that end, and so G was the senior staff branch. The division had three G staff officers: the General Staff Officer Grade I, or GSOI, a lieutenant colonel and effectively the chief of staff, who was assisted by a GSO II (major) and a GSO III (captain). A and Q matters were presided over by the Assistant Adjutant and Quartermaster General (or AA&QMG), also a lieutenant colonel, with two majors as assistants, one for A staff matters and one for Q, and another major who was the technical adviser and whose duties involved mainly ammunition and weapons, but increasingly motor transport as well. Medical services were overseen by a colonel of the Royal Army Medical Corps assisted by a lieutenant colonel, and veterinary services by a major of the Royal Army Veterinary Corps. In regard to the latter, one should remember that an infantry division of 1915 had almost 6,000 horses on strength, of which only 167 were the property of the cavalry squadron that formed an integral part of every division. The horse was still the fastest way of getting across country off roads, and was the equivalent of today's Land Rover, artillery prime mover and, hitched to a wagon, supply lorry.

The artillery of the division (up to fifteen field batteries) was commanded and coordinated by a Brigadier General Royal Artillery (BGRA) assisted by two officers, and the engineers by a lieutenant colonel Chief Royal Engineer with one assistant. Others not on the staff but attached to the headquarters were the commander's aide de camp (ADC) and the Assistant Provost Marshal, who in war was much more concerned with traffic control and all its problems, than with pursuing breaches of military law.

However fashionable it has become to tease the staff for their supposed comfortable existence compared to that of the fighting troops, the facts are that those few officers responsible for all that plethora of plans, orders, instructions, briefings and preparation, worked long into the night to get everything ready for the offensive. Not all could take the strain, and Major General Landon, commanding 9 (Scottish) Division, had to be sent home sick on 8 September, to be replaced by Major General Thesiger.

As the date for the assault grew nearer, commanders pored over air photographs, and peered through binoculars to see what the artillery had done so far. The results were mixed. From mid-morning on the first day, 21 September, the clouds of chalk dust made it very difficult for observers on the ground or in the air to see what had been achieved. The third day, 23 September, opened in cloud and drizzle, which did lay the dust and allowed some observation. It was obvious that by no means all the wire had been cut, especially on the reverse slopes where the wire could only be observed from the air. In some cases it was thought that the inexperience of those artillery batteries only recently arrived from England was to blame, as they had not yet reached that standard of precision firing required to deal with wire obstacles. Withal, such had been predicted – all were well aware that the artillery alone was insufficient for the job, but provided that gas could be used then all would yet be well. One spectacular hit was achieved by one of the heavy batteries on 23 September when they hit the *cité* of St Pierre, 3,000 yards behind the German first line and on the Franco–British boundary, setting the buildings on fire and causing a conflagration that burned for two days and nights, lighting up the area for hundreds of yards around. On the night of 23/24 September there were violent thunderstorms and heavy rain, making the chalk floors of the communication trenches slippery and almost impossible to move along. The guns kept firing but digging and the movement of stores and ammunition was slowed down considerably. On 24 September there was low cloud and mist, which prevented aerial bombing from taking place, but did not prevent the guns from firing on pre-selected targets. The counter-battery programme, the shelling of enemy gun positions, appeared to be going well, for batteries shelled lapsed into silence. Unfortunately it later transpired that very few of them had been knocked out: they had simply ceased firing when a British shell landed near them, lulling the British into thinking that they had been destroyed.

Zero Hour, although set for some time on 25 September, could not be fixed exactly until it was known whether or not gas could be used, and the use of gas depended entirely on wind direction. The wind had to blow from any point between south-west and north-west at a speed of around eight miles an hour at ground level, and for long enough for all the gas to be discharged and blown over the German lines. In making his decision as to Zero Hour, the Commander First Army, Haig, was in the hands of his weather forecaster. Armies do not generally worry too much about weather forecasting, which for most operations undertaken by infantry and cavalry does not need to be an exact science, but aviators do, for a knowledge of what the weather holds is vital to their operations. The Royal Flying Corps had a weather forecaster, or meteorologist, in the shape of one Captain Gold, who found himself attached to Army Headquarters and required to provide a daily weather forecast. If weather forecasting is a black art now, it was even more so in 1915. Gold prepared his forecasts from reports received from the Meteorological Office in London and from Paris. These told him the wind speed and direction in various places in the British Isles and in France every twelve hours. From these, and from about twelve places behind the British front and from reports filed by the forty gas officers stationed along the attack front and who had been trained to take meteorological observations, Gold compiled his forecasts. Unbeknown to Gold, General Haig had, for some weeks, been comparing Gold's forecasts with the actual observations filed by the gas officers. As Gold was not sacked and as Haig continued to consult him, we may assume that the forecasts were more often accurate than not.

The critical day for wind forecasts was 24 September. In the afternoon, once he had compiled his forecasts from the 0700 observations, Gold reported to General Haig, who had both his corps commanders, Gough and Rawlinson, with him. Gold told them that while he did not think there would be a favourable wind that night, there was a possibility – and it was no more than that – of a favourable wind the next morning. At 1800 hours that same day, having compiled his forecast from the 1300 hours observations, Gold reported that there was a better than even (but only just) chance of a favourable wind the next morning. At 2100 hours Gold had compiled a further forecast from the 1800 hours observations, which did not include observations from anywhere in France (they had not yet come in) except those from the gas officers in the British front line. He told Haig that the chances of a favourable wind were increasing, and that the wind that at 1800 hours was blowing from the south-east, would veer round to south-west to west by morning, and that the wind speed would be around twenty miles an hour twenty feet above ground, or ten miles an hour at ground level. At 2145 hours an order went out from First Army confirming the orders issued for the gas attack on the morrow, and saying that Zero Hour would be issued later.

Within the hour, the two brigades in each division of I and IV Corps detailed for the first assault began to move. From their billets in the villages behind the lines long crocodiles of men marched up to the jump off line. Traffic control was in the hands of the military police, and routes were taped and signed. There was almost no reaction from the Germans, and once the attacking troops reached the jump off lines the units that had been holding the front moved back down the communication trenches to assembly areas in rear, prior to going into billets. Incredibly, by 0245 hours on 25 September, the relief had been completed and First Army was ready in all respects. While First Army troops were moving into position the reserve divisions were being moved up under the direction of GHQ. 21 Division marched to billets in the Bethune area, about four and a half miles behind the northern end of the jump off line; units of 24 Division moved to Hallicourt, Houchin and Noeux les Mines and were now from eight to four miles behind the centre of the British front, and the Guards Division moved to Allouagne, about ten miles from the battle area.

North of the La Bassée Canal too, the divisions that would mount diversionary attacks were deploying their assault troops. The northerly division of I Corps, 2 Division, had one brigade north of the canal, and to its north was the Meerut Division of the Indian Corps. The Meerut Division was a regular division of the Indian Army and had arrived in France from India in October 1914, the second division of the corps to reach Europe. Like all the Indian Army, its soldiers were regular long service volunteers, but after taking part in the winter battles around the Ypres Salient, Festubert and Givenchy 1914, and Neuve Chapelle, Second Ypres, Aubers

Ridge and Festubert 1915, the men who had landed at Marseilles were now outnumbered by reinforcements and recruits from India, and had a British Territorial Force battalion in each brigade, in addition to the three Indian or Gurkha and one British battalions already established. Their role was to mount an attack from their positions north-east of Neuve Chapelle, going south-east through the German line, and on through the village of Mauquissart, finishing at the Moulin de Pietre, about 1,500 yards beyond the German firing line. If all went well, they might subsequently be able to push on to Aubers Ridge and link up with 8 Division, of III Corps, who would attack to the north of the Indians.

Like 7 Division, 8 Division had come into existence for this war to command regular units not included in the original six divisions of the BEF. It formed up at Southampton in September and the first formation to come under its command was the regular brigade garrisoning Malta, which had been replaced by Territorial Force units. On deployment to the Western Front in early November 1914, as part of IV Corps, the division was entirely regular except for the divisional cavalry squadron (Northamptonshire Yeomanry) and a Territorial Force signals company. It had fought around Ypres during the winter battles of 1914, and at Neuve Chapelle during the first attempt to capture that village in November and December 1914. It had taken part in the Battle of Neuve Chapelle in March 1915, where it was generally considered not to have done as well as it might have. Major General Davies, the then divisional commander, was almost sacked by his then corps commander, Rawlinson, but was reprieved, promoted and sent off to Gallipoli. By September 1915 and Loos the division was part of III Corps, and the regular element had been much diluted, while an additional four Territorial Force infantry battalions had been added. 8 Division's part in the Loos battle was to mount an attack from its front line 9,000 yards north-east of the Indian attack, from the direction of Bois Grenier towards the Le Bridoux Redoubt. Success there would allow the division to push on to Aubers Ridge and meet the Meerut Division.

At 0300 hours on the morning of 25 September General Haig and his chief of staff, Major General Butler, saw Captain Gold again. Gold was of the view that the wind would be at its most favourable early on, and Haig then issued orders that Zero hour would be at first light, or 0550 hours, with the main infantry assault beginning at 0630 hours. At 0500 Haig personally checked the wind direction again, and ordered no change to his previous instructions. At 0515 he mounted his observation tower. The die was cast.

Notes

1. The British front line between the La Bassée Canal and the junction with the French was not a straight line and followed the lie of the land for 12,000 yards. The frontage to be covered by the gas was 'as the crow flies' for 10,200 yards, needing 8,160 cylinders. Taking into account the 160 to be used by the Indian Corps, there were therefore only enough cylinders to produce twenty-seven minutes of gas, or a little over half that estimated.
2. The most effective way of producing instant, thick smoke, then and now, is by a phosphorus bomb, shell or grenade. It also causes severe burns and is therefore a very effective anti-personnel weapon for clearing buildings, bunkers and dugouts.
3. Each infantry battalion started the war with two medium machine guns (a modification of the Maxim, the British Vickers was water cooled and belt fed, with a cyclic rate of fire of 500 rounds a minute and a maximum effective range of 2,500 yards). In 1915 the establishment of guns was increased to four, with the intention of increasing it to six. By Loos some battalions had received four, but the formation of the Machine-Gun Corps at the end of the year saw the removal of all MMG from battalions, and their substitution by Lewis guns on a much more generous scale.
4. Perfectly legitimately, as Holland was neutral.

CHAPTER IV

The First Day

In the four days of the bombardment, the artillery had been subjecting the Germans lines to an unceasing pounding. Altogether the field guns had fired a total of 233,692 rounds, while the heavies had discharged 22,191. Now, at 0550 hours on 25 September 1915, they increased their rate of fire all along the front. High explosive and shrapnel shells were mixed with smoke, and at the same time gas officers and NCOs of the Special Companies RE began to open the taps on the gas cylinders. Soon a thick cloud of yellowish white chlorine gas began to build up and mix with the smoke from smoke candles lit and thrown over the parapet by the infantry. If the wind continued in the right direction and the right speed, the gas cloud, mixed with smoke, would drift gently over the German trenches. The result was mixed.

In the north, opposite 2 Division, the wind did not move at all, and neither did the gas, whereas the next-door division, 9 Division, found that the gas did exactly what it was supposed to do. In the centre of the attack, in front of 7, 1 and 15 Divisions the results varied widely: in some areas it did as expected, in others it blew back towards the British troops preparing to assault, and in some places it seemed to do nothing at all, save loiter for hours until eventually dissipating and floating away. To the south of the assault, opposite 47 Division, the gas again went exactly where it was wanted, except at the extreme south of the front, where even when all the cylinders had been discharged the cloud had still not reached the German firing line.

The divisions to the north who were to carry out the diversionary attacks also benefited from the four-day bombardment, although they had rather less ammunition than did their comrades who would launch the main offensive. On 8 Division's front a complete battery – six guns – of eighteen pounders had been manhandled up to the firing line and dug in with their barrels camouflaged and facing the German line. The assault here was to take place at 0430 hours, two hours before the main attack, and there was no gas allocated. There should have been smoke, but it was ineffective, due to the wind blowing in the wrong direction.

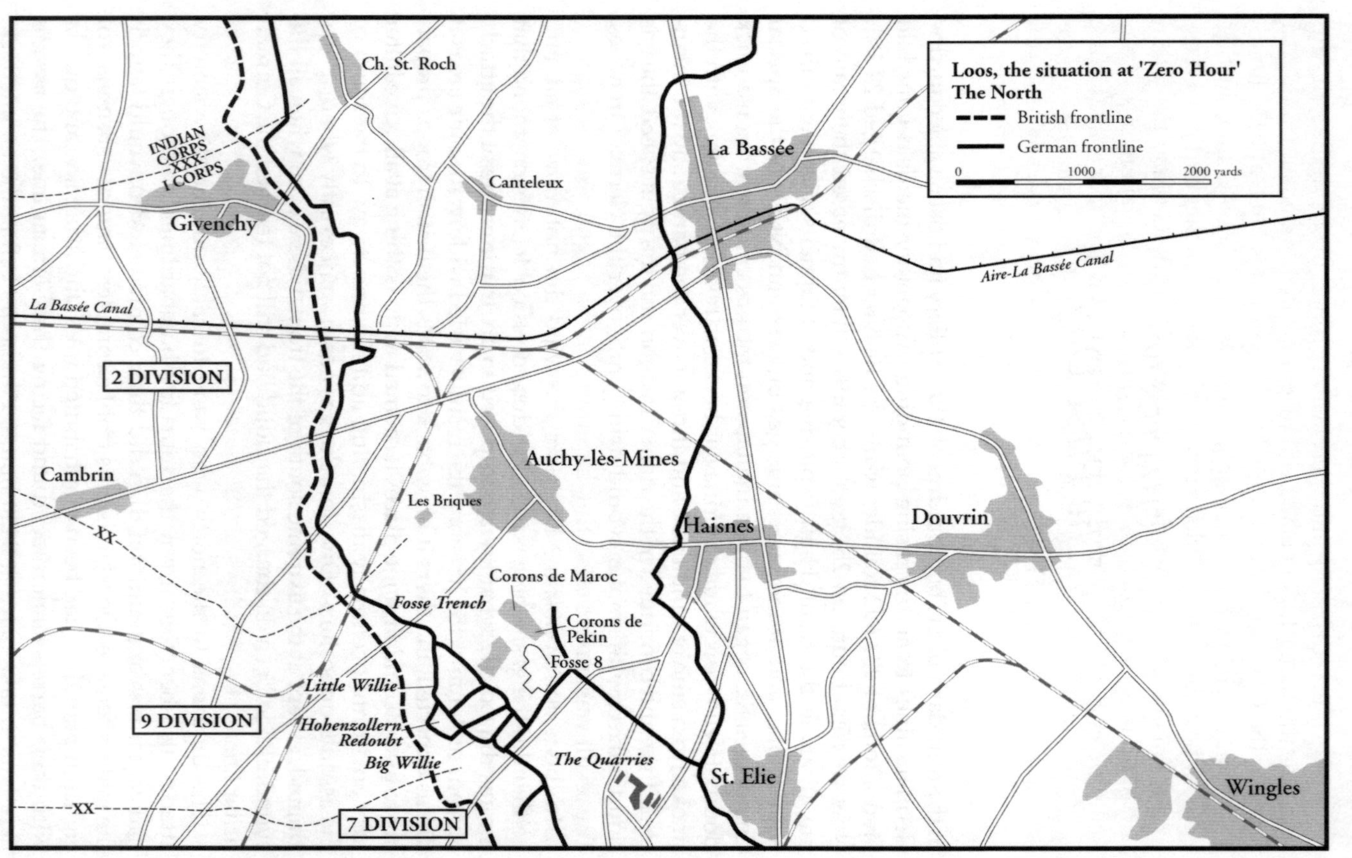
Loos, the situation at 'Zero Hour'
The North
British frontline
German frontline
0
1000
2000 yards
Ch. St. Roch
INDIAN CORPS
XXX
I CORPS
Givenchy
Canteleux
La Bassée
Aire-La Bassée Canal
La Bassée Canal
2 DIVISION
Auchy-lès-Mines
Cambrin
Les Briques
XX
Haisnes
Douvrin
Corons de Maroc
Fosse Trench
Corons de Pekin
Fosse 8
Little Willie
9 DIVISION
Hohenzollern Redoubt
Big Willie
The Quarries
St. Elie
Wingles
XX
7 DIVISION

At 0425 it was drizzling and there was a ground mist, but the guns dug in along the firing line belched out at point blank range and tore great holes in the German parapet opposite. Five minutes later, at 0430 hours, the assault companies of three battalions of 25 Brigade – 2 Lincolnshire, 2 Royal Berkshire and 2 Rifle Brigade – left their trenches and moved out into no-man's-land, as two mines, placed under the German line at the end of tunnels that had been dug laboriously by the Royal Engineers tunnelling companies, exploded with a muffled roar. The roar was muffled because due to a miscalculation the mines failed to break the surface, and craters that the British hoped to seize failed to appear. Even so, the Germans were unable to man their firing line before the British troops were upon them, and there was brief, and confused, bombing and hand-to-hand skirmishing before flares indicated that the British were in possession of the German front line, except for a gap of 200 yards between the Royal Berkshires and the Rifle Brigade.

By around 0600 hours the division had taken almost all of their assigned objectives, and the Rifle Brigade had even penetrated as far as the German support line. The 200 yards of uncaptured firing line now became critical, however, as it covered a communication trench up which the Germans began to feed troops as they got over the surprise of the initial assault. The British soldiers in the German support line could not hold, and withdrew to the captured firing line. German counter-attacks began to come in, crumbling the initial British lodgement area from both flanks. Much use was made of bombs, and while the supply of these items was maintained, there were no fewer than twelve different types on issue to the infantry, all needing different drills to operate them. Inevitably, in the heat of battle, men confused the methods of initiation, and many bombs did not go off, including some with fuses that had to be lit with a match, and which were thrown unlit. Eventually the remnants of the attacking infantry were forced to pull back to their own firing line, and by 1600 hours all the captured positions had been given up. The division had done what it had been asked to do, however: hold the attention of the Germans opposite them, and prevent them being switched to deal with the main offensive to the south.

Farther to the south-west, the Indian Corps diversion did not start so well. Zero Hour was the same as for the main attack, and gas was to be used, albeit only ten minutes of it. For an assaulting frontage of 1,900 yards, ten minutes' gas would have required 380 cylinders, but only 161 could be made available. The Special Companies' men were instructed to discharge all cylinders one after the other, with the gas cloud being thickened up by smoke. At around 0440 hours a German shell burst on the parapet of 3 London Regiment, the battalion holding the trenches to the right of the assaulting troops, and burst some of the cylinders. Some men were affected by chlorine before earth could be shovelled onto the damaged cylinders. At 0550 hours the gas taps were turned on by the Royal Engineers, but changes in wind direction led to many of them being turned off again. The smoke screen, augmented by phosphorus bombs fired by catapult, began to build up and at 0500 hours the assaulting battalions of the Garhwal Brigade moved off. Neither side could see anything through the smoke and the gas, but the Germans did man their front line, and firing through the smoke they could not fail to hit somebody. The two right-hand attacking battalions, 2 Leicesters and 2/3 Gurkha Rifles, hit the German wire, and found it uncut. Desperately trying to find a way round, through or over the wire, their momentum was lost and what had been two battalions operating as one deteriorated into small knots of men trying to work their way along the wire looking for a gap. Only on the left of the brigade did the 2/8 Gurkha Rifles find the wire cut. Bursting through it, they were into the German firing line and then on towards the support line. Unfortunately no one knew what was going on. Visibility was nil because of the smoke, and runners sent back to report never got there. Much the same happened to the Bareilly Brigade, the left-hand assault brigade. Only 4 Black Watch, the right-hand battalion of the brigade, found the wire uncut (it was the same gap as found by 2/8 Gurkhas) and by mid-morning only those two battalions were across the first German line. In fact elements of the division did penetrate the German firing line, did fight through the village of Mauquissart, did reach the German support line and were attacking the Moulin du Pietre – exactly as they had been told to do – but a breakdown in communications and the fact that the Indian right flank was completely exposed owing to what happened to parts of 2 Division astride the La Bassée Canal, made their situation precarious indeed. This narrow Indian salient was put under more and more pressure by the Germans on either side. As last light approached small groups of men fought their way back to their own lines, and by nightfall, all the gains of the day had been given up. Like 8 Division, the Meerut Division had achieved what had been asked of them, and had occupied the attention of large numbers of Germans who would otherwise have been available to oppose the main attack. It was, however, at the considerable cost of nearly 4,000 casualties. The 2/8 Gurkha Rifles were virtually annihilated; of the eleven British Officers of the 69th Punjabis five were killed and three wounded, and Vaughan's Rifles, that started the day with twelve British Officers and 550 Indian ranks, finished it with four British Officers and 299 Indian ranks fit for duty.

Farther south still, 5 Brigade of 2 Division, consisting of four regular and two Territorial Force battalions, was north of the La Bassée Canal and ordered to take the German firing and support lines to the brigade's front, and then to consolidate along the line Chapelle St Roch–Canteloux, or an advance of about 1,000 yards. At Zero Hour the gas duly spewed forth, but the wind had died, and even after the cylinders had been turned off, the gas hung about the British lines with the troops having to wear their smoke helmets. The smoke too depended on the wind, and did not build up where intended, but it and the clouds of gas were seen by the Germans, who had ample time to light small fires on their parapet[1] and put on their own gas masks well before eddies and small gusts of wind brought some of the gas in their direction.

North of the canal only ten minutes of gas, rather than forty, was to be discharged, and at 0600 hours the assaulting wave of 5 Brigade, 2 Oxfordshire and Buckinghamshire Light Infantry, 1 Queens and 2 Highland Light Infantry, left their jump off trenches and moved across no-man's-land towards the German firing line, between one and two hundred yards away. Despite a number of men in the attacking battalions having been affected by gas before putting their smoke helmets on, the two left-hand battalions, the Queens and the HLI, managed to get into the German firing line without too much difficulty, taking a good number of prisoners. Not so the Ox and Bucks, whose left-hand company was heavily affected by a well sited and operated German machine gun, and had to withdraw, eventually getting to the German firing line by a more southerly route, using old mine craters in no-man's-land as cover. Once in the German firing line, it was time to go for their support line, another 800 yards away, and it was at this point that things began to go wrong.

German snipers and machine gunners had recovered from the initial bombardment and began to cause casualties amongst the attackers, and the supply of bombs (hand grenades) carried by the bombing parties of each battalion, and an essential adjunct to fighting within trench systems, began to run out. Not only were there not enough bombs, but many of the 'cricket ball' type, which had to be ignited from a friction igniter carried by bombers before being thrown, would not ignite due to the damp weather. The troops did their best, but they could not secure a foothold in the German support line, and were soon driven back to the firing line. Even here they were unable to hold, and by 0930 hours those who were alive and able to move were all back in their original jump off trenches. The wind had let them down, 188 men had been killed, and there was neither smoke nor gas to cover them across open ground against objectives insufficiently damaged by such artillery as had been made available north of the canal.

Also north of the La Bassée Canal, and also part of 5 Brigade, was 1/9 Highland Light Infantry, a Territorial Force battalion, that was ordered to coordinate its attack along the canal with 6 Brigade, attacking as part of the main operation south of the canal. Despite protests from some of the infantry that the wind was in the wrong direction for gas, the cylinders were nevertheless turned on at 0550 hours. When it was obvious that the gas was not going to move towards the German lines the taps were turned off, leaving clouds of gas lingering menacingly close to the troops waiting to assault. Just five minutes before the Highlanders were about to leave their trenches, a gust of wind blew north, taking a cloud of gas over and into their trenches. The men of two lead platoons, and most of the battalion machine gun section, were caught unprotected with their smoke helmets rolled up on the tops of their heads. Within a minute or so only sixteen men out of the eighty were capable of any effort at all. Two reserve platoons were summoned, and although they came up the communication trench and were in position at the front in the remarkably short time of ten minutes, that they were unable to move until ten minutes after the troops to the south of the canal meant that the Germans facing the HLI were thoroughly awake. A small reconnaissance patrol was sent forward from the jump off line, but none returned. With the artillery bombardment having moved on, German retaliatory fire was now taking effect, and with the element of surprise lost the attack by 1/9 HLI was abandoned.

When 6 and 19 Brigades left their forward trenches at 0630 hours, they too had lost the element of surprise, due to the diversionary attacks to their north, and they too found the gas of little help – indeed in the 6 Brigade area it actually blew back over the assaulting troops. Several contemporaneous reports noted that almost as soon as the artillery bombardment lifted, the German firing line appeared to be fully manned and machine guns on fixed lines were firing across no-man's-land.

The ground between the La Bassée Canal and the Cambrin–La Bassée road, over which 2 Division had to attack, had been brickworks before the war. The opposing trench lines were only about 200 yards apart and there were numerous stacks of bricks, both in no-man's-land and just behind the German firing line. In these latter the Germans had placed their machine guns, and most had not been knocked out by the artillery. The area had been the scene of much local fighting earlier in 1915, and no-man's-land was pockmarked with mine craters and criss-crossed by abandoned sap heads. Brick stacks, craters and saps, to say nothing of German wire, prevented the attacking troops from advancing well spread out across the whole front. Instead they were channelled into a few restricted approaches with the inevitable results. The 2nd Battalion the South Staffordshire Regiment on the left and the 1st Battalion the King's Regiment on the right could make no headway, and although an attack from the canal towpath by C Company of the South Staffs led to a posthumous Victoria Cross for the company commander, Captain Kilby, neither that battalion nor the King's could make any progress, and by 0830 they were back in their own trenches. On 6 Brigade's right 19 Brigade, although less affected by the gas, fared no better. The 2nd Battalion Argyll and Sutherland Highlanders and the 1st Battalion The Middlesex Regiment also faced a fully manned German firing line and uncut wire. They too could not penetrate the first German line and by 0830 hours were either back in their own front line or under what cover could be found in no-man's-land. An attempt by the

2nd Battalion The Royal Welsh Fusiliers to advance where the Middlesex had failed petered out when the battalion lost thirty-six men dead.

So far 2 Division had achieved nothing, and the divisional commander decided to try again at 0930 hours. Men who could move were withdrawn from no-man's-land to allow the artillery to recommence firing, and the battalions that had advanced in the initial attack were withdrawn and replaced by the units in each brigade that so far had not been involved. It soon became apparent, however, that deploying fresh troops and organising a second attack was going to take far longer than at first thought. Major General Horne, commanding 2 Division, consulted with his corps commander, and cancelled the proposed second attack, although the artillery was told to go on bombarding the German firing line until 1130 hours.

For 2 Division, that was the end of the first day of the Battle of Loos. Of the battalions that had spearheaded the attack, the Highland Light Infantry had nine dead, the South Staffords forty-seven, the King's sixty-seven, the Argylls 116 and the Middlesex had fared worst of all with 152 men dead, in a series of actions that lasted little more than two hours.

Next door to 2 Division the experiences of 9 (Scottish) Division were quite different. Here the frontage over which the division would advance was 1,300 yards, mostly dominated by a formidable defence system starting with the Hohenzollern Redoubt. The redoubt was a mass of bunkers, dugouts and machine gun nests, many of them concreted in, and surrounded by wire. It was but 200 yards from the British jump off line, and sat forward of the German firing line, to which it was connected by two communications trenches – North Face and South Face to the British. Preventing the redoubt from being attacked in rear were two flanking trenches, Little Willie, which ran north from the redoubt and connected with Fosse Trench, the main German firing line, and Big Willie, running south-east to the German firing line at Quarry Trench. If 9 Division could take the Hohenzollern Redoubt, it would then have to contend with the German front line 300 yards beyond it, and even if that could be captured the attackers' troubles would by no means be over, for 100 yards behind the German firing line sat The Dump, a huge slag heap that dominated the entire area, and just beyond and to the north of that was Fosse 8, the pithead whose gantry and towers could see well beyond the British line. Connected with Fosse 8 were the Corons (miners' cottages) de Pekin and the Corons de Maroc. 9 Division was being asked to fight its way through a 600-yard deep defensive complex, and even then would still be 500 yards from the German second line. This was nevertheless a critical area. Whilst the Hohenzollern Redoubt was a very tough nut indeed, its nuisance value did not extend much beyond 9 Division's area. The Dump and Fosse 8 however, along with the double Crassier to the south of the British front, could bring direct or indirect fire down anywhere in the area of the offensive, and until those objectives were in British hands, no artillery could be safely moved forward to support a British advance beyond the first German defence line. An awful lot was being asked of a New Army division in its first battle.

At first it seemed as if 9 Division would repeat the misfortunes of 2 Division to their north. The left-hand brigade, 28 Brigade, attacked with the 10th Battalion The Highland Light Infantry on the left and the 6th Battalion The King's Own Scottish Borderers on the right. The HLI found the wind hardly moving at all, and the commanding officer was gassed very early on and the adjutant killed. No sooner had the men crossed their own parapet than the German machine guns began to cause casualties, and while those who could pressed on to the German wire, they found it uncut, were unable to get through and eventually had no option but to withdraw back whence they came. It was unfortunate that the commanding officer and the adjutant of 6 KOSB were both killed by a German shell before they even left the jump off trenches, and here too the wind failed to oblige and the forward companies could only lie down and wait for the gas to move forward. When it did, and the troops got to their feet to follow, they came under heavy German fire, again found the German wire uncut and could only straggle back to their own trenches.

The right-hand brigade of the division, 26 Brigade, attacked with two battalions forward, 5th Battalion The Cameron Highlanders on the left and 7th Battalion the Seaforth Highlanders on the right. Their task was to take the Hohenzollern Redoubt, the German firing line, Fosse 8, the Corons de Pekin and a crossroads north-east of Fosse 8 known as Three Cabarets. Once these objectives were secure, the other two battalions of the brigade, 8th Battalion the Black Watch and 8th Battalion the Gordon Highlanders, would pass through and attack the German second line.

On the right the Seaforths found the smokescreen provided sufficient cover for the leading companies to get into the southern portion of the redoubt, from where they bombed their way up the South Face communication trench to the German firing line, and from there to Fosse 8, the Corons and the Three Cabarets. An hour after leaving the jump off line, the battalion had captured all its objectives and was reorganising along the northern edge of the Corons de Pekin. In its first action the battalion could not have performed better.

On the Seaforths' left the Camerons had an appalling baptism of fire. Firstly they were held up by gas hanging about their own front line, and then when they did advance they came under very heavy fire from their left, where 26 Brigade had been unable to progress. Taking heavy casualties the while, the battalion pressed on through the northern part of the Hohenzollern Redoubt, through the German firing line and up to Fosse 8. Fifteen minutes after the Seaforths the Camerons too were reorganising north of the Corons. They had also done all that had been asked of them, but at a terrible price. Of the 800 men who had left the British line, only around 100 were still able to fight, and only two of the twenty officers.

Now was the time to capitalise on success and push the third brigade of the division, 27 Brigade, on behind 26 Brigade, but there was fire coming from the left, where 28 Brigade should be. Had that brigade's attack failed? Nobody knew, and with the smoke, the gas and the dust raised by the artillery, nobody could see either. No information was coming back from 28 Brigade to 9 Division's headquarters, as even that brigade's headquarters was unsure of what was going on to its front. All this was nobody's fault, but an inevitable result of developing weapon technology having forced dispersion on the battlefield, while communications technology had failed to keep pace. Although nobody on the British side knew it then, the village of Haisnes, on the other side of the second line of German defences, was but lightly held, and could probably have been taken if attacked by the fresh battalions of 27 Brigade.

As it was, it was not until 0910 hours that information eventually reached the headquarters of 9 Division that the attack by 28 Brigade had failed, with no ground captured. The brigade was ordered to attack again, at 1215 hours, after a thirty-minute artillery bombardment. Exactly as ordered, the 9th Battalion The Cameronians (Scottish Rifles) and the 11th Battalion The Highland Light Infantry, the two battalions of the brigade that had been in support for the first attack, moved out of the British trench and started across no-man's-land. They had no chance. Heavy German rifle and machine gun fire began to take its toll as the leading waves emerged from their own trench, and those few men who reached the German wire found it uncut. The brigade commander, Brigadier General Scrase-Dickens, had no option but to order his battalions to withdraw back to the jump off line, which they were barely able to hold, such were the casualties. Of the four battalions in 28 Brigade, 10 HLI and 6 KOSB had lost seven officers and 265 soldiers and nine officers and 261 soldiers killed in the first attack; and in the second attack 9 Cameronians and 10 HLI had seven officers and 235 soldiers killed between them.

It was 28 Brigade's misfortune that they had attacked the only portion of 9 Division's front where the German wire could not be seen from the British lines. As the 18 pounders seemed to have cut the wire satisfactorily elsewhere, it was assumed that they had done so here too. The division should have ordered 28 Brigade to send patrols out at night to check, but they did not as they did not wish to risk casualties from their own shelling. This was understandable, but wrong. Brigadier Scrase-Dickens, 53 years old, personally brave and very experienced, should have insisted that his battalions in the line send out patrols, but he did not. There might have been some friendly fire deaths,[2] but they would have been far fewer than actually occurred through the failure to find out that the wire had not been cut.

Once the divisional commander realised that 28 Brigade was now incapable of any further action, he ordered his third brigade, 27 Brigade, forward to reinforce 26 Brigade. The plan had been that the brigade would wait in the support trenches and then move up into the firing line as soon as the troops occupying it had moved off into the attack. There were two communication trenches for that purpose, but when 27 Brigade began to move forward they found these trenches blocked with wounded being brought down them. There were frequent hold ups and the trenches were under constant German shell fire, with the result that casualties began to occur before the battalions even got to the firing line. Despite German shelling, the lead battalions of 27 Brigade, 11th and 12th Battalions The Royal Scots, reached the area of Fosse 8 and advanced towards Haisnes. But it was now too late. The Germans had brought up reinforcements and heavy fire was coming down. The Scots tried to advance using fire and movement, with short sharp rushes, and although some soldiers did get into the outskirts of Haisnes, they could neither hold nor be reinforced, and eventually they were forced to pull back to the area of Fosse 8. The important thing now was to keep what had been gained, and the infantry and the divisional engineers set to to improve and reverse the captured trenches. It was now raining hard, and rifles were beginning to clog while the fuses of the locally made grenades would not light. Help was forthcoming from the artillery, however, and a mountain battery of the Royal Garrison Artillery managed to get right up to Fosse 8, where it provided invaluable fire support for the infantry.

As night fell, 28 Brigade had made no progress at all, but 26 Brigade held Fosse 8 and the Dump, while 27 Brigade was also forward and in touch with 7 Division on the right. The day had cost 26 Brigade twenty officers and 561 Other Ranks dead; while in 27 Brigade the butcher's bill was six officers and 201 Other Ranks.

7 Division were to attack a frontage of 1,200 yards from the south of the Hohenzollern Redoubt as far as the east-to-west running Hulluch Road. Here too the gas had not performed as was hoped, and while the wind was blowing in the right direction it was not nearly strong enough, and many soldiers of the first wave, despite taking anti-gas precautions, were affected. The left-hand brigade, 22 Brigade, found the gas either not moving at all, or drifting along the British trenches, and they found the smokescreen of much more help. The two lead battalions, the 2nd Battalion the Royal Warwickshire Regiment and the 1st Battalion The South Staffordshire Regiment came under heavy fire from the Pope's Nose Redoubt, but they did get to the German wire. Unfortunately the wire was partly hidden by long grass, and had not been cut in nearly enough places. A few men did force their way through and did get into the German firing line, but there were not nearly enough of them, the commanding officer of the Royal Warwicks was killed and for a while it seemed as if

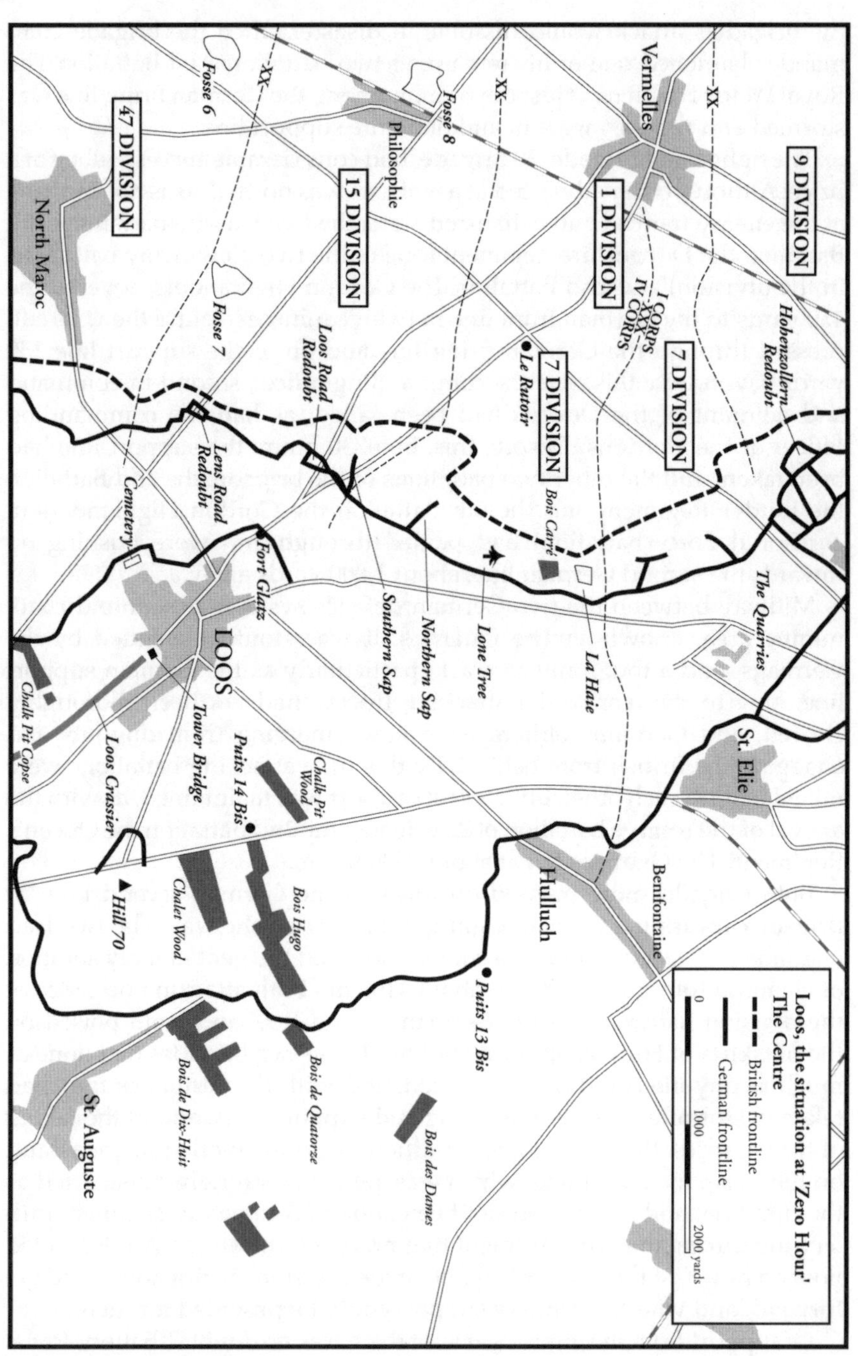
Loos, the situation at 'Zero Hour'
The Centre
British frontline
German frontline
0
1000
2000 yards
9 DIVISION
1 DIVISION
7 DIVISION
7 DIVISION
15 DIVISION
47 DIVISION
I CORPS
IV CORPS
XX
Vermelles
Philosophie
Fosse 8
Fosse 6
Fosse 7
North Maroc
Hohenzollern Redoubt
Le Rutoir
Loos Road Redoubt
Lens Road Redoubt
Cemetery
Fort Glatz
Bois Carré
La Haie
The Quarries
Lone Tree
Northern Sap
Southern Sap
LOOS
Tower Bridge
Loos Crassier
Chalk Pit Copse
Chalk Pit Wood
Puits 14 Bis
St. Elie
Hulluch
Benifontaine
Bois Hugo
Chalet Wood
Hill 70
Puits 13 Bis
Bois de Quatorze
Bois de Dix-Huit
Bois des Dames
St. Auguste

the brigade's attack would dissolve in disaster. Then the brigade commander launched one of his remaining two battalions, 1st Battalion The Royal Welch Fusiliers, at just the right moment, the German firing line was stormed and the men were in and on to the support line.

The right-hand brigade, 20 Brigade, had considerable success, albeit at a price. Although they advanced at a walk, as was normal so as not to arrive at the enemy trench in an exhausted state, the two leading battalions, 8th Battalion the Devonshire Regiment (one of the two New Army battalions in the division) and 2nd Battalion The Gordon Highlanders, covered the 450 yards to the German front line in twelve minutes, found the wire cut, pressed through the German firing line and on to the support line 150 yards beyond. By this time the commanding officer, second-in-command and adjutant of the Devons had been killed, as had the commanding officer of the Gordons. Despite this, by 0730 hours the support line had been taken, and the other two battalions of the brigade, the 2nd Battalion the Border Regiment and the 6th Battalion the Gordon Highlanders (a Territorial Force battalion) had passed through and were pushing on towards the second German line, about 1,000 yards away.

Midway between the two German defence systems was an old chalk mining area, known as The Quarries. It was stoutly defended by the Germans, and a tough nut to crack, particularly as the German support line, now to the rear of the attacking troops, had not been thoroughly cleared, and German soldiers were now emerging from dugouts and engaging the British from behind. By this time attacking battalions were mixed in with each other, but control of a sort was maintained, as with the arrival of the reserve battalion of 22 Brigade, the 2nd Battalion the Queen's Regiment, The Quarries fell at about 0930 hours.

Both brigades now pressed on towards the German second line, 20 Brigade capturing a German eight-gun battery on the way. The two lead battalions – 8 Devons and 2 Gordons – adopted the gentlemanly solution of claiming four guns each. By about 1100 hrs both attacking brigades of the division had reached the German second line, and were poised on the outskirts of Hulluch and Cité St Elie. These two brigades had done as much as anyone could have expected, and with the casualties they had taken in storming the German firing and support lines, and in the taking of the Quarries, they were in no condition to mount another major assault on the German second line, which was almost as strongly constructed as the first line, and which had not been subjected to nearly as much artillery fire during the bombardment that preceded the attack. All depended now on how fast the reserve brigade of the division, 21 Brigade, could get forward, and whether artillery support could be provided for them.

Of support from the gunners at least there was no doubt. T Battery, Royal Horse Artillery, had managed to get an artillery observation officer up to Gun Trench, about 500 yards south-west of Cité St Elie, and over a telephone line strung out behind him he was able to direct the fire of his battery onto the German line. Soon the whole battery appeared, coming straight up the Hulluch road at the gallop, to the cheers of the British infantry and too fast for German artillery to react. In minutes all six eighteen pounders[3] were safely ensconced in Gun Trench ready to support the next advance.

The units of 21 Brigade had begun the day between two and three miles behind the British front line, with orders to move forward once the attacking troops left their jump off lines. To begin with the battalions moved along communication trenches, but these were rapidly becoming congested and the brigade commander found it faster, and no less safe, to order his men out of the communication trenches and to advance over open ground. By 0930 the whole brigade, less the 2nd Battalion Royal Scots Fusiliers who had not yet arrived, was assembled in the old British front line. There was then some confusion as to what exactly was happening, and after several false starts two battalions, 2nd Battalion The Green Howards and 4th Battalion The Cameron Highlanders (Territorial Force), were sent off to support 22 Brigade, and Brigadier General Watts, commanding 21 Brigade, now set out to do with his remaining two battalions what should have been done by four. At around 1130 hours these two battalions left the old British front line, intending to pass over the first German line, cross Gun Trench, and then attack Cité St Elie. They moved off with 2nd Battalion The Wiltshire Regiment on the left and 2nd Battalion the Bedfordshire Regiment on the right. Each battalion covered a frontage of 250 yards, with the Bedford's right on the Hulloch road. Each battalion moved with two companies forward, each company in column of platoons with a fifty-yard gap between each. This meant that the two battalions were advancing in eight waves, and the whole was occupying an area 500 yards wide by around 350 yards deep.

At first all went well, and only a few stray artillery or mortar rounds came anywhere near. Then, as the battalions were crossing the increasingly open ground on the approach to Gun Trench, German fire increased and men began to go down. Try as they might neither battalion could get beyond Gun Trench. It was soon clear that unless the defence of Cité St Elie could be reduced drastically by artillery, there was no point in further infantry attacks. The other two battalions of 21 Brigade, 2 Green Howards and 4 Camerons, had also come to a halt, being unable to advance much beyond The Quarries. There would be no further progress that day, in daylight at least.

The Northern division of IV Corps, 1 Division, was to attack on a 1,400-yard front south of the Hulluch road (which was the inter-corps boundary). On the centre of the advance, and about two thirds of the way across no-man's-land, was a cherry tree. Marked on the British maps as 'Lone Tree', despite the artillery and small arms fire to which the area had been subjected since the front settled down here in 1914, the tree not only survived, but had actually flowered in May 1915. By the time of Zero Hour for Loos it had undergone another intensive shelling, and while most of its branches and all of its flowers had gone, fifteen feet of trunk was still there, and while of no tactical significance, it did act as a reference point for troops navigating in smoke and gas.

Jump off trenches for 1 Division had been dug 300 yards forward of their firing line, and about 500 yards away from the German first line. Between the British and the Germans was Grenay Ridge, which prevented the German firing line from being seen until the British breasted the high ground. It was known from air reconnaissance, however, that the Germans had pushed out two saps, Northern Sap and Southern Sap, which ran into no-man's-land for 400 yards or so, and it was thought that these saps probably held machine guns, thus dominating the area between the saps. Northern Sap was on the southern boundary of 1 Division, while Southern Sap was in the 15 Division sector, 300 yards farther south. Rather than attempt to attack the German trench between the two saps directly, and thus have to cross this killing zone, the plan was for this portion of the trench to be dealt with by 15 Division, who would send bombing parties from south to north up it, once the trench to the south of Southern Sap had been taken. For 1 Division, this meant that there was a risk of flanking fire coming at them from their right, at least until 15 Division had captured the southern portion of its frontage.

The attacking brigades of 1 Division would be 2 Brigade on the right and 1 Brigade on the left, with 3 Brigade in reserve. Once through the first German line the direction of advance of each brigade would change. 2 Brigade would veer south-east to link up with 15 Division, poised to assault the second German line, while 1 Brigade would keep going east. There would therefore be an increasing gap between the two brigades once they started to diverge, and to fill it a two-battalion ad hoc unit was created by removing the fifth (Territorial Force) battalion that was attached to each of 1 and 2 Brigades. Consisting of the London Scottish[4] and the 9th Battalion The King's Regiment, plus a field company Royal Engineers, Green Force – from the commander, Lieutenant Colonel Green of the Royal Sussex Regiment – would come under command of divisional headquarters and move behind the leading brigades, ready to fill the gap once the attacking troops crossed the Lens–La Bassée road.

Once again, gas for 1 Division was, at least initially, more of a hindrance than a help. The wind, blowing towards the German lines when the order to switch on the cylinders was given, quickly veered round until it was coming from the south, and drifted along the British trenches. In 2 Brigade the two leading battalions, 1st Battalion the Loyal North Lancashire Regiment and 2nd Battalion The King's Royal Rifle Corps each had around 200 men affected before the cylinders could be switched off, and while most would speedily recover, they were unavailable for the initial assault. The wind then changed again, blowing in more or less the correct direction this time, and the taps on the cylinders were opened once more. Because of the delay, however, when the men left their jump off positions they found that they were keeping pace with the gas and again numbers of soldiers were coughing and spluttering before they donned their smoke helmets. It was 2 Brigade's misfortune that as they breasted the gentle rise of Grenay Ridge, they came under sustained machine gun fire from guns not identified by air reconnaissance, and from enfilade fire directed from that section of German trench to the brigade's right, which was so far untroubled by 15 Division.

Soon the gas and smoke began to disperse, and without the cover from view they provided, the casualties inflicted on the brigade increased. Worse was to come, for when the leading companies at last hit the German wire, they found that it was uncut and that they were unable to get through it. Initially men took such cover as they could find, while they attempted to cut through the obstacle belt, but the German fire was too intense and eventually, in dribs and drabs, individuals and small groups of British soldiers began to extricate themselves and make their way back to their own trench line.

Ironically, where the regulars of 2 Brigade had failed, the New Army battalions of 1 Brigade succeeded, albeit at a price. The lead battalions, 8th Battalion The Berkshire Regiment and the 10th Battalion The Gloucestershire Regiment were also affected by the gas but not as badly as their comrades in 2 Brigade. On the right 10 Glosters took the German firing line and pressed on to the support line. The battalion came under very heavy fire from the support line, and took many casualties, before the Germans holding the line broke and ran back along the communication trenches to Hulluch village. With not much more than half the battalion left capable of doing their duty, the Glosters consolidated their position in the support line. On the left the 8th Berkshires did even better, pushing on through the firing and support lines until by 0800 hours they had reached the southern limits of Gun Trench. At this point the reserve battalion of the Brigade, 1st Battalion The Cameron Highlanders, came up and with the Berkshires pressed on up and through Gun Trench, capturing three German artillery pieces on the way, which went to join those captured by 7 Division.

The two battalions pressed on to the Lens–La Bassée road, and could see the village of Hulluch, from where it appeared that German troops were withdrawing. What happened next is unclear. Whether or not some independent spirits had actually penetrated Hulluch, brigade headquarters got the impression that Hulluch was about to fall to the British. In reality, the commanders of the remnants of the three battalions facing that village with several dead were united in thinking that a coordinated attack by them had no realistic prospects of success, and they decided to wait for the arrival of the reserve brigade, 3 Brigade, and Green Force.

At this stage 1 Brigade's attack had come to a complete halt, with increasing numbers of men making their way back to their own trenches. The brigade commander ordered the so far uncommitted 2nd Battalion The Royal Sussex Regiment with two companies of the 1st Battalion The Northamptonshire Regiment to advance across the British jump off line, collect whatever was left of the Loyals on the way and attack the German firing line. The KRRC, more heavily hit by the first attack than the Loyals, were ordered to remain in the British front line.

Now occurred a period of uncertainty and confusion inevitable in conditions of wide battlefield dispersion, restricted visibility and no means of instant long-distance communication. Initially a report was received by Headquarters 2 Brigade that the Royal Sussex had reached the German wire and were through it and into the trenches beyond. This was duly passed back to divisional headquarters, to be contradicted when it was discovered that the first message was incorrect. To the divisional commander, Major General Holland, it appeared that while his 1 Brigade had made substantial progress, 2 Brigade had not moved forward at all. If this situation was not rectified, then the chances of the division to Holland's right, 15 Division, being able to bomb up as far as Northern Sap were slim, and – worse – a gap in the British line of over 1,000 yards from Lone Tree down to Southern Sap could prevent any general First Army advance beyond the first German line. As the intelligence summary compiled before the offensive had suggested that the area in front of 2 Brigade was relatively lightly held, it seemed that one more hard knock could collapse the German defence. Stressing the importance of closing the gap, Holland ordered 3 Brigade to attack to the left of 1 Brigade, while Green Force were to assault the German line to the right of 2 Brigade.

Once again, the difficulties of communication made themselves felt. Headquarters 1 Division was located at Marsden's Keep, 3,500 yards behind the jump off line. Green's Force had originally been at Le Rutoire, but had started moving east behind and between 1 and 2 Brigades once the infantry attack started. General Holland sent his order to Colonel Green at 0910 hours. It did not reach Green until 1055 hrs, having taken an hour and three quarters to travel 2,500 yards. The message was sent by runner and successive runners were hit by German fire or got lost. Even once Green received the order, it still took another hour to get to his two battalions, a few hundred yards away, such was the effect of the German retaliatory artillery that swept the open ground with shrapnel.

Green attacked with a battalion either side of Lone Tree but could make no impression on the German wire, covered as it was by intense fire from the defenders. To their north 3 Brigade found it equally difficult to penetrate the German line, and it was not until the reserve battalion of that brigade, 2nd Battalion the Welch Regiment, and the divisional reserve, 1st Battalion the Gloucestershire Regiment, were fed into the battle that the Welch did manage to get through the German firing line and took the surrender of a group of Germans in the support line. Elements of 1 and 3 Brigade now pressed on towards the German second line, stopping to reorganise on the Lens–La Bassée road. Farther south a battalion-sized group of Germans, commanded by a captain and holding their firing line, finding themselves outflanked by the British infantry along the road, surrendered to Green's Force. This allowed Green and 2 Brigade to push on across the German front and support lines, and by about 1730 hours they too were digging in along the Lens–La Bassée road. On the right of 2 Brigade the Northamptonshires had made contact with the left-hand battalion of 15 Division, 6th Battalion the Cameron Highlanders, in Bois Hugo on the inter-divisional boundary. Ahead of 1 Division there seemed to be hardly any Germans manning the second defence line, although men on the division's right-hand boundary could see groups of Germans moving to the rear and north of Hill 70, in the 15 Division area.

Now was the time for 1 Division to surge on over the German second line, capture Hulluch and menace Wingles, where there were a number of German headquarters. That was not to be, for 1 Division now had only about a quarter of its Zero Hour strength, and there were gaps between brigades and between battalions within brigades. There were no fresh troops instantly to hand, and all the soldiers could do was to dig themselves in along the road, while sending patrols out to establish contact with flanking units and formations. By the time night fell, the divisional commander was aware that there were gaps in his frontage, but he was not aware that there was still a 1,200-yard gap between the inner flanks of his two leading brigades, 1 and 2. This had come about because Green's force had perforce been directed to help 2 Brigade, rather than filling the gap, and because 1 Brigade were trying to support 3 Brigade. Neither 1 nor 2 Brigade seems to have been aware of the whereabouts of either Green's Force or that the Northamptonshires, of 2 Brigade, had managed to establish themselves in Bois Hugo. This ignorance, which extended to Headquarters IV Corps, was to have repercussions the next day.

The men of 15 (Scottish) Division were rather more fortunate than the formations to their north, in that over their 1,500-yard front the wind blew more or less where it was supposed to, and the gas did roll slowly towards and over the German first line. Even so, there was some hesitation amongst the leading British infantry during the gas discharge, when at first it seemed to hang about on home territory, rather than move across no-man's-land. At 0630, when Second Lieutenant Young, the officer commanding the lead platoon of 7th Battalion the King's Own Scottish Borderers, ordered the advance, nobody moved. Young turned to the company piper, and ordered him to play. Piper Daniel Laidlaw climbed out of the jump off trench and joined Young on the parapet, where he proceeded to march calmly up and down the parapet playing 'Blue

Bonnets over the Border', despite German harassing fire coming through the gas and smoke. The men of the battalion, and men of other battalions nearby, Scottish martial ardour aroused and mixed, perhaps, with some embarrassment, reacted, and swarmed out and over the parapet and on towards the German lines. Laidlaw followed them up, piping as he went, and despite being wounded at least twice, only returned to his own lines once he was sure the men had taken their first objective. There is a special deity that looks after the very young, the simple minded, the drunk and the unbelievably brave, and it was looking after Laidlaw that day, for he survived both the battle (to be awarded the Victoria Cross), and the war.

In many ways Laidlaw was an unusual recipient of the Victoria Cross, for while extreme bravery is often shown by the very young or the very inexperienced, who may not realise the consequences of their actions, Laidlaw was an old soldier and must have known exactly the risk he was taking. Aged 40 at the time of Loos, Laidlaw had joined the Durham Light Infantry as a regular soldier in 1896, and served with its second battalion until transferring to the KOSB in 1898 as a piper. He completed his sixteen-year regular engagement in 1912, still a private soldier, when he was discharged and transferred to the reserve, until being mobilised in 1914.

Despite the gas being more helpful to 15 Division than to most others, the division was nevertheless required to advance five miles, taking redoubts and trench systems on the way. In the German first line of defences there were two strong redoubts, the Loos Road Redoubt, just south of the Southern Sap, and the Jew's Nose Redoubt,[5] towards the right (southern) end of the division's front. Then there was the town of Loos itself and, beyond Loos and about 1,000 yards forward of the German second line of defences, Hill 70, so named by the French because it was seventy metres above sea level. This feature dominated the battlefield between the two German lines, and was assumed by the British to be well fortified and garrisoned.

The division attacked in five columns, each forward brigade – 46 on the left and 44 on the right – providing two columns and the reserve brigade – 45 – furnishing one. Numbers One, Two, Three and Four Columns each consisted of one battalion of infantry with a section of Royal Engineers and a platoon from the divisional pioneer battalion. This particular grouping was decided upon because of the large number of German fortifications spread over the divisional frontage. Number Five Column, directed to bomb up Southern Sap, was composed of two companies of 12th Battalion The Highland Light Infantry and the machine gun section of that battalion, with 63 Trench Mortar Battery in support. The remaining two battalions of each brigade were in support and reserve.

Once Piper Laidlaw and Second Lieutenant Young (who, unlike Laidlaw, did not survive the battle) had got the leading infantry moving, the division made good progress. As the gas and smoke rolled over the German first defence line the volume of fire from it slackened noticeably. By 0705 hours most of the German firing line had been occupied, but not without cost: the Jew's Nose was a hard nut to crack and the 9th Battalion the Black Watch had two officers and 233 soldiers killed taking it. On the extreme left of the division, Number Five column found that the Southern Sap was, after all, but a dummy trench, which would give them no cover at all, and which was covered by very heavy fire from the German firing line behind it. As we have seen, 2 Brigade of 1 Division was initially unable to get forward, and this meant that Number Five Column also came under enfilade fire from the German line to the north.

An officer who witnessed 15 Division's attack described how the soldiers, despite having a maximum of only twelve months' service and training, moved calmly and without fuss across no-man's-land. 'I saw one man whose kilt had got caught in our wire as he passed through a gap; he did not attempt to tear it off, but, carefully disentangling it, doubled up to his correct position in the line and went on.'[6] It might be unkind to remark that having to pay for damaged kit sometimes has more effect than conventional discipline.

Pushing on down the slope the advancing infantry came up against uncut wire in front of Loos village. Fortunately the British artillery, while it had not cut the wire, had done considerable damage to the German communication trenches, and 9 Black Watch and 8 Seaforths, reinforced by 10 Gordons and 7 Camerons, were able to get through the wire and into the village. Here the Germans were defending, using houses, cellars and makeshift barricades, and some vicious hand to hand fighting took place. After the expenditure of prodigious amounts of grenades, 44 Brigade had fought their way through the village and by 0800 hours some of their men had reached Hill 70, albeit not having cleared all the cellars and houses in the village. On the left 46 Brigade too were approaching the hill, although Number Five column was still held up at the junction of Southern Sap and the German firing line. Once through Loos village the division was supposed to attack Cité St Auguste, about 1,000 yards due east, but in fact most of 44 Brigade, deflected towards the south-east by the lie of the ridge of which Hill 70 was a part, became deflected from their proper objective and caught up in the attack on Cité St Laurent, south-east of Loos and actually the responsibility of 47 Division. Withal, 15 Division had done well, but now they were to be the victims of their own success. On their left the right-hand brigade of 1 Division had been unable to get forward, and on their right 47 Division was still west of Loos. This meant that 15 Division's advance had outstripped that of the troops on its flanks, and was therefore in danger not only of coming under enfilade fire, but of being counter-attacked from the north and from the south.

In the meantime, men swarmed up the western slope of Hill 70. Unusually, the Germans seemed to have fallen below their normally high standards in the construction of defence works, for far from Hill 70 being strongly fortified and garrisoned, the Scots found a mixture of German infantry and pioneers trying to complete a partially constructed redoubt on the top of the hill. The British infantry passed over the hill, driving the Germans before them. Then, as they reached the slopes leading down towards Cité St Auguste, things began to go wrong.

Looking only at the map and at the objectives gained by 15 Division, the impression gained is of an orderly advance, well under control and with commanders at all levels aware of what was happening. The reality was very different. By the time the leading waves of the division had reached Hill 70 most of the officers and senior NCOs of the leading waves had either been killed or incapacitated. Platoons and companies within battalions had become mixed up and battalions themselves were no longer coherent formations, rather men followed the nearest officer or NCO, regardless of what battalion he belonged to, and headed for landmarks that they could see and recognise. Once over Hill 70 familiar features on the ground disappeared, and the landscape was unfamiliar and known only from the map.

At the southern bottom of Hill 70 was a group of houses known as the Dynamitière, originally used to store explosives for the mines, and into these went the Germans driven off Hill 70 who, supported by their comrades in the Cité St Auguste, began to bring down rifle, machine gun and mortar fire on the British infantry descending the slope. The men of 44 Brigade, 200 yards down the slope, were stopped in their tracks and began to take what cover they could. On the division's left, 46 Brigade could still not make contact with 1 Division, thus leaving their own flank in the air.

At around 1100 hours both leading brigades began to retire. Captain Strong, the only officer of 8 Seaforths still alive and unwounded, and Lieutenant Johnson Royal Engineers tried to organise the occupation of the incomplete German redoubt on the top of the hill, but machine gun fire and artillery were sweeping the crest line, and the best that could be done was to improvise a shallow firing line to the west.

At around 1200 hours the divisional commander, Major General McCracken, ordered his third brigade, 45 Brigade, forward to hold the village of Loos. The division had now committed all its reserves save some machine gun sections and the cavalry squadron, and a message was sent to Headquarters IV Corps advising that corps or army reserves should be committed. This was a sensible recommendation: 15 Division had penetrated deep into German territory, but were now effectively used up. If the momentum of the attack, lost around Hill 70, was to be regained, then fresh troops were needed. There were no corps reserves, nor any army reserves, but a brigade from the reserves under the command of the Commander-in-Chief, Sir John French, was sent. That brigade, 62 Brigade of 21 Division, did not begin to arrive until 1700 hours, by which time the initial initiative had been lost, and it was too late to do very much that day anyway. The whole question of the employment of the reserves will be examined later.

By last light 46 Brigade had at last made contact with the right-hand troops of 1 Division, who had finally managed to deal with the Germans holding them up and had got forward level with 15 Division, and 15 Division had joined up with 47 Division to the south. The men of 15 Division had been fighting for twelve hours; they were exhausted, but they had got farther forward than anyone to their north on that first day of the battle.

The southernmost division attacking along the British frontage, 47 Division, had spent the days before the attack rehearsing its part in it. All officers and NCOs down to and including sergeants were taken up to the firing line to look over the ground across which they would advance; all platoon commanders and platoon sergeants were given a panoramic sketch of their area, and areas behind the lines were taped out to resemble the real objectives so that troops could practise their part in the offensive. All this undoubtedly helped on 25 September, although perhaps some time should have been spent on traffic control, for on the night before the attack one battalion took nine hours to move the nine thousand yards from Noex Les Mines to the jump off line.

As with 15 Division, the gas in the 47 Divisional area was more use than it was to the north. Casualties to the leading waves caused by their own gas were kept to a minimum by making all those waiting to jump off in the first wave wear their smoke helmets until the gas had drifted on, rather than having them rolled up on top of their heads as was the case in other divisions. The extreme right-hand flank of the division, and the boundary between the British and the French, was held by the 21st and 22nd Battalions of The London Regiment, otherwise known as the 1st Surrey Rifles and the Queen's. These two battalions were not to take part in the initial attack but rather operated a system of dummies, worked by a system of strings and pulleys, and designed to make the Germans think that a full-blooded infantry attack was coming at them through the smoke and the gas. The ruse seems to have worked, at least for a time, for fire at the real infantry noticeably slackened, whereas that at the dummies intensified.

The division attacked with 141 Brigade on the left, 140 Brigade on the right and 142 Brigade in reserve. On the left the London Irish, or 18th Battalion the London Regiment, demonstrated what to the English newspapers was a fine example of British pluck, and what to the German newspapers was a fine example of British stupidity, by kicking a football ahead of them as they advanced. Plucky or stupid, 141 Brigade made good progress against their objectives, the Loos/Bethune road along to Loos cemetery, the Chalk Pit, 'Garden City', the south end of Loos village (the north end was the responsibility of 15 Division), Tower Bridge and the crassier running from it south-east towards Lens. Despite German resistance – and the gas appears to have inconvenienced rather than

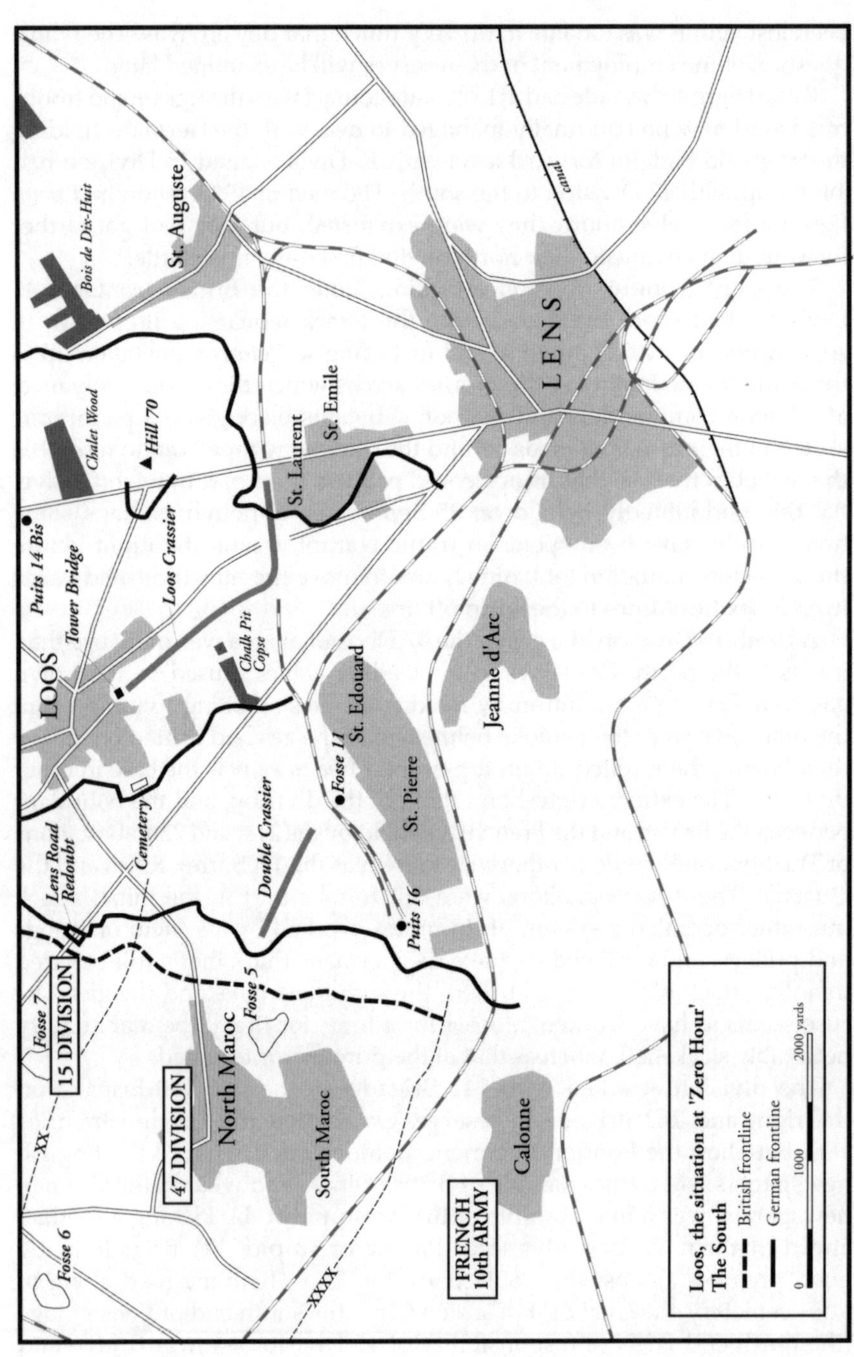
Loos, the situation at 'Zero Hour'
The South
British frontline
German frontline
0
1000
2000 yards
LENS
LOOS
St. Auguste
Bois de Dix-Huit
canal
St. Emile
St. Laurent
Hill 70
Chalet Wood
Puits 14 Bis
Tower Bridge
Loos Crassier
Chalk Pit Copse
St. Edouard
Jeanne d'Arc
St. Pierre
Fosse 11
Double Crassier
Cemetery
Lens Road Redoubt
Puits 16
Fosse 5
Fosse 7
15 DIVISION
47 DIVISION
North Maroc
South Maroc
Calonne
FRENCH 10th ARMY
Fosse 6
XX
XXXX

incapacitated the defenders – 141 Brigade was on all its objectives except one by 0900 hours. The last to fall was Tower Bridge, taken by 19 London, although their commanding officer, Lieutenant Colonel Collison-Morley, was killed in the action. Under the tower of Loos church, also captured by the 19th Battalion, was found a large mine, with the fuse already burning. Despite German shell fire, presumably trying to detonate the mine, Major Blogg, commanding 4th London Field Company Royal Engineers (Territorial Force), exposed and cut the fuse.

The one exception to the success of 141 Brigade was the western end of a narrow wood that ran south-west from the Chalk Pit. This contained a maze of interconnecting trenches which were stoutly defended and which would not be captured for another forty-eight hours.

On the right 140 Brigade advanced on the Double Crassier, and despite some uncut wire and at least one German counter-attack, they too had all their objectives by 0800 hours, including the capture of three field guns and 300 prisoners of war. The rest of the day was spent in consolidating that which had been gained and in joining up the captured trenches to the old British front line by means of communication trenches dug under the supervision of the divisional pioneer battalion and the Royal Engineers. The first day of the battle was coming to a close.

Notes

1. The theory was that the fires caused an updraught of warm air that would carry the gas above the defenders' heads. It sometimes worked.
2. Deaths due to friendly fire, or a 'blue on blue' as it is known now, are not peculiar to 21st century warfare. When decisions have to be made in split seconds and when the fog of war allows only a very incomplete picture of what is going on, such sad but inevitable casualties will always occur.
3. RHA batteries were normally equipped with thirteen pounders because they had to be able to move as fast as the cavalry whom they normally supported. Because this battery was supporting an infantry division, they had been re-equipped with eighteen pounders in June 1915.
4. Actually the 14th Battalion the London Regiment (London Scottish), but always known by the latter title.
5. So called because from the air it resembled a hooked nose. No doubt if it was so named in modern operations, some politically correct Prodnose would cry racism and anti-semitism. In fact there was a lot less anti-semitism in 1914 Britain than in anywhere else in Europe, largely because British Jews saw themselves as Englishmen first and all else second.
6. Stewart, Lt Col J DSO and Buchan, John, *The Fifteenth Scottish Division 1914–1919*, London: Blackwood, 1926.

CHAPTER V

The Reserves

As night fell on 25 September 1915 commanders at all levels surveyed the results of the day's efforts. North of the canal no ground had been gained, but these had been but diversionary operations, and they did prevent the Germans from switching troops or artillery south. That said, the diversionary attacks had not forced the Germans to shift reserves to face them, so their success can only be described as partial. Astride the canal 2 Division had gained no ground at all, but south of that division the other five divisions had made some progress. All had crossed the first German line of defences; 7 Division was poised just short of the second line, while the others were not far short of it. The gas had not, perhaps, been as decisive as had been hoped, partly because of the fickle wind and partly because there was not enough of it, but it had played its part in helping the troops to get forward with insufficient artillery to support them.

All in all it was a good start, but it was not without cost. In total 6,011 infantrymen in the six divisions undertaking the main attack were killed, ranging from the relatively inexpensive 391 deaths in 47 Division to 1,562 in 9 Division. The butcher's bill was not evenly spread amongst battalions either, for in nine battalions nobody had been killed at all, while eight battalions – all of them Scottish – had more than 200 men killed.

The first day of the Somme offensive, 1 July 1916, is generally seen today as the benchmark of British military slaughter, with its 19,000 dead on that first day. The first day of the Loos battle was not much less bloody. Overall the average number of deaths per division on Day One of Loos was 1,001, compared to 1,266 on Day One of the Somme, but 9 (Scottish) Division and 15 (Scottish) Division at Loos with 1,562 and 1,547 were well over the average for the Somme. Of the total dead 1,423 were regular soldiers, from a dwindling band of regulars who had been out since August 1914 or shortly after, and this was one more factor towards the metamorphosis of the British Army from an all regular volunteer force in 1914 to the citizens' army which it became by the later stages of the war.

There were periods in the morning when it looked as if just one more push would see the whole of the German second line collapse – which would have had consequences reaching well beyond the British sector, as it would have forced the Germans to withdraw from in front of the French too. The capture of Fosse 8 and the Dump by 9 Division; 7 Division's occupation of The Quarries; 15 Division's chasing of the Germans off Hill 70 and 47 Division's seizing of the Double Crassier were all significant gains, valuable not just for the sake of capturing them but because of their dominating influence on the ground around and beyond them. All this was achieved relatively early in the day: why then was more advantage not taken to sweep on and capitalise on the disorganisation and confusion that had been sewn amongst the German defenders?

It is axiomatic in all forms of warfare that success must be exploited. This nearly always means the deployment of fresh troops, because those who have captured the first objective are often too tired, or have taken too many casualties, to continue the movement. Fresh troops means reserves, and commanders at all levels will always keep some of their troops back to be used to exploit advantage, or to deal with disaster. In this war, with the inherent difficulties of communication during an attack, the only way a commander could influence the battle once his lead troops had left their jump off positions, was in the timely and judicious employment of his reserves. As a very rough rule of thumb, between one quarter and one third of available troops would generally be held in reserve: a battalion would have a reserve company (of four), a brigade a reserve battalion (of four), a division a reserve brigade (of three). At corps and army level, the size of the reserve would depend on the number of divisions in the corps and the number of corps in the army, but both corps and army commanders would certainly have them.

In the Loos battle each division assaulted with two brigades, leaving the third brigade in rear. This third brigade was not a proper reserve, however, as it was always intended to deploy it for a specific task. Neither of the two corps had any reserve, and First Army had virtually nothing. The reason for this was quite simply because there were no troops to spare to form reserves. As we have seen, to ensure success across the frontage over which the British were to attack required far more than the six divisions allocated, but there were no more divisions available – the British Commander-in-Chief considered that the front could not be thinned out elsewhere any more than it already had been. If only six divisions were available for the assault, then overwhelming artillery would be needed, but that did not exist either, so gas was used to compensate, with mixed results.

There was, of course, a reserve available for this offensive. It consisted of three divisions, or one third of the attacking force, and the Cavalry Corps. The three divisions were the Guards, 21 Division and 24 Division. The Guards held, and hold, a unique position in the British Army. They are the monarch's personal troops, were until recently forbidden to serve farther away from the United Kingdom than Suez (in case the monarch

1. Field Marshal Sir John French. Aged 63 when the Battle of Loos opened, French had been CIGS, the professional head of the army, before resigning as a result of the 'Curragh Incident' of March 1914. Recalled at the outbreak of war, as he had been unofficially assured that he would be, he commanded the British Expeditionary Force until being relieved of command in December 1915, partly because of his handling of the Loos battle. A dashing and thoroughly competent cavalry commander in the South African War, French was too emotional and lacked the robustness and mental resilience needed for this, the most intensive war in Britain's history. (IWM Q48355)

2. Men of the 1/8 London Regiment, otherwise known as the Post Office Rifles, carrying out signals training before deployment to France as part of 140 Brigade 47 (London) Division (Territorial Force). Although by Loos there were three entirely Territorial Force divisions in France only 47 Division went into action in the initial attack. In general Territorial soldiers were good material, but at the beginning of the war much of their equipment was obsolete, they could not be compelled to deploy overseas and they were short of training. The Territorial Force was, however, the best reserve the British were likely to get, and by September 1915 almost half the infantry in France was Territorial, and the deficiencies were being rectified. The main method of communication was still by telephone, and these soldiers are practising CW (Morse), which worked well in defence but was more difficult in an attack. (IWM Q53714)

Opposite: **3.** General Sir Douglas Haig. Aged 54 when Loos opened, in the years before the war Haig had already proved himself as a thoroughly professional commander and staff officer. Largely responsible for creating the Expeditionary Force and the Territorial Force that supported it, he started the war as one of French's two corps commanders, becoming commander First Army at Christmas 1914, by which time the build-up of the BEF justified the creation of two armies. The obvious successor to French, he started the war in command of two divisions and ended it in command of sixty-one. Traduced by self-serving politicians, Haig never received the credit that he deserved as the man who expanded, trained and deployed the BEF until in 1918 it was the only army capable of defeating the German army in battle. This photograph was taken later, sometime after February 1917, when he was Commander-in-Chief of the BEF. (IWM Q23636)

4. HM King George V, accompanied by FM Sir John French, inspecting 1st Battalion Scots Guards prior to their deployment to France. The officer to French's left is of the newly raised (March 1915) Welsh Guards. Often envied and sometimes teased by the rest of the army, the Guards were (and still are) the backbone of the Infantry. (IWM Q48355)

Opposite: **5.** On deployment to France battalions were initially supplied with interpreters, although these became rarer as the size of the BEF increased. Interpreters tended to be either conscripted students or teachers who were bilingual, or old soldiers whose commanding officers wanted rid of them and who spoke a few words of English. These may not have been much help linguistically, but were of enormous assistance when it came to scrounging food or comforts from the locals. This one would appear to be of the latter category. (IWM Q57452)

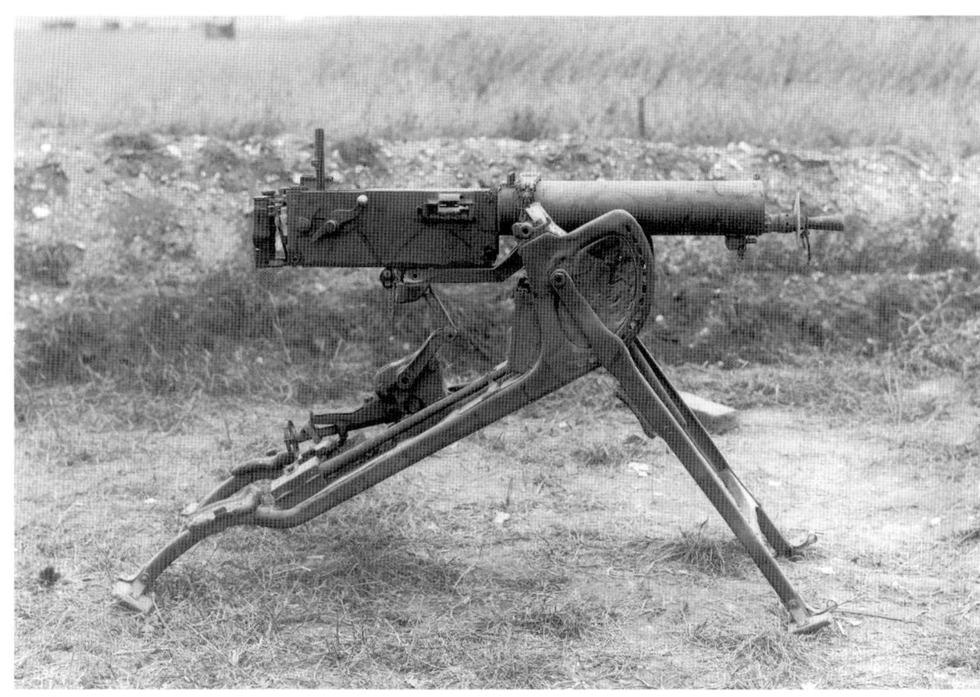

6. A German Medium Machine Gun as used at Loos. Both the British and the Germans employed versions of the gun designed by Hiram Maxim in the 1890s. This one is the 08 pattern with a cyclic rate of fire of 300 rounds per minute (later increased to 450) and a range of 2,500 yards. Machine guns were sited in enfilade, that is they fired not directly at an enemy but diagonally across his front. The Germans considered the machine gun as a support weapon and concentrated them in regimental (British brigade) machine gun companies, whereas the British version (Maxim–Vickers) was initially a battalion weapon, two to a battalion. At the end of 1915 battalion guns were withdrawn and replaced by Lewis Light Machine Guns, and the Machine Gun Corps was formed.

7. The Cyclist Section of the Post Office Rifles (Territorial Force) behind the lines in France. Each division had a cyclist company, which usually functioned as a message delivery service but sometimes fought as mobile infantry, and some battalions had a section. The army bicycle was remarkably robust, if a little heavy, and remained as an item of British military equipment until the 1970s. There was a laid down bicycle drill, based on that for cavalry, and including such words of command as 'prepare to mount … Mount!' and 'Half Sections right … Walk March!' Saluting on a bicycle was eventually abolished, after generations of cycling soldiers had fallen off trying to do the right thing, and from then on cyclists passing officers merely 'sat to attention'. (IWM Q54345)

8. Two officers of the Scots Guards in trench kit at Loos. The sheepskin jackets tended to be turned inside out when near the enemy, to hide the white wool. The officer on the right is wearing pre-war officers' breeches, while his companion is wearing the OR pattern. Swords have now all but disappeared and these two have both armed themselves with rifles. All participants started the war in soft caps until the French introduced steel helmets, followed by the British and the Germans. The British began to issue them as trench stores (that is remaining in the trench and taken over on arrival) in 1915 and by 1916 the helmet was an individual issue to every man in the BEF. On 16 October 1915 issues to 1 Scots Guards began. (IWM Q17393)

9. The Vermelles to Hulluch road running roughly west to east was the inter-corps boundary. On 25 September 7 Division attacked to the left of the road and 1 Division to the right. This photograph was taken on 27 September and shows abandoned and damaged transport wagons and dead horses. The road itself has been cleared to allow passage along it, and its surface is typical of the roads in the area. Today it is the tarmac D 39, and runs past the cemetery where John Kipling is alleged to be buried. (IWM Q17350)

10. 'Tower Bridge' was the name given to a pair of pithead winding towers at the south-west of Loos. In this photograph, taken from the outskirts of Loos, the right-hand tower has collapsed, due to the September fighting. The left-hand tower eventually came down too. The difficulty of moving around while the Germans could observe from Tower Bridge is obvious, as is the difficulty in swift movement over the boggy ground. This side of tower Bridge can be seen the houses of Loos, and behind it is the Loos Crassier, a long slag heap. This portion of the sector was eventually taken over by the French. (IWM Q49287)

11. Looking along the road running south-west from Vermelles to Loos, after the attack on 26 September by 21 and 24 Divisions, the old German support line can be seen zigzagging on the forward slope on the right of the photograph. The abandoned vehicles are mostly British machine gun limbers. The New Army divisions were not ready to go into action, and suffered accordingly. (IWM Q17378)

12. Loos on 30 September 1915, a few days after its capture by the British. Although the houses would not attract the attention of predatory estate agents, they are considerably less damaged than other villages subjected to shelling would be later in the war, when the British had remedied the shortage of artillery ammunition that still prevailed even in September 1915. Tower Bridge can be seen in the background.

13. A bombing party of the Scots Guards in 'Big Willie', the German trench to the east of the Hohenzollern Redoubt. There were a plethora of different types of grenades in use by the British at this time, and the Guards were fortunate in receiving a good quantity of the new Mills Bomb (later the 36 Grenade, still in service until the early 1980s). The Mills Bombs came with their detonators in a separate box and here the men are inserting the detonators in the grenades. Most, if not all, of these men are probably pre-war regulars. (IWM Q17390)

14. Looking from Vermelles north-east towards the Hohenzollern Redoubt, as the British made one last attempt to capture it on 13 October 1915. The chalk spoil from successive lines of trenches can be seen, as can the exploding British shells over the redoubt. (IWM Q29004)

15. British walking wounded coming back through Vermelles after the attack on the Hohenzollern Redoubt on 13 October. Vermelles was always well behind the British lines so had suffered little from shelling, although by this stage most of the civilian population had left. (IWM Q29005)

16. The Guards Division went back into the line on the night of 16/17 October, and one company of the Scots Guards had six men killed and fifteen wounded in this sap on 17 October, from shelling, sniping and bombing. The Germans were only just the other side of the sandbags.

needed them), their commanding officers had and have the right of direct access to the monarch in all matters affecting their regiments, and, again until recently, Guards battalions, except in emergency, had to be in brigades commanded by Guardsmen. Officers of the Guards are selected from the very best public schools, are beautifully groomed and impeccably mannered. They are a privileged elite, and suffer the leg pulling of the rest of the army because of it, but, at least in the opinion of this author (a Gurkha with no axe to grind), richly deserve what status they may have. Some Guards regiments – the Grenadiers, Coldstream and Scots – were more than two hundred and fifty years old in 1915; the Irish Guards on the other hand had been formed but fifteen years previously, while the Welsh Guards were the babies of the bunch at just seven months. It did not matter. However young the regiment it had absorbed the Guards ethos: the highest standards of military professionalism, combined with a fierce pride, the whole kept in order by a system of discipline which may often have strayed from the strictly legal, but which was accepted by those upon whom it bore.

Guards regiments did not have any Territorial Force battalions, nor did they raise any New Army units. They did, of course, expand during the war, but were always selective and, while they no longer insisted on their recruits being six footers, they did manage to avoid any degrading of the Guards mystique. The Guards were better than others because they believed they were and because they had a superb system of delegation, trusting subordinates to get on with what they were trained and paid to do, rather than stifling initiative by over supervision. Guards NCOs were, and probably still are, quite simply the best in the world.

The Guards Division itself was relatively new. Six battalions of Guards went to France with the original BEF in August 1914, and two more followed on 7 October. They were in three brigades (1 Guards, 4 Guards and 20 Infantry) spread amongst three divisions (1, 2 and 7). On 6 February 1915 Lord Kitchener ordered the raising of a brand new, one-battalion regiment – the Welsh Guards. It says a great deal for the Guards system that the new battalion mounted guard at Buckingham Palace on Saint David's Day, 1 March!

The idea of forming a Guards division also seems to have come from Kitchener, and did not meet with universal approval. There were many who thought that the best way of stiffening the rest of the army, and in particular the New Army units, was to spread the Guards battalions amongst them, rather than concentrate all the excellence in one division, and there were those officers of the Guards who thought that the expansion that would be necessary to man a complete division would dilute the existing high standards. Kitchener convinced the King, however, and that was that. An order for the formation of the division was issued in July 1915, with a view to its becoming operational in August.

The infantry required by a division was twelve battalions and a pioneer battalion, but there were only ten battalions of Guards in existence (eight with the BEF, one in UK and the brand new Welsh Guards),[1] so also in July approval was given for the raising of a fourth battalion for the Grenadiers, a fourth battalion for the Coldstream (which would be the division's pioneer battalion), and a second battalion for the Irish. This provided the thirteen battalions needed for the Guards Division, with the Household Cavalry providing the divisional cavalry squadron and the cyclist company. There were of course no Guards artillery or engineer regiments, but those to support the new division were carefully selected, as were the logistic units and the divisional staff, the latter being almost all officers of Guards regiments. Apart from each Guards regiment forming a reserve battalion (a holding and training unit) and the Guards Machine Gun battalion, part of the Machine Gun Corps formed in late 1915, there were no other Guards units raised in the war, thus maintaining the unique high standards of those regiments.

The two other divisions of the reserve, 21 and 24 Divisions, were very different from the Guards. Both were New Army formations raised as part of the K3 expansion – the third hundred thousand – in September 1914. Of the six brigade commanders (three per division) four were retired officers re-employed, and of twenty-six battalion commanders all except one was a retired officer (and some were retired Territorial Force). No battalion had, apart from the commanding officer, more than one regular or retired officer, all the rest were newly commissioned. There were only a handful of old soldiers and recalled NCOs spread around the two divisions, and both formations had been in theatre for only three weeks and had not yet fired a shot in anger. They were well motivated, enthusiastic and keen, but the lack of training and experience made them a twin disaster waiting to happen.

The reserve was held under the command not of the officer commanding the offensive – Haig – but of the Commander-in-Chief of the BEF, Field Marshal Sir John French. If there were other major operations taking place at the same time as the Loos offensive – if for example Second Army was launching a wholesale attack out of the Ypres Salient, or Third Army was to attempt to advance north of the Somme – then retaining the reserves in the hands of the Commander-in-Chief would have made eminent sense, as there could come a time when all three armies might need reinforcement, and the Commander-in-Chief would have to decide who should have them. In September 1915, however, the British were capable of only one major operation – Loos – and anything else that the BEF might undertake would be in support or as a diversion. That being the situation, it would have been much tidier to allocate the reserves directly to Commander First Army at the outset, allowing him to decide when and where they should be used.

In the planning stage of the operation Haig and his staff were unhappy that First Army had no integral reserve apart from a cavalry division, and were only mollified when they were assured by French that two of the reserve divisions – 21 and 24 Divisions – would be given to Haig as soon as he needed them. If this is so, then why did French insist on retaining control of them? Why not simply allocate those two divisions to First Army and allow that formation to decide where they should go and what they should do? As it was, the implication that the reserves would be deployed when needed was not clearly laid down in black and white, but was an arrangement between the Commander-in-Chief and his subordinate army commander. Worse still, Haig assumed that 'when needed' would be as defined by him, whereas French intended that the decision to deploy the reserve would be his. Certainly some of Haig's subordinate commanders were confused. Rawlinson's operation order for IV Corps says: 'The 3rd Cavalry Division and XI Corps will be in army reserve and will be held behind I and IV Corps and will be brought forward in support as occasion demands.' Similarly Major General Barter, commanding 47 Division, says in his operation order that: 'XI Corps and the 3rd Cavalry Divisions are in army reserve.' On the other hand Gough, in I Corps, got it right when he said in his orders that the 3rd Cavalry Division less one brigade would be in army reserve.[2] The 3rd Cavalry Division less one brigade could produce the equivalent of two battalions dismounted: not much of a reserve for an army.

On September 12 Haig told General Foch, commanding the French attack under Joffre, about his concerns as to the placing of the British reserves. The French general agreed and made the point to Field Marshal French that the reserves must be close behind the assaulting troops – close behind the corps reserves, as he put it. As there were no corps reserves, the need for the general reserve to be close at hand was even more important. The British Commander-in-Chief cannot have been entirely happy that his junior had importuned a foreign general to lobby for him, but at a meeting at St Omer on 18 September, when Haig asked that two of the reserve divisions should be at Noeux les Mines and Verquin, about four and a half miles behind the jump off lines, when the offensive began, Sir John French thought that was too far forward, but eventually agreed.

As the fallout from the deployment of the reserves at Loos was a major factor in French's removal as commander-in-chief, and as it caused considerable bad blood between Haig and French, it is probably quite impossible at this range to know what was in Sir John French's mind before the battle, as opposed to after it when he had to justify his actions. French was not an idiot, nor did he consider that Haig was tactically so incompetent that he could not be trusted with taking the two reserve divisions under command from the outset. Sir John had been told quite unequivocally by Lord Kitchener that the French must be supported, and that the BEF must play a full part in the coming offensive, regardless of the very large numbers of casualties that would undoubtedly ensue.

French's previous form indicates that whatever he had been told by the Secretary of State, he had severe reservations about the wisdom of launching British troops across this particular stretch of front, gas or no gas. During the retreat from Mons French had at one stage threatened to take the BEF out of the line altogether, even considering withdrawing to the Channel Ports ready for an evacuation if needs be, and was only dissuaded from doing so by the personal intervention of Kitchener. There can be no doubting French's personal courage. He had displayed leadership and bravery of a high order throughout his service. On occasions, indeed, in this war he was too dismissive of danger, going forward to visit the troops when he would have been better employed at his headquarters where he could communicate and control the battle. French, however, like every other British commander from Harold Godwinson to Robin Brims, was very well aware that there was only one British army, and if he broke it there would not be another one. Britain did not at this stage have the luxury of being able to conscript those whom she wanted. While the expansion of the army was well under way by 1915, the BEF was still only thirty-seven divisions at the opening of the Loos offensive, and of those six were Territorial Force divisions with hardly any experience, and six were New Army divisions with none at all. The employment of six divisions to attack at Loos, almost negligible by French standards with their ninety-eight divisions on the Western Front, was a considerable commitment for the British: their loss would be a disaster. French knew that Haig, while also doubtful about the wisdom of the coming offensive, would fight the battle to the utmost of his considerable ability. Haig spoke French well enough to discuss operational matters in detail with his French opposite number, unlike his commander-in-chief who had to work through an interpreter, and was more understanding of the French point of view. Perhaps French thought that by retaining control of the reserve himself, he could save something from what he considered to be the looming debacle, whereas if he gave them to Haig they too might be wasted to no good effect.

If that was Sir John French's attitude it makes his insistence on retaining control of the reserve understandable, but not excusable. In battle there can be no half measures, and if the British were to attack, and whatever the views of the generals it had been agreed that they would, then there can be no good military reason for not giving 21 and 24 Divisions to First Army from the outset, even if there might be a case for Sir John retaining control of the Cavalry Corps and the Guards as the *ultima ratio regis*.

Even more extraordinary were the command and control arrangements. At this time General Headquarters (GHQ) of the BEF was at St Omer, about thirty miles from the Loos battle front. A headquarters – any headquarters – must be situated where the commander can control the battle, and in modern war that does not necessarily mean close to the fighting – although it might – but rather where communication with the fighting formations can be established. St Omer was a well-established headquarters, it had all the necessary means of communicating with any part of the British sector of front, and it had secure telephone lines to the headquarters of each army, including, of course, First Army. Given that Sir John French would personally decide when to release the reserves, and was therefore in a position to influence the battle, it might be thought vital that he could talk directly to the man fighting the battle – Haig. On the evening of 24 September Sir John French, taking with him only a skeleton personal staff, left St Omer and moved into a chateau at Philomel. As this was south of Lillers and only some ten miles behind the front, and only about six miles from First Army headquarters at Hinges, it might be thought that Sir John could more easily keep in touch with the battle as it developed. Philomel, however, lacked that essential for a headquarters – communications. All that was available to Sir John was the French civilian telephone system. He could not speak directly to Headquarters First Army, and any communication with Haig had therefore to be relayed through St Omer.

At 1900 hours on the night of 24 September 21 and 24 Divisions began to march up to the battle area, 21 Division to Noeux les Mines, and 24 Division to Beuvry. From their previous concentration area this was but a short march of between eight and twelve miles, depending on the particular unit, and under normal conditions and at the usual marching speed of two and a half miles per hour, should have got them into position by midnight at the latest, allowing a good night's rest before the attack. As it was, conditions were not normal. Try as the staff and the military police did to control traffic, the available roads were simply not sufficient, nor were they good enough, to take all the troops and transport using them that night. The men marching up to the front ran into men who had been relieved by the attacking troops and who were marching back to billets. Halts were frequent and roads were only just wide enough to take a column marching in fours. There were wide ditches on either side that made passing or being passed by horsed transport a difficult business. There were hold ups at nearly every crossroads and at railway level crossings; march discipline in the two New Army divisions was not good – hardly surprising when one considers that they had only been in the country a matter of weeks – and there were instances of over zealous military policemen stopping marching units because the commanders lacked the necessary movement orders.

The soldiers of the two divisions did not reach their allotted positions until 0200 hours if they were lucky, and 0600 hours if they were not. The leading units of 21 Division were at Noeux les Mines, and the rearguard was near La Buissière, four miles back. The head of 24 Division was at Beuvry, and its tail three miles behind near Béthune. The lead battalions of both divisions were now about four and a half miles from the British front line, or less than two hours marching for fresh troops. Unfortunately these troops were not fresh. They were exhausted by marching, not helped by the wet weather, and there were no billets available for them. Men lay down in fields off the roads and tried to get some sleep under their groundsheets. As the artillery bombardment was still going on, rising to a crescendo from 0400 hours, there was little rest for anyone.

As we have seen, the initial attack by the British infantry advancing behind gas and smoke was, with the exception of 2 Division astride the canal, largely successful. It may not have achieved all that had been hoped, but real inroads had been made into German territory and early on the leading battalions of I and IV Corps were poised within striking distance of the German second line. Soon divisions had committed their third brigades, and the time for fresh troops to push on through the German second line had come. At this stage the leading units of the two divisions of the first reserve – 21 and 24 – were five miles from where the fighting was, tired, wet and uncomfortable. As the deployment of the reserves was so crucial to the success or otherwise of the Loos battle, it is worth examining what happened in detail. From an examination of the Official History, Divisional and Regimental Histories, despatches and war diaries, what seems to have happened on the morning of 25 September was:

0700 hrs Haig sends a staff officer in a motorcar to French at Philomel, to tell the Commander-in-Chief that the attack is going well and asking that XI Corps might be released to under command First Army.

0845 hrs Having received no answer, Haig sends another messenger to tell French that all divisions have now deployed their third brigades, that all are either on the German second line or on their way to it, and once more asking for XI Corps.[3]

0930 hrs French sends a message to Commander XI Corps (Lieutenant General Richard Haking) ordering 21 and 24 divisions to move forward to First Army trenches 'as soon as the situation requires and permits', and saying that on arrival in those trenches the divisions will come under command First Army. XI Corps is to arrange the move with First Army accordingly. There is little urgency in the phraseology (no 'now', 'immediately' or 'as soon as possible'), and command does not devolve to First Army until the divisions are actually on the battlefield.

0930 hrs + As soon as Haking (at his headquarters at Noeux les Mines) receives the message above from French, he sends a message to 21 and 24 Divisions ordering them to move to the line Mazingarbe/Vermelles (about two miles from the two divisions' present position and a mile and a half behind the British jump off line).

0950 hrs Haig informed of above.

1030 hrs Haig orders his own army reserve, the two brigades of 3 Cavalry Division, forward to Corons du Rutoire, two miles behind the jump off line. They are to be prepared to advance and take the high ground overlooking the Haute Deule Canal, about five miles inside German territory.

1030 hrs 21 and 24 Divisions receive Haking's message.

1115 hrs 21 and 24 Divisions begin to move. They are still seven miles from where the battle has now moved to.

1130 hrs The Commander-in-Chief arrives at First Army HQ at Hinges, and confirms that he has ordered 21 and 24 Divisions to move to the battle area.

1230 hrs The Commander-in-Chief arrives at XI Corps HQ, briefs Haking, confirms that the Guards Division is to move to Noeux les Mines but remain in general reserve (i.e. under French).

1240 hrs Haig orders 3 Cavalry Division forward. Major General Briggs, the divisional commander, says that it is not yet possible to advance but that he will do so as soon as possible.[4]

1320 hrs First Army receives message from XI Corps saying 21 and 24 Divisions now under command First Army, marching to battle area but delayed on the road.

1435 hrs Haig orders Haking to detach one brigade to each of I and IV Corps and to push on with the rest and occupy the high ground between Hulluch and St Auguste, relieve the cavalry (who would push on to Carvin), and seize the crossings over the Heute Deule Canal. 62 Brigade of 21 Division is told to report to 15 Division in Loos, 73 Brigade of 24 Division is told to report to 9 Division west of the Hohenzollern Redoubt.

1700 hrs The commanding officer 8th Battalion the East Yorkshire Regiment, part of 62 Brigade of 21 Division, reports to Commander 44 Brigade of 15 Division in Loos. At about the same time units of 73 Brigade are reporting to 9 Division. The first of the reserves are arriving.

1800 hrs Troops of 62 Brigade arrive and are deployed under instructions of Commander 15 Division, whose own troops are exhausted.

If we now zoom in to battalion level of the reserves, we find 8th Battalion the Somerset Light Infantry, part of 63 Brigade of 21 Division, bivouacked for the night of 24/25 September at Houchin, seven miles as the crow flies behind the jump off line. Only at 1130 hrs on the morning of 25 September did they receive orders to march to Noyelles les Vermelles, five miles away and by now nearly three miles from the fighting. They got there at 1430 hours, not bad going given the state of the roads. At 1600 hours the brigade started to move again, this time in the direction of Fosse 7, on the Loos road, a distance of four miles which took them four hours. Having reached Fosse 7 at 2000 hours, two companies were sent to the Lens/Hulluch road, where they went into defence for the rest of the night, while Battalion HQ and the other two companies were warned for a night attack on Hill 70.

Had the two reserve divisions arrived on the battlefield ready for action at 0900 hours on 25 September then they might have been able to carry the initial attack forward and have broken through the German second line. Five miles behind the jump off line was a perfectly acceptable concentration area for them, and once orders were given for them to move, there was not much time wasted. That 21 Division received the order to move at 1030 hours, forty-five minutes or so after it left HQ XI Corps is reasonable, and that 8 Somerset were ordered to move an hour after that is about right given that orders had to be absorbed by the HQs of divisions, converted into orders for brigades and in turn into instructions to battalions. We would do it rather more quickly now, using radio and computers, but not much. Again, a speed of between one and two miles an hour for troops moving through a battle area is not at all bad, particularly for inexperienced troops who were already exhausted from the trying approach march of the night of 24/25 September.

Speculation can be dangerous, but at a distance of ninety years perhaps we may be forgiven on this occasion. We do not know why Sir John French did not react to the staff officer sent to report progress to him at 0700 hours, and it would be uncharitable to suppose that the Commander-in-Chief was in bed. A staff car would take a maximum of forty-five minutes (and probably a lot less) to complete the twelve-mile journey from Hinges to Philomel. If Sir John had immediately agreed to release 21 and 24 Divisions, then assuming that the orders would have travelled at the same speed as they did in reality, the two divisions would have started to move at 0930 hours, and marching at one and a half miles per hour through the rear areas and at one mile an hour in the battle area (as they did on the day), the lead battalions would have arrived where they were needed at 1230 hours at the earliest. This would have been five and a half hours earlier than they did arrive, but still much later than the ideal moment for their deployment against the German second line – 0900 hours. The only way the reserve divisions could have been launched against the German second line at 0900 hours or thereabouts, would have been if they had begun their approach march from their bivouac area at 0500 hours, an hour and a half before the jump off time for the six divisions in the main attack.

As Sir John French was only going to deploy the reserve divisions if and when he thought they were needed, he would hardly have agreed to them leaving their concentration area before the main assault even began. If the reserve, or at least 21 and 24 Divisions, had been placed under First Army in the first place, it is unlikely they could have been held any farther forward than they were – there was no room for them nearer the British front and bivouacking in the field within range of German heavy artillery would have been a risky business. Haig himself had asked that the heads of the divisions should be at Noeux les Mines and Annequin by the morning of 25 September, and that is where they were, although had they been under his command he might have moved them there a day early, to allow some rest before the offensive began. If they had been under command First Army, then in his operation order for the attack Haig might have ordered that they begin to move forward as the attacking divisions left the jump off line, at 0630 hours, in which case both divisions might have been approaching the German second line by 1030 hours, later than the ideal time for their use, but still early enough to take advantage of the German defenders having been knocked off balance. All the foregoing is an attempt to second-guess Commander First Army. We today would say that 21 and 24 Divisions should have been placed under command First Army from the outset, and had they been so, they could have arrived on the battlefield in time to achieve something. They might, of course, have achieved very little – they were desperately inexperienced – but at least the opportunity would have been there.

It was not the refusal of the Commander-in-Chief to place the reserves under First Army from the outset that infuriated Haig and his staff. They had reluctantly accepted – as they had to – that Sir John French would retain control initially, although they assumed that once First Army asked for the reserves it would get them. The bone of contention was French's statement in his dispatch (which went to King, Cabinet and ultimately the Press) implying that he had handed over command of 21 and 24 Divisions at 0930 hours on the morning of 25 September, when in truth he had only issued an order to the two divisions to move. They would not come under command First Army until much later. The impression created, however, was that First Army received the two New Army divisions at 0930 hours and then took eight and a half hours to deploy them into battle less than six miles away. In fact, it made little difference. Even if command had changed at 0930 hours, the divisions would not have arrived very much earlier than they did. The major error made by French was to insist on retaining control of 21 and 24 Divisions himself: after that it was only a matter of compounding the error.

During the planning stage of the Loos offensive it had always been assumed that when and if 21 and 24 Divisions were deployed, it would be in pursuit of a beaten enemy and as reinforcements to I and IV Corps. It had never been the intention to employ XI Corps as a separate corps, and that Haig now decided to use those two divisions as a corps in its own right may perhaps, with hindsight, be seen as an error by a man not generally prone to getting it wrong. There was confusion as to exactly what was required, there were communication difficulties, there was still doubt as to exactly how far the British had advanced – both First Army and IV Corps thought that Hulluch (on the corps boundary and inclusive IV Corps) was held by the British, whereas it most definitely was not. The two divisions, less one brigade each, were not able to move from the Vermelles / Mazingarbe area until it was nearly dark, and they were being asked to cross ground that they had not seen, marching on a compass bearing, with only maps and out of date air photographs to guide them and in a steady downpour of rain. Each division set off with one brigade in the lead and the other following up, and progress was painfully slow. It soon became apparent that there could be no question of seizing the Haute Deule Canal that night, a fact that Haig realised early on, and which prompted him at 2027 hours to issue orders to 21 and 24 Division to take up a position between Hill 70 and the west end of Hulluch, and to be prepared for an advance next morning.

As it happened, Haig's orders did not reach 24 Division until 0200 hours, and it was even later arriving at 21 Division. The two divisions did not reach their final position for the night until even later, and by the time they had sorted themselves out and dug a rudimentary trench line, it was nearly first light on 26 September. Commander First Army assumed that both divisions, with only a few miles to go, had been able to get a good night's rest and would be ready for anything in the morning: the truth was that the men of both divisions, having been asked to do far more than they were capable of and exhausted by a trying night, were hardly ready for anything.

The first units of 21 Division to arrive in the battle area were battalions of 62 Brigade, detached to 15 Division. The brigade commander, Brigadier General Wilkinson, had been told about midday, before he left Mazingarbe, that his men were wanted at Hill 70, although whether to reinforce troops already there or to attack it was unclear. He decided to send off two battalions immediately, and to follow with his remaining two battalions an hour later. The two lead battalions, 8th Battalion the East Yorkshire Regiment and 10th Battalion the Green Howards, duly marched down the Lens road, reached the old British front line, crossed it, and carried on in column of fours. They had no guides, only 1 / 100,000 maps (far too small a scale for accurate navigation), and continued in their column of fours with their battalion transport following behind them, until German artillery in Cité St Pierre found them far too tempting a target to ignore and shelled them with shrapnel. Both battalions had a number of men killed and wounded and their transport destroyed, the road now being blocked by upturned carts and dead horses and mules.

The two battalions should then have turned left and gone north-east into Loos village, where they would have had their objective, Hill 70, pointed out to them. Instead, shocked and disoriented by their first exposure to enemy fire, but still, perhaps surprisingly, coherent units, they moved south of Loos, along the edge of Loos Crassier, and found themselves approaching Chalk Pit Copse. The Chalk Pit had been captured by 47 Division that morning, but they had been unable to drive the Germans out of the copse, and now the two 21 Division battalions came under machine-gun fire from there. Trying to move away from the hostile fire the two battalions now came under fire from British troops in Loos Cemetery, who thought that the figures moving towards them were part of a German counter-attack. It was a shambles, but one of the lessons that would come out of this war was that if Britain eschewed compulsory military service in peacetime, and then had to expand its army hugely in the event of war, heavy casualties amongst under trained and inexperienced troops, led by equally inexperienced officers, were inevitable.

About this time the other two battalions of 62 Brigade, 12th and 13th Battalions the Northumberland Fusiliers, with Brigade HQ, arrived where they should be – in Loos village. Contact with the 8th East Yorkshires and 10th Green Howards had been long lost, so Brigadier General Wilkinson, with understandable caution, sent one company of 12 Northumberlands to Hill 70. The arrival of these men on the slope short of the ridge was assumed by the current occupants to mean a general relief, and at 2300 hours the two battalions on the hill, 9 Black Watch and 10 Gordon Highlanders, upped sticks and withdrew. The Northumberland company now found itself the sole guardian of the approaches to Hill 70.

The last battalion of 62 Brigade, 13 Northumberland, was now sent off to assist 46 Brigade, where here too some units assumed a general relief and began to withdraw. Some were stopped by the commander of 46 Brigade, others went back to the original British jump off line, and it was not until well after first light on 26 September that some sort of control was restored. It was indeed fortunate that despite control on 15 Division's front having been largely lost during the night, individual officers and NCOs did use their common sense, and while the line reached during the day was much weaker than it had been and should have been, there were always some troops manning it.

During the night the Germans launched two counter-attacks on 7 Royal Scots Fusiliers, one of the battalions of 45 Brigade that Commander 15 Division had deployed to hold Loos after his other two brigades had taken it. Both were beaten off. A New Army battalion might be inexperienced, but put in a defensive position and with clear instructions, they could fight well. The situation around Loos and Hill 70 and the right flank of First Army did not change very much throughout the night. This was not so elsewhere on the British front.

The brigade detached from 24 Division, 73 Brigade, had been instructed to place themselves under command 9 Division, and while on the road at Sailly Labourse received orders from that division to assemble in the original British front line opposite the Hohenzollern Redoubt. This is a march of only three miles, and guides were provided by 9 Division, but such was the state of the ground and the congestion behind the battle area that the leading troops of the brigade took until 1600 hours to arrive, and the rear elements were not present until 1900 hours. Once in the old British line, the brigade was ordered to relieve the now seriously understrength 26 Brigade at Fosse 8. Again, guides were provided, and although the distance was less than a mile, there was a whole series of German trench lines to be crossed, some bridged others not, wire to be negotiated, some cut some not, the whole to be done in failing light and then in the dark, and in pouring rain. The men of 73 Brigade did not begin to file into the trenches round Fosse 8 until 2200 hours. The relief was a long process, and had not been completed when the Germans counter-attacked at around 0100 hours on 26 September. The right of the counter-attack fell on Fosse 8, but, despite the inevitable confusion with one defending brigade in the process of being relieved by another, the fosse was held.

This counter-attack was a major affair, delivered over a frontage of a mile by a reinforced German division. At the crossroads where the north/south Hulloch to Loos road crossed the west/east Vermelles/Hulloch road, the Germans were able to approach to within bombing distance before the alarm was raised, and the British were pushed back 400 yards or so into what had been the German Gun Trench. This did not matter very much – nothing of any great tactical importance had been given up – but rather more serious was the loss of The Quarries a few hundred yards away, when the Germans managed to get in through a gap to the north, while the British defenders were carrying out a relief of the forward units. Not only did the Germans recapture The Quarries, but they also bagged the Commander 27 Brigade, Brigadier General Bruce, and only just missed getting two of his battalion commanders too. The British managed to halt any more progress on the part of the Germans, but had to pull back and establish a line in the old German front-line trench about 500 yards back.

Farther north Gun Trench itself had already been counter-attacked in the 1 Division area, when at about midnight the 1st Battalion the South Wales Borderers, a regular battalion, had not been caught napping but acquired a great many German helmets as souvenirs.

Meanwhile, the nineteen-division French Tenth Army, to the right of the British, had attacked at 1245 hours on 25 September, but with the Territorial (older reservists) division on the extreme left flank, next to the

British and facing Lens, not leaving their trenches but only firing at the German positions. This had always been the plan, and was dictated by the French wanting four hours of daylight for a final bombardment of the German second line, but it did mean that the French moved far too late to be able to take advantage of the initial success of the British. Across their front very little was achieved: the German first line was penetrated in a few places, some wire was cut, some prisoners were taken, but Vimy Ridge, a major objective, could not be captured. Nevertheless, the French were encouraged by what the British had done, and at around 2100 hours that night General Foch, commanding the French northern group of armies, summoned General d'Urbal, commanding the French Tenth Army, and ordered him to switch his main effort to his left flank and support the British First Army by attacking the following morning.

In Champagne the French Second and Fourth Armies had attacked with twenty divisions, followed up by seven more, at 0915 hours. At first it looked as if real gains could be made, and in the early stages a large number of prisoners and some guns were captured. Then the attack began to get bogged down under heavy fire from German artillery, most of which had been pulled back to behind the German second line. The French had penetrated the first line in a few places, but could make no impression on the second line, taking many casualties in the trying.

All in all, 25 September had been a lot less disastrous than some had forecast. Once the German counter-attacks had petered out, by 0400 hours on the morning of 26 September, the British line now ran from 47 Division's defensive flank on the Double Crassier, north-east though the Chalk Pits, then turning north short of Hill 70 and running west of the La Bassée/Lens road to where Gun Trench cut the Vermelles/Hulluch road, before cutting back short of The Quarries to the old German first-line position, working round the salient that the German counter-attack had created before going north-east again through The Dump and then turning north-west and west back to the original British front line in the 2 Division sector. From the First Army perspective much had been achieved; the two reserve divisions were in the field and poised ready to do great things on the morrow, and the Germans appeared to be holding only a thin line between Haisnes and Cité St Auguste. A determined attack by 21 and 24 Divisions in the morning of 26 September should be able to pierce that line and rupture the whole German defence plan for the area. It might even capture Lens itself.

It was not the fault of Haig or his staff – reports took time to be compiled and come in – that they did not know of the many gaps in the British line, particularly where 7 Division had been forced to abandon The Quarries, nor of the very high casualties so far incurred, nor that the 21 and 24 Divisions had been marching and digging all night.

Notes

1. 1st and 2nd Battalions Grenadier Guards, 1,2 and 3 Coldstream Guards, 1 and 2 Scots Guards and 1 Irish Guards in France, and 3 Grenadier Guards in London. Nobody quite knows why a regular battalion of Guards was retained in London: it was not, as is sometimes supposed, that the King demanded it (quite the reverse – he made it clear that he did not require it), but it may have been for the protection of Parliament in the event of something dreadful happening (invasion? revolution?).
2. Edmonds, J E, *Military Operations France and Belgium 1914*, Vol. II, London: Macmillan, 1928.
3. A bit of a porkie pie here as the situation was not quite as rosy as painted, but nevertheless all was going pretty well.
4. Briggs himself had gone forward (the Official History says 'galloped' but trot and canter are more likely) and visited the headquarters of 1, 7 and 15 Divisions. He realised that first reports were too optimistic and that the British infantry was not as far forward as had been thought.

CHAPTER VI

The Attack Continues

At 2330 hours on the night of 25 September First Army issued its orders for the following day. Still not fully aware of the results of the fighting on 25 September, and still under the impression that they were better than they actually were, Haig was nevertheless concerned about what the French might or might not do. General d'Urbal, commanding the French Tenth Army, had assured his British opposite number that he would attack vigorously on the morrow, but as his army had made virtually no progress on the first day of the offensive, it would have to advance about four miles through German-held territory just to get level with the new British front. If the French could not do that, but the British did advance farther east, there was a risk that the British thrust might be nipped out by attacks on its flanks. The plan, therefore, was for the British to attack at what seemed to be the weakest point, that is between Cité St Elie and Hill 70, along the front of what had been the 7, 1 and 15 Divisional fronts the previous day. In the north I Corps were to capture Cité St Elie and IV Corps Hulloch, while in the south IV Corps was also instructed to capture Hill 70 and then establish a defensive flank guard in case the French on the other side of Lens did not manage to come up level with the British. In between, that is over the two miles between the south of Hulloch and Hill 70, IX Corps with 21 and 24 Divisions (each less one brigade detached to IV and I Corps respectively) would drive over the German second line and on to the Haute Deule Canal, a distance of about three miles. The attack on Hill 70 was to be carried out at a time to be decided by Commander IV Corps, while everything else was to happen at 1100 hours after an artillery bombardment.

As German troops on Hill 70 could see and direct fire on almost the whole of the intended advance, it had to be in British hands before the general advance began, that is before 1100 hours. General Rawlinson, commanding IV Corps, allocated the task to 15 Division, stipulating that Zero Hour was to be 0900 hours, after an hour's bombardment by the divisional artillery. HQ 15 Division in turn gave the job to 45 Brigade (their own) and 62 Brigade (on loan from 21 Division), the orders arriving at both brigade headquarters at around 0500 hours 26 September.

Both brigade commanders now consulted, agreed a plan and sent out orders to battalions – which reached them about 0700 hours. If the impression is given that information was taking an awfully long time to be passed on, then that impression is correct, but it must be emphasised that written messages (such as the orders for the attack on 26 September) had to be delivered by hand, over unfamiliar ground, at night and under enemy fire, and that in 62 Brigade there were very few men who had any experience at all of active service.

Fortunately, at this stage of the war operations involved the coordination of a maximum of five arms only: cavalry, artillery, engineers, infantry and the air. On this night there was no role for the cavalry or the air (the latter had its tasks but they involved interdiction behind the German lines and were irrelevant to the attack on Hill 70) and putting together the infantry assault was a relatively simple affair. After the artillery had done its work 45 Brigade would make an attack astride the track which ran just south of east from Loos to the La Bassée/Lens road, and then would be followed up by 62 Brigade. Once Hill 70 and its redoubt had been taken, the troops would be responsible for digging in and facing south and south-east to prevent any interference with the attack to its north.[1]

The artillery plan to support the attack included using two field batteries and two howitzer batteries which had come forward during the night and were now at the cemetery just west of Loos. The difficulty was that the road from Béthune to Loos, along which the batteries' ammunition wagons would have to come, was blocked by battle debris and under constant German shellfire. These batteries, the closest to the German positions, would probably be able to fire only the ammunition carried in their limbers, and the rest of the divisional artillery would have to do the best it could from Mazingarbe, Fosse 7 and North Maroc, up to 7,000 yards away from the target and therefore getting near the field guns' extreme range.

Due to battle debris and the shell-pitted ground, the darkness, the mist and the shortage of good maps, orders from the two brigade headquarters took a long time to get down to the soldiers on the ground. Battalion commanders received their instructions at around 0800 hours, and some soldiers did not receive their orders until after the artillery barrage had started, only an hour before they were expected to attack. The confusion of war, allied with the difficulties experienced by the artillery observation officers in clearly identifying targets in the mist, led to a number of shells falling on the British front line, which the artillery had been told would be evacuated. Orders to evacuate were either unclear or had not been received, with the result that a number of British soldiers were killed or wounded. Casualties caused by friendly fire, as it is termed today, that is fire from one's own side, has always been a risk and always will be. Every effort was (and still is) made to identify without any doubt the exact location of one's own units, but reports are not always accurate; not everyone is an expert map reader every time; reports get lost or are late arriving, and not every artillery round will drop unerringly where it is aimed.[2] The numbers killed or injured were not great; experienced soldiers who survived it would have cursed the gunners and put the incident behind them, but to the inexperienced New Army men the effect was unsettling, and – understandably – did have an adverse effect on their morale.

Once the artillery bombardment had finished, the three battalions of 45 Brigade began to move forward. Here the mist, which had been a hindrance to the gunners would have been an advantage to the infantry, and it was their misfortune that it now cleared, and the attackers could be seen clearly by the Germans ensconced on the top of the hill. The redoubt on Hill 70 had been reinforced during the night, and although damaged by the artillery it had not been rendered uninhabitable. Despite casualties on the approach, men of 13 Royal Scots, 11 Argyll and Sutherland Highlanders and 7 Royal Scots Fusiliers did get into the redoubt, and they did succeed in killing a number of its German occupants and in driving more out and back towards their own second defence line, in front of Cité St Auguste. Try as they might, however, they could not force the defenders out of the central part of the redoubt, which meant that any attempt to push on to the east, towards the second line, was met by fire not only from St Auguste to the east and St Emile to the south, but from Hill 70 as well. As German artillery and mortar fire increased in intensity, and the toll of dead and injured attackers mounted, the survivors of 45 Brigade found themselves forced to abandon the redoubt and fall back to the western slopes. The two battalions of 62 Brigade, 12 Northumberland Fusiliers and 10 Green Howards, following up 200 yards behind 45 Brigade, had problems caused by bad light and inadequate maps, and initially veered way off to the right and began to attack Loos Crassier. Once the error was realised the commanding officers did get their men pointing in the right direction and the two battalions reached the ridge and swept over it, either side of the Hill 70 Redoubt. They still could not take the redoubt, however, and they too were soon driven back to the western slopes.

Now the inexperience – and naïve gallantry – of the New Armies began to show. Officers of the Green Howards and Northumberlands tried to get their men to go forward for another try. From the Green Howards, one after another, beginning with the commanding officer Lieutenant Colonel Hadow and continuing in order of seniority, four officers got to their feet and tried to lead by example. It was in vain, no shouts of 'charge' nor personal example could drive the men forward in the teeth of German rifle and artillery fire, and all four were killed. With most of the officers who had accompanied the troops dead or wounded, the men began to fall back and take shelter in the shell scrapes and hastily dug shelters from where they had started. Units of the two assaulting brigades were hopelessly intermingled, and more attempts by the surviving officers to renew the attack came to nothing. The Germans were now able to reoccupy the outlying arms of their redoubt and at about 1100 hours they began a heavy bombardment of the British line, using a mix of shrapnel and high explosive with the occasional gas shell thrown in.

After all the efforts of the past two days this was just more than the exhausted troops could take. In the words of the Official History, 'this had a most unsettling effect on the men'. To put it bluntly, many of them ran away; or rather slipped back from where they were supposed to be and made off rearwards through the village of Loos, regardless of their officers' attempts to stop them, and oblivious to the catcalls of the Royal Engineers who were working away to put Loos in a state of defence. Given their inexperience, their exhaustion and the very heavy German fire to which they had been exposed, it is difficult to blame those who were simply unable to stick it out. Fortunately not all abandoned the battle, and a thin khaki line held out from the 6th Cameron Highlanders opposite Chalet Wood on the left along the western slope of Hill 70 and cutting across Loos Crassier to a polyglot group of stragglers collected by 20 Londons on the right, who were in contact with the left flank of 47 Division. Despite this being the 6th Camerons' first battle, they fought with great determination under the leadership of the 54-year-old Lieutenant Colonel Angus Douglas-Hamilton. The battalion lost four officers and ninety-five men killed – including Douglas-Hamilton, who was awarded a posthumous Victoria Cross, and Lance Corporal Brown[3] – but they did stem the German advance.

The attempt to neutralise Hill 70 before the main attack had failed, but Haking, XI Corps Commander, decided to press on nevertheless. His view seems to have been that the main attack on the German second line would perforce outflank Hill 70, which would be thus rendered useless to the Germans. If this was so, one has to ask why he wanted to attack it separately in the first place. Phase Two of the operation required the attacking infantry of 21 and 24 Divisions on a frontage of just under a mile to ascend a gently rising slope for about a thousand yards, when they would come upon the German second line of defence. This was only one trench, without the usual support or reserve lines, but it was strongly held and well protected. Reinforcements of men had been fed in during the night and they had thrown up a barbed wire entanglement four feet in height and up to twenty feet deep. There would be a preliminary artillery bombardment lasting an hour.

If the bombardment went according to plan, it would be carried out by the artillery of both divisions plus two heavy batteries. This was little enough to blast a mile of German line that had not yet been subjected to any artillery at all – the bombardment prior to 25 September being aimed at the first line of defences only – and the heavy batteries were allocated only 200 6-inch shells, and ninety of 9.2. The bombardment did not go according to plan. During the night of 25 September the artillery of 21 and 24 Divisions should have been pulled out of their existing positions and moved forward to the rear of Lone Tree, where they would have been nicely sheltered on a reverse slope unseen by German spotters. As it was, the area between the original British front line – the jump off line – and where the battle had got to at last light on 25 September, was a parking attendant's nightmare. The normal procedure was for administrative transport – carrying a resupply of rations, ammunition, water and all the other bits and pieces that soldiers need in order to carry on making war, and including the wherewithal to produce a hot meal – to move forward and make contact with their parent units at night. As no proper traffic plan had been laid down, and as there were insufficient movement control officers and military police to impose compliance even if there had been, it was every quartermaster for himself. There were few maps of the scale needed and throughout the night horse- and mule-drawn vehicles floundered about trying to find their owners. As Le Rutoir was one of the few easily identifiable landmarks on what had been no-man's-land, nearly every brigade sent their battalions' wagons there. The inevitable grid lock, with roads and tracks blocked with lost transport or transport all trying to get to the same place, inevitably affected the artillery move, which had been predicated on the basis of unclogged roads and the normal traffic priority for artillery. Navigation was not helped by a thick mist that covered the battlefield

With all the movement difficulties met during the night the artillery could get no farther forward than the western side of Le Rutoir, or about a thousand yards short of where they should have been. This in itself would not have mattered – the second German line was now well within the range of both field and heavy guns – but it meant that instead of being nicely sheltered behind Lone Tree the guns were now on the forward slope, and as soon as the mist lifted, which it did at about 0900 hours, they were clearly visible to the Germans from their positions. Attempts by the gunners to camouflage their guns were useless, and the Germans were soon able to bring down counter-battery fire from their own artillery, and some guns even suffered the indignity of receiving infantry rifle fire. It is hardly to be wondered at that the bombardment was even less effective than that originally planned – which itself would have been far from devastating – and that little damage was done to the German trench before the infantry advanced to attack it.

While final preparations for the attack were going on, the Germans counter-attacked on Bois Hugo, on the right flank of 21 Division, then held by 63 Brigade. It could have been a total disaster for the British: the 12th Battalion the West Yorkshire Regiment, caught by surprise in the flank, broke and ran back to the Lens road. This sort of herd instinct is infectious: the 10th York and Lancaster Regiment, and the 8th Lincolns began to pull back too, and the brigade commander, Brigadier General Nickalls, running forward to try to rally the men, was killed instantly. A battalion from 64 Brigade, 14 Durham Light Infantry, sent forward to help, saw the retreating British soldiers and, assuming they were attacking Germans, opened fire on them. The panic did not spread to the whole brigade, however, and in the Chalk Pit two companies of the fourth battalion in the brigade, 8 Somerset Light infantry, held their ground and brought fire down on the advancing Germans. The counter-attack was eventually brought to a halt by artillery fire, but it was not a good start for young soldiers in their first battle.

The men who were to carry out the 1100 hours attack were tired, hungry, wet and, no doubt, frightened. They had spent the last two nights marching, and of the six brigades of the two divisions only one (72 Brigade of 24 Division) had been able to provide their men with a hot breakfast, all others having to make do with their emergency rations – perfectly nourishing but neither hot nor appetising. It should have been an attack by twenty-four battalions, and it should have driven through the German defence line and sent the enemy reeling. As it was, due to orders arriving late or not at all, and the difficulty in moving over the ground, it was carried out by six battalions of 24 Division on the left, and two battalions and the intermingled remnants of four others of 21 Division on the right. Despite the problems, at first all seemed to go well.

At exactly 1100 hours the leading troops – two battalions – of 24 Division left their trenches. They shook out into extended order and moved off across the La Bassée to Lens road. As they did so they had to change direction half left to line up on their objectives, and this too was completed smoothly and without fuss. The German survivors of their earlier counter-attack were driven off in confusion, and the determined image of the division had a steadying effect on the retreating troops of 21 Division, many of whom turned about and began to retrace their steps. Things rapidly began to go wrong, however. On the extreme left of the attack 1 Division was supposed to attack the village of Hulluch, strongly held by the Germans and able to direct fire into the flank of the attacking troops. Due to a mixture of muddle, misunderstanding and severed telephone wires, this attack was uncoordinated and half hearted. It failed to capture or neutralise Hulluch from where both artillery and rifle fire began to take its toll on 24 Division. There were huge gaps in that divisional frontage and so battalion after battalion was fed in by the divisional commander, until six battalions now led the division, and by 1300 hours the survivors of the leading waves were a mere fifty yards from the Germans second line.

Now, however, came disappointment and disaster. The German second line was well protected by wire; the artillery bombardment, such as it was, had damaged it not a jot, and to add to the wretched infantry's misery their own artillery shells began to fall amongst them instead of in the enemy trench. Try as they did no one could get through the wire and the division's advance ground to a halt, under fire from in front and from their left.

On the right of the attack 21 Division fared even worse. Orders did not get through to some battalions until ten minutes before Zero Hour, and many of the soldiers had no idea what their objectives were or where they were to go. The division had already suffered heavy losses in its attempt to capture Hill 70 and in repelling the German counter-attack; 14 Durham Light Infantry had lost its commanding officer, all its company commanders, the machine gun officer and the adjutant, and when its sister battalion, the 15th Battalion, came forward it too met a hail of German fire from Bois Hugo and Hill 70. The few – very few – soldiers of 21 Division who managed to get anywhere near the German line found it impossible to get through the wire and gradually groups of men began to fall back towards the Hulluch–Grenay road.

Over on the 24 Division portion of the front no advance was possible, and the troops were horribly exposed in front of the German trench. Should they hang on where they were, avoiding giving up the ground that they had taken, as some officers averred, or should they accept that they had done all that they possibly could (as Major General J E Capper, who took over command of the division shortly after the battle, said later) and withdraw? The sight of 21 Division pulling back on their right was another pressing influence, and as the senior officers began to be killed or wounded, command devolved on company and platoon commanders or on NCOs. Of the eight battalions available to 24 Division that morning, the commanding officers of three of them – 8 Buffs, 8 Queens and 11 Essex – were killed in front of the German line, and two – of 8 Royal West Kents and 9 Suffolks – were wounded, and many other officers were killed or rendered incapable of carrying on. The loss of Lieutenant Colonel Romer of 8 Buffs was particularly sad. Originally an officer of the Militia, he was aged 61 when he was killed; not the oldest death on the Western Front, but certainly the oldest commanding officer of an infantry battalion.

Officers were dying; units were intermingled, communications to the rear were non-existent, and then somebody – nobody knows who – shouted 'Retire'. Back went the men of 24 Division, and now both divisions were retreating as best they could, back across the open, bullet-streaked no-man's-land, to the Grenay–Hulluch road and the trenches of the old German front line, from where they had started that morning. There the few officers and senior NCOs still on their feet ran themselves ragged to rally the remnants of the two divisions. The Germans did not press home their advantage by a major counter-attack, but, proving that gentlemanly conduct had not been entirely eradicated from modern warfare, they sent out medical orderlies to minister what attention they could to the British wounded, sending all those who could walk or crawl back towards the British line unmolested. It was at this point that the Chalk Pit had to be given up. The tiny force of Somersets holding it was now unsupported on both flanks, and terribly vulnerable to being surrounded and defeated in detail. The men were ordered to withdraw, which they did with a creditable steadiness.

It would be wrong to say that the two New Army divisions broke and ran, but they were certainly disorganised, confused, badly cut up and in no state for further action. Regular troops might have got to the German line with fewer casualties, and might have retired in better order, but it is difficult to see how even they could have broken the German position given the paucity of artillery support and the lateness of the attack. Had the reserves been available on the previous evening and had the attack been mounted then, and had the German second line been subjected to accurate and sustained bombardment, things might have been different. As it was Sir John French could take some small comfort from apparently being proved right in his assertions that it was always a mistake to push reserves forward through a narrow gap.

Lieutenant General Haking, commanding XI Corps from his headquarters at Noeux les Mines, five miles behind the jump off line, simply did not believe it when the first news of the disintegration of his two New Army divisions began to trickle in. It must, he thought, be a message sent by an alarmist. Commander First Army, Haig, present at Haking's headquarters, also refused to believe it, and it was not until a staff officer sent forward to ascertain exactly what had happened had returned and submitted his report that the last spark of hope was extinguished. Thus, at around 1615 hours on 26 September, Haig knew without a shadow of doubt that the attack on the German second line had failed.

More bad news was to follow. Although the summit of Hill 70 and the redoubt were still occupied by the Germans, troops of 15 Division were firmly entrenched on the western slopes of the hill, and their position, while precarious, was by no means untenable. As the day wore on, however, casualties began to mount, ammunition was running short and carrying parties with resupplies were unable to get up. The sight of the men of 21 Division retreating was naturally unsettling, and at about 1300 hours on 26 September the men on the slopes of Hill 70 began to pull back down the slope westwards to Loos. Communications were virtually non existent, but the order to hold Loos at all costs was passed around, and those commanding officers of battalions who were able to talk to one another debated the wisdom of further retiring to the old German front-line trenches – which would have meant giving up Loos altogether. Such was the confusion that proper orders could not be promulgated, and some groups – for battalions were mixed up by now – withdrew from Loos while others did not.[4] Fortunately 7th Royal Scots Fusiliers did not retire but stayed where they were east of Loos until, finding themselves the only battalion still on the approaches to Hill 70, they too withdrew to Loos, where they met the commander 6th Cavalry Brigade, who had been sent up to hold Loos with his own brigade and with instructions to take under his command any men of 15 Division still in Loos. A cavalry brigade had three regiments of cavalry (as compared to four battalions in an infantry brigade) and a cavalry regiment had fewer men than an infantry battalion (600 compared to 1,000). As one man in four was a horse holder, looking after his own horse and those of three of his comrades when the regiment dismounted, the two regiments available to hold Loos – 3rd Dragoon Guards and the 1st Royal Dragoons – were equivalent only to one infantry battalion, but they managed to rally many of the 15 Division men streaming back through Loos, and by around 2000 hours the trenches on the western slopes of Hill 70 were reoccupied.

When the news of what was happening to 21 and 24 Divisions was brought home to the Army Commander, there was but one reserve division which might be made available to him: the cream of the British infantry – the Guards.

Earlier in the morning of 26 September, when the attempt to capture Hill 70 had failed, Haking had already sent a warning order to the Guards Division, which was still under command GHQ and not yet released to First Army, that their services might be needed, and ordering them to move from their overnight locations of Noeux les Mines (1st Guards Brigade), Houchin (2nd) and Hallicourt (3rd) to positions between the Le Rutoir / Loos and the Vermelles / Hulluch roads, about 1,200 yards behind the original British front line. Due to the traffic chaos in the area the order did not reach the Guards brigades until 1200, by which time the attack by 21 and 24 Divisions was already in trouble. The Guards began to get on the road at 1300 hours, but at 1410 hours, by which time Haking was beginning to appreciate the enormity of what had happened to his two New Army divisions, even if it was yet to be confirmed, he sent another order to the Guards telling them not to stop behind the original British front line but to carry on to the old German front line, and strengthen the position as best they could.

The Guards had not yet been released to under command First Army. Haking was assuming that they would be, but already expediency was taking over from principle. In the original planning it had been assumed that the reserves would be used to exploit success: the initial attack would breach both German lines of defence, and the reserves would then erupt through that breach, with the Guards taking the Heute Deule Canal. Now they were to be used merely to plug a gap. Congested roads and tracks, desultory German shelling including gas shells, and the general confusion of the battlefield meant that the Guards did not reach the British jump off line until around 1800 hours, and by the time they got to the old German line it was very nearly last light.

Now the Guards Division was firmly under command Haig and First Army, but as with the two New Army divisions, the matter of command of the Guards would lead to acrimony. Sir John French in his despatch said that the Guards Division was placed under command First Army 'on the morning of 26 September', whereas the message handing over command from GHQ was timed at 1500 hours and received by First Army sometime after 1600 hours. In practice it made little difference. Even if Haig had been given control of the Guards in the morning, they would still have been unable to get to the battle area before late evening: only their being placed under First Army from the outset could have affected their availability.

No sooner had the Guards begun to turn the old German trenches that they now occupied into something resembling a defensive position facing east rather than west, when more orders arrived. Major General the Earl of Cavan, commanding the division, arrived at the headquarters of each of his brigades and explained that his division was to relieve 21 and 24 Divisions during the night. Lord Cavan's orders were given to commander 1st Guards Brigade at around 2145 hours, and to the other two brigade commanders some time after that. Despite the obvious difficulties the Guards began to move out and to take up their new positions, allowing the remnants of the two New Army divisions to be pulled out of the battle. By 0600 on the morning of 27 September 1st Guards Brigade had 3 Coldstream on the left, in touch with 1 Division, and 2 Coldstream on its right, and covered a frontage of round 1,400 yards from about 800 yards south-west of Hulluch, running just south of west to a point 600 yards south-east of Lone Tree, where they joined with 2 Irish Guards of 2 Guards Brigade. That brigade's sector ran south-west for 1,800 yards to Fort Glatz, a redoubt on the old German Loos defences, where 1 Scots Guards linked up with the 6th Cavalry Brigade holding Loos.

As the men of the Guards worked to improve and consolidate their new positions, the Commander First Army considered how he might consolidate the new British line in order to renew the attack from it. Orders went down to General Haking, the corps commander, and from there to Major General the Earl of Cavan. At 1350 hours on 27 September Cavan's orders went out to his three brigade commanders. The Guards Division was to attack and capture, from north to south, the Chalk Pits, Puits 14 (a factory building with a tall chimney), and Hill 70. The Chalk Pits and Puits 14 would be the objectives of the 2nd Guards Brigade, while Hill 70 would be taken by the 3rd. Even as the orders were being given out, events were happening that would render the information upon which the plan was based out of date, for at around 1430 hours the Germans counter-attacked Fosse 8 and The Dump, recapturing both of these key points.

For their attack the Guards would have the support of not only their own artillery, but that of the no longer effective 21 and 24 Divisions too. In all 640 field guns and ninety-six howitzers would be available, and had they been able to fire an unlimited number of rounds they would have struck a mighty blow. As it was there was insufficient ammunition, and the bombardment, with a final five minutes of intense fire to precede Zero

Hour at 1545 hours, was insufficient. It would have been insufficient even if the situation to the Guards' north had been unchanged, but now the news came in that the Dump and Fosse 8 had been lost.

It will be recalled that 73 Brigade, lent to 9 Division from 24 Division, had relieved 26 Brigade at Fosse 8. The relief had taken a long time – hardly surprising as 73 Brigade had no experience of such an operation – and there had been a German counter-attack during it, but since then three battalions of 73 Brigade, 7 Northamptonshire, 12 Royal Fusiliers and 9 Royal Sussex, had been holding the line from the Fosse eastwards to Fosse Alley trench. The men were exhausted by marching and digging, and had been under sporadic German fire for most of the 26th. It was not surprising that the brigade commander, Brigadier General Jelf, who visited all three battalions in their firing line on the afternoon of 26 September, considered the situation to be 'serious'. Things got worse for these inexperienced and undertrained battalions. By the morning of 27 September the men had had little or no sleep, only irregular and cold meals, and were still being subjected to shelling.

It is hardly surprising that when the Germans counter-attacked, firstly against the troops on 73 Brigade's left and then against the brigade itself, the men began to fall back and the Germans established infantry and machine gun positions on the Dump. The brigade commander considered that there was no point in trying to regain the Dump – the approaches to it were open and swept by German fire – and decided to establish a new defence line along the east of the Hohenzollern Redoubt, abandoning Fosse and Dump trenches. It was at this time that the commander 9 Division, Major General Thesiger, realising that things were not going well for 73 Brigade, came forward to assess the situation for himself, and was killed along with his ADC and a staff officer from his divisional headquarters.

Further reinforcements were now being made available, however, for 28 Division was moving to the battle area. 28 Division was a regular division formed to take under its command regular battalions returning from overseas garrisons having been replaced by Territorial Force or local units. It had taken a severe hammering at the Second Battle of Ypres, April/May 1915, and had been in Second Army reserve until ordered to reinforce I Corps and then subsequently to relieve 9 Division. As no transport was available the division had to march the fifteen miles from Bailleul, and arrived too late to save Fosse 8.

Major General Butler, chief of staff to the commander First Army, was at Headquarters XI Corps when the news of the successful German counter-attack on the Dump and Fosse 8 came in. Butler passed the news back to Haig, who ordered that the attack by the Guards should be cancelled. It was too late. By the time the order not to proceed had got down to General Cavan, the Guards had left their jump off line.

On the left 2nd Guards Brigade was to attack the Chalk Pit with 2 Irish Guards supported by the 1st Coldstream, while 1 Scots Guards would take Puits 14. The 3rd Grenadiers would be in reserve, ready to reinforce the Scots Guards if required. The brigade was assisted by a smoke screen deployed by 1 Guards Brigade from south-west of Hulluch. The Chalk Pit was quickly taken, but the men advancing on Puits 14 came under withering machine gun fire. The Scots Guards were reinforced by men of the Irish Guards from the Chalk Pit, and a detachment of the 4th Grenadier Guards, which had become separated from its parent formation, 4th Guards Brigade, and was lost, but had nevertheless marched to the sound of the guns and joined in 2 Guards Brigade's battle with great gallantry. Despite this, eleven of the Scots Guards officers, including the commanding officer, became casualties and only a small group of men under Captain Cuthbert could get into the Puits, where, for the moment, they held on doggedly. One platoon of the 3rd Grenadiers managed to join them, but after they too began to take casualties it became clear that the approaches to the Puits were far too open, and that the cover in the building itself was so sparse, that to persist in trying to hold it was doomed to failure, and those who could withdrew. A temporary firing line was established from the Chalk Pit running south to Loos, along the lower slopes leading to Puits 14.

In giving his orders for the attack to the brigade commander, Lord Cavan had said that the 3rd Guards Brigade were only to attack Hill 70 once the Chalk Pits and Puits 14 were in the hands of the 1st Brigade. The reason was self evident: from the Chalk Pits and, particularly, from Puits 14 heavy flanking fire could be directed against anyone approaching Hill 70, and to assault that feature without having first eliminated the threat from the north would be hazardous indeed. The Chalk Pits had been captured, but Puits 14 had not, although Brigadier General Heyworth, commanding the 3rd Guards Brigade, saw some men of the 1st Scots and 3rd Grenadier Guards enter the building and assumed that it had been captured, unaware that the Puits would be in British hands for only a short period before perforce being abandoned

The 4th Grenadier, 1st Welsh, 2nd Scots and 1st Grenadier Guards of 4 Guards Brigade moved off 'as if on parade',[5] down the exposed, mile long slope to Loos village, through which they would have to pass to get at Hill 70. At once they were met by a hail of high explosive and shrapnel shells from the German artillery, but by making use of the maze of old German communication trenches battalion and company commanders managed to reduce the effects of the shelling considerably. As the leading battalion, 4 Grenadier Guards, began to emerge from the east end of Loos a salvo of gas shells fell among them. There was some confusion as the men halted and scrabbled in their packs to find and don their gas masks, and the commanding officer, Lieutenant Colonel Hamilton, on his way up from Brigade Headquarters to rejoin his battalion, was badly affected and unable to continue. It is unclear as to exactly what was in these gas shells: the Germans were certainly capable of discharging chlorine gas from cylinders, and there is some evidence to suggest that even before their use of chlorine at the Second Battle of Ypres in April 1915 they had experimented with tear gas delivered by shell. Whether it was chlorine or tear gas that fell around the Grenadiers as they emerged from Loos is not known, but in any event it was during the confusion so caused that two companies of the battalion, under Captain Morrison, took a wrong turning, became detached and ended up with the 2nd Guards Brigade attacking Puits 14.

The brigade commander was close enough behind his troops to discover fairly quickly that half of his lead battalion had disappeared, he knew not where, and so he readjusted his plan and ordered 1 Welsh Guards to attack Hill 70 supported by the remaining two companies of the 4th Grenadiers. At 1730 hours the men of the Welsh Guards swarmed up the slopes of Hill 70. All went well until they reached the crest of the hill, when they came under vicious machine gun fire from Puits 14, now regained by the Germans, and from the redoubt on the hill itself. Try as they might, neither the Welsh nor the Grenadiers could get over the crest and into the redoubt. At around 2300 hours the 2nd Scots Guards were sent forward and they began to dig in about a hundred yards down the slope. Wisely, the Welsh Guards commanding officer ordered his men to withdraw to this new line, but had great difficulty in persuading them to do so, such was their reluctance to give up ground won, regardless of its exposed location. The Welsh Guards had experienced their baptism of fire, and while they had not been able to take the hill, they had, in the words of their commanding officer, Lieutenant Colonel Murray Threipland, borne themselves 'up to the best Brigade of Guards standards'. As the night wore on it was apparent that while Puits 14 and Hill 70 were still in German hands, there was nevertheless a far stronger British line now than had existed at the beginning of the day, and the British position in Loos was far more secure than it had been earlier. On their right the Guards linked up firmly with the cavalry holding Loos, and on their left they clung to the Loos–Hulluch Road.

While the Guards Division had been attacking on their front, 47 Division, south of the Loos crassier, attacked Chalk Pit Copse (not to be confused with Chalk Pit Wood to the north) and a strongpoint known as Sitzpunkt 69. This was completely successful, indeed British casualties amounted to two men killed and fourteen wounded, while the attackers found around 150 German corpses. On the 2nd Division front, on the other hand, an attack on Cuinchy was cancelled, as the discharge of gas that was to precede an infantry assault was rendered ineffective by changes in wind direction.

At 0645 hours on the morning of 26 September 7 Division had mounted a counter-attack against The Quarries, which they had lost during the night, using the 9th Battalion the Norfolk Regiment, lent to them by 71 Brigade of 24 Division. The counter-attack achieved nothing, except the deaths of four officers and fifty-nine Other Ranks of the battalion, with another 350 wounded or missing. If a brigade had been unable to hold them the previous night, it should have been apparent that a battalion was unlikely to recapture them, and it has to be said that this operation was misconceived. Another attack on the same objective was mounted at 1600 hours the same day, using the 2nd Worcesters and elements of 1 KRRC from Carter's Force. These were regular battalions and advanced using fire and movement, with two sections of a platoon lying down and firing while the other two advanced, then providing covering fire in turn, but while it made considerable progress it was stopped a few hundred yards short of the objective when the divisional commander 7 Division, General Capper (brother of Major General J E Capper who took command of 24 Division on 3 October) was killed.

To the south of the British front, despite assurances by General d'Urbal, commanding the French Tenth Army, very little happened. While d'Urbal did intend to launch an attack with the French XXI Corps, the one nearest to the British, and while he did augment it with an infantry division and much heavy artillery, an attack planned for 1200 hours was postponed to 1400 hours, then made very little progress, and was finally halted at 1500 hours, being put off until the French could capture the northern portion of Vimy Ridge (which in the event they were unable to do).

During the night of 27 September Lord Cavan visited the headquarters of both his forward brigades. In discussions with the brigade commanders he agreed that any further attempt to take Hill 70 was pointless, at least for the moment, but First Army insisted that another attack on Puits 14 should be mounted the next day, on the grounds that it was this position that very largely contributed to the Germans' ability to defend Hill 70, and that as long as Puits 14 remained in German hands the new British line could not be wholly secure.

While Lord Cavan was converting First Army's orders to the Guards Division into instructions to his brigade commanders, the Commander-in-Chief of the BEF, Field Marshal French, was taking stock. The whole of the reserve corps for the Loos battle had now been released to First Army. The two New Army divisions, 21 and 24, had disintegrated and were unfit for any military task until they had been brought up to strength, retrained and re-equipped; the Guards Division was already holding a considerable stretch of front and was not therefore available to exploit any breach of the German second line that might be achieved. First Army had no reserve left, and a commander with no reserve is unable to affect the course of a battle. Not only were there no reserves to meet any eventuality that might arise, but as General d'Urbal had been unable to get forward, the right flank of First Army, 47 Division, was 'in the air', that is to say there were no friendly troops to its immediate right, or south, which made the division's positions horribly vulnerable to counter-attack from the flank or rear.

French pointed all this out to General Joffre, the French Commander-in-Chief, explaining that in view of the exposed right flank the British might have to stop the offensive unless the French could do something in that area. Foch agreed that during the night of 28/29 September, the French would relieve the British 47 Division, thus allowing that division to be brought into reserve, and that they would also take over the village of Loos and Hill 70 – provided the British captured it first – thus allowing the British to shorten their line even further.

In the Guards Division General Lord Cavan's order for the 2nd Guards Brigade to attack Puits 14 at 1545 hours was not greeted with universal acclaim. Brigadier General Ponsonby, commanding the brigade, thought that as it had not been possible to capture it the previous day, with more artillery than was available on 28 September, it was most unlikely that the task could be achieved now, particularly when his brigade had sustained 1,200 casualties, or over a quarter of its strength. He sent off a message to the headquarters of the Guards Division suggesting that the attack should be postponed until after dark, but having received no reply had no option but to carry on as ordered.

After a preliminary bombardment by as much heavy artillery as could be made immediately available, and a five-minute 'hurricane bombardment' by the divisional guns, the 1st Coldstream, supported by the brigade machine guns and the rifle fire of the 2nd Irish Guards, attacked Puits 14 from the southern edge of Chalk Pit Wood, about 400 yards away. The men did their best, and a small group led by two subalterns did, briefly, penetrate the Puits, but there was just too much machine gun fire, from a defilade position in Bois Hugo, and when nine officers and 250 men of the Coldstream had become casualties, Brigadier General Ponsonby called off the operation.

For the rest of that day and night the men of the Guards Division dug to improve their positions, and it was as well that they did so, for on the 29th they were subject to prolonged and accurate German shelling. It killed the commanding officer and the adjutant of the 1st Coldstream, but the toll could have been far greater. Shells also fell on Loos village, but again good work by the soldiers in digging themselves in saved lives. On 30 September the Guards Division, still in the line, was ordered to prepare a new jump off line for a renewed attack, provisionally planned to be launched on 3 October. All night the men laboured. As they were digging in chalk it was, said those who were there, the hardest digging of the war, but by 0400 hours on the morning of 1 October, a new fire trench ran parallel to the Lens–La Bassée road south to Chalk Pit Wood. For the next two nights men of 12 Division, which had relieved the Guards, continued to work to develop the new jump off line.

With the agreement by the French to take over part of the British line, some formations could now be taken out of the line, and on the night of

29/30 September 3 Guards Brigade was relieved by 47 Division, themselves and 2 Brigade of 1 Division being replaced in turn by elements of the French IX Corps. By first light on 1 October the Guards were out of the line, and by 3 October the French IX Corps, which had been required to move from the right (south) of the French 10th Army to the left (north) of it in foul weather and over congested roads and tracks, had taken over Loos village and the sector north as far as the Puits 14 track.

Between 26 September when the Guards were first ordered into action, and 29 September when their first elements began to be relieved, the Guards Division had lost nineteen officers and 414 Other Ranks killed, and around three times that number wounded, from twelve battalions. To put this into perspective, the table below shows the total death toll in the regiments of Foot Guards from the outbreak of war until their commitment to the Battle of Loos, compared to their losses by death in that first deployment.

Regiment	Number of battalions on the Western Front	Average number of OR[6] killed per battalion from outbreak of war until 25 September 1915	Average number of OR killed per battalion 26–29 September 1915
Grenadier Guards	4	218	32
Coldstream Guards	4	268	18
Scots Guards	2	594	63
Irish Guards	2	274	20
Welsh Guards	1	Raised in 1915	48

The Guards lost an average of thirty-two men per battalion killed in that four-day deployment, whereas 21 Division, in a one-day deployment, lost an average of fifty-three men per battalion, or a death rate of nearly seven times that of the Guards. The intensity of the fighting was just as great when the Guards went into action, and the situation just as dangerous. The difference is that the Guards, even with their casualties to date, were led by officers and NCOs who, by and large, knew what they were about. Dilution there had surely been, but enough regular expertise remained to keep the death rate as low as it could be given the task to be carried out.

It was now time to take stock, and to decide what should happen next. What should be done was a simple enough conclusion to come to: when it should, or could, be done was another matter.

Notes

1. The original orders were for the two brigades to attack side by side, with the track as the axis. Both brigade commanders realised the difficulty of moving their troops to the laid-down jump off line, and agreed with each other to attack from the positions they occupied when the orders came.
2. The modern term 'blue on blue' to indicate a friendly fire incident, comes from the custom of marking on the map friendly and enemy positions. Today friendly forces are shown in blue, enemy in red. At this stage of the war the French used that convention (historically French soldiers wore blue, while the traditional enemy, England, dressed its soldiers in red) and the British did the opposite (for the same reason). Later in 1915 the British changed their colour coding to conform to the French system.
3. Who, as we have seen, was finally laid to rest in October 2004.
4. The Official History says that a message purporting to come from HQ 15 Division ordered a withdrawal, later considered unnecessary, but that a subsequent inquiry failed to discover the source of the message.
5. Headlam, Cuthbert DSO, *The Guards Division in the Great War*, London: John Murray, 1924.
6. At this time the lowest rank in the Grenadier and Scots Guards was Guardsman; in the Coldstream, Irish and Welsh Guards it was Private. Now all are Guardsmen.

CHAPTER VII

Reflection

Amongst the casualties of the Guards Division was a young officer who was to be, and remains to this day, the subject of considerable argument. Lieutenant John Kipling, only son of the bard of Empire Rudyard Kipling, was missing believed killed on 27 September, during the attack on Chalk Pit Wood by the 2nd Battalion Irish Guards. The young Kipling should never have been in the army at all. While at school (Wellington, whence came many British Army officers, then and now) he had briefly considered applying for Sandhurst, but his low academic achievements and poor eyesight made it very unlikely that he would be accepted.

When war came John, like thousands of other young men who thought it would all be over by Christmas and who were anxious to do their bit before it was, applied for a temporary commission in the New Armies. On 10 August 1914 and again on 19 August, just after his 17th birthday, he failed. This time it was not his education that let him down (academic standards for temporary gentlemen were much lower than those required for potential regular officers), but his eyesight, and he failed the medical examination. By the way in which the army measured (and still measures) eyesight, his left eye was found to be 6/36, improved to 6/9 with spectacles, and his right eye 6/36 corrected to 6/6 with spectacles. What this meant was that even with his glasses Kipling would have had difficulty reading and deciphering maps in bad light, and without glasses would have had difficulty in finding his way about. This might not have mattered too much if John had wanted to work in the world of military ration accounting or the postal service, well behind the lines, but in the infantry – and a Kipling could hardly serve anywhere else – wearing spectacles, even if they could give the wearer perfect vision, which in this case they could not, was a risk. Glasses could easily be broken or knocked off, and a platoon commander who cannot see where he is taking his men is a risk to himself and to those he commands.

John did, briefly, consider enlisting as a private soldier, before it was pointed out that the eyesight standards for officers in the infantry are actually slightly lower than those for Other Ranks (because of the requirement for the latter to be able to shoot well and accurately). It seemed that the only eligible representative of the Kipling family was destined to miss the opportunity to take part in military service, as opposed to just writing about it, when father took a hand.

Lord Roberts, 'Bobs Bahadur', military hero of the Victorian era and one time commander-in-chief of the British Army, was 82 in 1914 but still sprightly and still with much influence. Amongst his many connections with British and Indian regiments, Lord Roberts was the Colonel of the Irish Guards. The Colonel of the Regiment was (and still is) an honorary appointment. It carried no financial rewards and no operational authority, but its holder (usually for five years, extendable in multiples of five) wielded great influence over the way in which the regiment did its business, and he had the final say as to who should be commissioned into the regiment. Roberts had been one of those few men in the public eye who had been convinced that a war between France and Germany was bound to come, and that when it did Britain should be unequivocally at the side of France. He had caused much displeasure in Parliament when he had supported the National Service League (when a motion to reduce his field marshal's half pay was tabled), and he had spoken publicly in favour of its platform of compulsory military service in peacetime. Rudyard Kipling had agreed with Lord Roberts' views, and had appeared at public meetings in his support. It was time to call in past favours.

John Kipling, despite his eyesight, was gazetted as an ensign (second lieutenant) in the Irish Guards, with seniority backdated to his 17th birthday, 17 August 1914. After a hurried stop in London to be fitted for his uniforms he joined the Second Battalion at its training camp in Essex. At only five feet six and a half inches in height, bespectacled and frequently ill with colds, influenza and other minor ailments, he cannot have been an impressive looking Guards officer. Pre-war the Irish Guards had but one regular battalion, Kipling's being originally a reserve battalion, but, as we have seen, the pressure to find enough battalions to form the Guards Division led to the reserve becoming the Second Battalion and being designated a regular battalion by the King, with Lord Kitchener as colonel of the regiment in place of Lord Roberts who died while on a visit to the Indian Corps in France. The Second Battalion went to France in August 1915, and with them went John Kipling, only just 18 years of age.[1]

The baptism of fire for 2nd Battalion Irish Guards was the Battle of Loos, when on 27 September their brigade, 2 Guards Brigade, was ordered to capture Chalk Pit Wood and Puits 14 Bis. Kipling was the platoon commander of 5 Platoon of Number 2 Company, and he and another subaltern had got to the far side of the Puits building, along with some of their own men and some of the Scots Guards, when both young officers were seen to be wounded. The Puits area could not be held, and when the Guards were forced to fall back through Chalk Pit Wood both officers were missing, and reported as such. As the Red Cross was not given Kipling's name by the Germans as being a prisoner of war, in October he was included in the official list of those 'Missing', but not in the list of those 'Missing, believed killed'.

All fathers are, of course, dismayed if their sons are missing in action, but the loss hit Rudyard particularly hard. Partly this would have been because John was an only son, doted on and spoiled by his parents, and perhaps partly because it was Rudyard's string pulling that had got John into the army, when he was manifestly medically unfit and would not have been accepted had not his father arranged it. Rudyard spent much time and money trying to discover what had happened to his son. He or his wife wrote to or interviewed numerous men of the battalion to try to find out exactly what had happened – with little result.

Eventually Rudyard Kipling had to accept, albeit reluctantly, that his son was dead. He became a member of the Imperial War Graves Commission, an appointment which he took very seriously and discharged until his death in 1936.

Once the war was over the army mounted a huge operation to find and recover bodies that had not been found, or could not be recovered, immediately after death. There were all sorts of reasons for this: the man might have been blown to bits by shelling, and there was nothing left to recover; or have died in a shell hole or trench that collapsed; or in a portion of no-man's-land that was not occupied long enough for the body to be recovered – by friend or foe. Post-war clearing up also saw the exhumation of bodies from temporary cemeteries and their concentration into permanent ones, under the auspices of the Imperial War Graves Commission (now the Commonwealth War Graves Commission), and the erecting of memorials to the missing. As the bodies of nearly half of all British and Empire dead on the Western Front were missing – either never found at all, or if found not identified – these memorials were important, and Rudyard was very much involved in their design and in deciding what wording should be placed on them, and on the grave stones of unidentified bodies. As more previously unknown graves were located, and as the chaotic state of post-war Germany abated and more information about prisoners of war who had died in German hands became available, Rudyard's hopes would be temporarily raised, but when a second search of the Loos area in 1921 failed to find any trace that could be connected with John, Rudyard had to accept that his son was dead, and that his body would probably never be identified. In due course Lieutenant John Kipling's name was inscribed on the memorial to the missing at the Battle of Loos, located at 'Dud Corner', originally the site of the German Lens Road Redoubt.

And there the matter rested until 1992, when Norm Christie, a records officer of the Commonwealth War Graves Commission and himself a respected author and historian of Canadian actions on the Western Front, announced that he had identified the body of 'A Lieutenant of the Great

War Irish Guards', found during battlefield clearance in September 1919 and buried in a Commonwealth War Graves Cemetery, as being that of John Kipling. A new headstone was erected with Kipling's name on it, but at the time of writing (July 2005) his name has not been removed from the memorial to the missing. Christie based his finding on the fact that only one lieutenant of the Irish Guards was unaccounted for – Kipling – and that this must therefore be him. That the body is recorded as being found at a considerable distance from where Kipling would have been is explained by an error by the fatigue party who found him. It is not the purpose of this book to become embroiled in the argument as to whether the grave is or is not that of John Kipling. Suffice it to say that there is considerable doubt about whether he was wearing the rank of lieutenant on the day he was killed (the promotion, backdated to June 1915, was not gazetted until after he went missing), and the suggestion that the location of the body may have been wrongly recorded is unconvincing. That the matter should be the subject of heated debate ninety years after John Kipling's death is an indication of how deeply the Western Front is engraved upon the national psyche.[2]

It was not only subalterns that were being killed at Loos; the toll of senior officers was heavy too. In the first two days of fighting two had been killed, and a third would be. By the end of the battle of the nine major generals commanding divisions (six in the initial attack and three reserve divisions), three, or one third, would be killed. It is not the task of divisional commanders to get killed; rather they should be sufficiently forward to know what is going on and to get the feel of the battle, but not so far forward that they get tied down by involvement with the doings of the leading units. The trouble was that British officers believed in leading by example, and this was particularly important in an inexperienced Territorial Force or New Army division.

Major General Sir Thompson Capper was just a few days short of his 52nd birthday when he was killed. An infantryman, he had served in Africa, India, the Sudan and in the South African War before taking over command of 7 Division, which he took to the Western Front in 1914. He had to relinquish command of the division in April 1915, when he was badly injured by an 'own goal' during a grenade demonstration, but he resumed command of the division in July. When the division had lost The Quarries to a German counter-attack on the night of 25 September, it had tried to recover them on the morning of 26 September, and when that failed an infantry battalion and elements of a second from Carter's force were ordered to mount another attack that would be preceded by an artillery bombardment at 1600 hours. Capper accompanied the assault on foot, and was shot by a sniper as he was going back to his own headquarters down a communication trench that was overlooked by German positions (it had originally been a German trench). Capper's ADC dragged him to safety but he died of wounds the following day.

Major General Thesiger, originally of the Rifle Brigade, was another very experienced regular officer who was killed at Loos, just a few days short of his 47th birthday. Thesiger was very young for his rank, and perhaps epitomises the regular officers' toast (then and now) 'To a Sudden Plague and a Bloody War', as being the only way to fast promotion. On the outbreak of war in 1914 Thesiger was a lieutenant colonel commanding the Fourth Battalion of his regiment in India, whence he and the battalion returned to UK and were then posted to France in December 1914. Thesiger was promoted to brigadier general in May 1915 and placed in command of 2 Brigade, earning further promotion to major general in August and appointed GOC 33 Division and then 9 (Scottish) Division. In twelve months he had gone from commanding a thousand men to commanding ten times that number. On 27 September, it having been reported that 73 Brigade, lent to 9 Division from the reserve 24 Division, was 'unsteady' in the area of Fosse 8, Thesiger, with one of his staff officers and his ADC, went forward to assess the situation for himself. At the Hohenzollern Redoubt, now in British hands and just short of Fosse 8, where the fighting was, Thesiger and the two officers with him were killed. Neither the war diary of 26 Brigade (the unit that reported the death) nor that of 9 Division, nor indeed the Official History, tells us how Thesiger died, saying simply that he was killed, but as neither his body nor that of his staff officer, Major Le Mottee of the Gloucestershire Regiment, was ever found, or if found was never identified, it would seem that he was probably killed by a shell bursting very near him. The body of his ADC, Lt Burney of the Gordons (the 24-year-old son of a brigadier general), was found and buried.

The oldest of the three divisional commanders to be killed at Loos was the 55-year-old Major General Wing. Wing was an officer of the Royal Artillery and started the war as a brigadier general, in charge of 3 Division's artillery, being promoted to major general in October 1914 and moving to First Army as Major General Royal Artillery, before taking over command of 12 Division in March 1915.[3] He had been wounded at least twice in the war, and on 2 October, when returning from visiting front-line positions near Mazingarbe, he and his ADC were killed by a German shell.

As well as the three major generals who were killed at Loos, two brigadier generals were killed, three wounded and one was taken prisoner.[4]

One might well argue that Capper, Thesiger, Wing and the rest had no business to be where they were, but all commanders, at whatever level, prefer to see for themselves, rather than taking what might be the more sensible approach and relying on reports from units or from staff officers sent forward. There is no doubt that British senior officers were far fonder of getting up to where the action was than was wise; and one of the reasons for Sir John French's dilatory reaction to being asked by General Haig for the reserve corps to be placed under command First Army, was French's insistence on being close to the front, where communications with First Army and with his own main headquarters were poor. Equally, there can be no doubt that the popular image of generals lounging in safety well behind the lines while their men died needlessly, is pure fiction.

Nowadays it is unquestioned that the media – press, television, radio – have a huge impact on the conduct of a military operation. In a totalitarian regime the media can be controlled and fed with stories that support the government. What the papers might say was never a worry to Hitler, Stalin or Ho Chi Minh, and only rarely a matter of concern to the Kaiser, King Ferdinand of Bulgaria or the Sultan of Turkey. In a democracy the media are far more of a problem, as while they can be censored they cannot be instructed what to publish, and as journalists are not known for their military understanding they will often write articles which are either untrue (through malice or ignorance), dangerous to national security, damaging to military or public morale, or a combination of all three.[5] By the time of the Second World War proper regulations to ensure that the media did not betray any forthcoming operations were in place, and a form of censorship acceptable to both government and media was implemented, but in 1914 the British government and the British Army were still very much novices in what is today known as Media Operations. At first the authorities strove to keep the press as far away as possible from the front line, making them rely on handouts and published dispatches, but it was soon realised that this was counter-productive. As the army got bigger and bigger, and absorbed more and more of the nation's manpower, the public naturally wanted to know what was going on. Sir John French had already made a quite disgraceful use of his friends in the press to plant stories highlighting the shortage of ammunition, and by 1915 it was realised that a carefully managed press, kept informed and 'on side', could be a major asset in the management of information.

The opening phase of the Loos battle, 25 September 1915, was a Saturday, and on the following Monday, 27 September, *The Times* carried a leader headed 'The German Line Pierced in the West'. Factually the leader was absolutely accurate:

> … Formidable French forces penetrated the German entrenchments in Champagne over a front of over fifteen miles … Simultaneously the British Army broke the German line south of La Bassée on a front of five miles, and advanced a distance which extended at some points to well over two miles … The British are able to report the capture of over 2,600 prisoners and nine guns. In yesterday's fighting [26 September] all our gains were maintained except at one point north of Loos. Loos itself is in our hands …

The leader column went on to speculate that 'if the successes gained can be vigorously developed we may be on the eve of signal changes in the military situation'.

The following day, 28 September, *The Times* again carried a leader about the fighting at Loos. By now of course the situation on the ground was less rosy than that on the first day, and the paper warned its readers not to expect too much, while still remaining optimistic:

> The rush of good news from France has necessarily been followed by less stirring dispatches, but there is no sign of a set-back. A dispatch received late last evening from Sir John French records further progress of the British offensive east of Loos, while the inevitable counter attacks have been repulsed elsewhere with 'heavy loss'. The same apparently holds true for the French … Meanwhile the dominating factors must be constantly borne in mind. There have been tremendous storms of rain which may check the advance. Again, the second and third line of German entrenchments have to be treated with respect. It will take time to get the heavy guns into fresh positions, and we may be certain that the Allies are not going to throw away their new opportunities by impetuous recklessness … The present operations may last for several days. Their first stages must not be overrated, nor must we speak of the prologue as though it constituted the entire drama …

All this was perfectly true, and with hindsight was warning the paper's readership that a great and glorious victory was not, perhaps, inevitable. The following day, Wednesday 29 September, under a sub heading 'Third Line Breached', *The Times* quoted Sir John French's despatches, which accurately reported the number of guns captured and prisoners taken, but went on to say:

> We now hold all the ground north of Hill 70, which the enemy retook on the 26th … We are now closely engaged with the enemy's third line.

In reality, of course, the British did not hold all the ground north of Hill 70, for Puits 14 Bis, Bois Hugo and Chalet Wood were firmly in German hands, despite the best efforts of the Guards to re-take them. This misreporting is, however, far more likely to be due to ignorance at GHQ as to exactly what the situation was, than to any attempt to mislead. French's despatch was timed at 2258 hours 28 September, from reports received during the afternoon when the attack by the Guards Division on Puits 14 Bis was still going on. Optimism may have coloured the report.

As for the statement that the British were closely engaged with the enemy's third line, this was misleading and probably due to the reporter assuming that the Loos defences – a line of defences about 800 yards east of the first German line and 3,000 yards short of the second German line – were actually the second German line, and that the second line, which the British were indeed engaging, albeit perhaps not all that closely, was a third line.

On Thursday 30 September *The Times*, in the person of the great John Buchan, no less, gave way to wishful thinking, for under a sub heading 'The New Army's First Success' and dated 28 September, Buchan says:

> ... When it is possible to tell the full story of Saturday's doings [i.e. the opening of the Loos offensive] the British people will find that they have good cause for pride in the New Armies they have raised since last September. Old Regular battalions and Territorials played their part in the advance but the central movement on Loos was entrusted to one of the new divisions ... but Loos was its [the New Army's] first clear success

Pride in the undoubted courage and overwhelming desire to do well was certainly justified, and the two New Army divisions – 9 and 15 – that took part in the opening phase on 25 September had initially done well. 15 Division had indeed participated in the taking of Loos, but by the time Buchan filed his despatch, GHQ was certainly aware of the collapse of 21 and 24 Divisions, even if they had neglected to inform the press.

While the French were taking over part of the British line to allow First Army a reserve, discussions were taking place between Field Marshal Sir John French and General Sir Douglas Haig for the British, and Generals Joffre, Foch and d'Urbal for the French. The original idea had been to renew the attack almost immediately, or at least on 3 October, but the weather and the roads caused the French to take longer than intended to extend their line, and the renewal of offensive operations was delayed to 4 October, then 5 and then finally 6 October. In the wider picture, the French had, against expectations, managed to secure a toehold on Vimy Ridge on 28 September, expanding it to include the highest point of the ridge and holding on to what they had gained during the night. The French now decided to suspend all operations until a joint attack with the British could be mounted, and this included putting a temporary stop to operations in Champagne. In modern warfare doctrine would indicate that success should be reinforced by switching the main effort to Vimy Ridge, but the ability to react with the speed that would be required did not exist in 1915 – particularly in regard to communications, which, as we have seen, were unavoidably slow. The delay not only allowed the Allies to prepare for a renewed offensive, but also gave time to the Germans to prepare resistance to it. It also meant that the Germans could mount counter-attacks on Vimy Ridge, and by 30 September the French had lost their hold on the top of the high ground, although they did manage to retain positions on the western slopes.[6]

At the same time Sir John French had ordered 12 and 46 Divisions south to replace 21 and 24 Divisions. 12 Division was also of the New Army, being part of that first Hundred Thousand, and was recruited from

Norfolk, Suffolk, Essex, Berkshire and London. The infantry consisted of battalions of The Queen's (Royal West Surrey), East Surrey, Queen's Own (Royal West Kent), Buffs (East Kent), Sussex, Berkshire and Middlesex Regiments from the counties, and battalions of the Royal Fusiliers from London. Men initially formed up at their county recruiting depots, were formed into battalions and underwent some basic training, mainly with dummy wooden rifles like most of the early New Army units, and then moved to brigade camps at Shorncliffe, Colchester and Purfleet. Then, in November 1914, the whole division came together at Hythe, moving to Aldershot in February 1915. In March Major General Wing took over command of the division, which, along with three other New Army divisions in Aldershot, was now considered ready for the front. At last, after months of rumours, musketry training, route marches and practice embarkations, the order finally came and on 29 May 1915 the first units of the division entrained for France. The men left by way of Folkestone and Boulogne, while the cavalry and transport horses and those in charge of them travelled by the Southampton–Le Havre route. By 1 June all were in France and the division moved to the Armentières area, where serious training for trench warfare began. On 23 June the division took over their first sector of front, from Ploegsteert Wood – known inevitably as Plugstreet Wood – on the left to the Lys river on their right, or south. The frontage was about 6,000 yards, a lot for a single division, but this was a quiet sector, although the men of the 6th Queens, 6th Buffs and 11th Middlesex, the first battalions to occupy the firing line, may not have thought so, as thirty high explosive shells fell on them on the first day.

Thirty shells was, of course, a mere bagatelle compared to what they would have to face very soon, and the main form of warfare met by the battalions of 12 Division in those early days at the front was sniping. Plugstreet Wood had not yet been reduced to matchwood, and as the opposing lines lay through the middle of it, there was plenty of scope for camouflage and concealment. Both sides displayed much ingenuity and the most popular method was for snipers to work in pairs, with one up a tree armed with binoculars or a telescope, spotting for the other who lay in a concealed firing position below.

As the area was rather better drained than the Ypres Salient itself, the division had its introduction to mining, something that both sides indulged in and which involved tunnelling under the opposing trenches, placing as much explosive as could be crammed into the chamber at the end of the tunnel, and exploding the resultant mine. Whether the effort expended in tunnelling and mining was cost effective is debatable (the British eventually had the equivalent of two divisions of men burrowing away under no-man's-land towards the German trenches), but the fear that one's world would suddenly, and without warning, dissolve in a great gout of fire from below did concentrate the mind wonderfully. A number of mines were exploded by the Germans in the vicinity of 12 Division, but as the miners' underground navigation was never sufficiently accurate to place the mine correctly, not much harm was done.

On 15 July the division extended its sector even farther, to due east of Armentières, and the division now held 7,000 yards of front. This meant putting all three brigades into the line, and while there were no major operations on its front, 12 Division nonetheless had seven officers and sixty-four Other Ranks killed in July from the steady attrition of shelling, sniping and patrolling. There was a certain amount of live and let live, which the men of the division thought was because the troops opposite them were Saxons – 'non aggressive unless provoked' – as the Divisional History remarks,[7] and notices were put up in the German trenches advising of the capture of Warsaw and offering to send over German newspapers in rifle grenades with their explosive content removed. The British retaliated by catapulting over news of Royal Naval victories in the Baltic, and by stealing the German notice boards.

The other division now made available for Loos was 46 Division, marginally more experienced than 12 Division in that it was of the Territorial Force, so that its units had at least trained together before the war, and it had been on the Western Front longer. Originally based in the North Midlands, 46 Division was the first Territorial Force division to be sent to the Western Front as a division, and was composed of men from Derbyshire, Lincolnshire, Leicestershire, Nottinghamshire and Staffordshire, and commanded by Major General the Hon. E H Montagu-Stuart-Wortley. It was not originally intended to send the division to France so early in the war, but when the only remaining regular division, 29 Division, was warned for the Dardanelles, instead of being sent to the BEF, Sir John French was told he could have instead 46 Division, considered to be the best of the Territorial Force divisions at that time. That division duly arrived in late February 1915, and was part of Sir John French's GHQ reserve for the Battle of Neuve Chapelle in March, although it was not committed. It first went into the line in the Ypres Salient in April, but was largely untroubled by the Second Battle of Ypres.

Shortly before these two divisions were added to those available for the Loos offensive, there was an outbreak of spy mania in and around the Ypres Salient. These outbreaks were frequent, and largely fuelled by rumours, the sources of which were never identified. On this occasion suspicion took the form of tales that German spies were wandering around behind the British lines in disguise. The first manifestation was that the spy was dressed as a staff officer – staff officers' lives became almost impossible until the reports changed to that of a spy dressed as a brigadier general and moving around in a motorcar without a number plate. Average speeds of brigadier generals in their staff cars, with or without number plates, slowed markedly as they were repeatedly stopped and questioned, until the finger of suspicion shifted to a spy dressed as an officer of the Royal Engineers, leading to mass arrests of perfectly genuine engineer officers sketching enemy positions, including one Royal Engineer officer of 46 Division who was arrested four times in one day. One cannot help but wonder whether the humour of the private soldier was at work.[8]

12 Division moved to the Loos area by train and bus on the night of 27/28 September, and went into billets south of Béthune on the morning of 29 September, while 46 Division arrived in Béthune itself on 3 October.

The plan agreed on between the British and the French was sound enough. There was now a German salient which poked out into Allied-held territory south of Loos, and which included Cité St Pierre, Cité St Edouard and the Double Crassier, objectives for the British in the original attack on 25 September. The renewed offensive would be a pincer attack on this salient, with the British attacking south-east over a three-mile front, while the French would attack north-east over a similar frontage. Before this could happen, however, the existing front line had to be tidied up, and this included the problems of The Dump, Fosse 8 and The Quarries, now back in German hands, and the redoubt on Hill 70 which despite the best efforts of the British still held out. At first the British proposed that they should attack The Dump, Fosse 8 and The Quarries on 4 October, with the French assaulting Hill 70 on the same day. The French were not happy with this plan, considering that until the British objectives were taken, fire from them would make any approach to Hill 70 impossible, and after discussion it was agreed that the British would deal with their objectives on 5 October, while the French would deal with Hill 70 as part of the main offensive on 6 October.

The Dump was originally to be attacked by 28 Division at 0230 hours on the morning of 28 September, but such was the state of the ground and the congestion in communication trenches that only one battalion (1 Royal Berkshire, a regular battalion of Carter's Force), actually attacked at that time. It was a bright moonlit night, and after losing seventy-eight men killed with no ground gained, the battalion withdrew. At 0930 the same morning, 28 Division attacked with six regular battalions, but despite desperate fighting, and the deaths of two of the commanding officers, no headway could be made. The next day, and the day after that, attacks on The Dump continued, but again there was no progress. On 30 September the British stopped attacking The Dump, but that night a German local attack from Cité St Elie captured 250 yards of Gun Trench, between The Dump and the Hulluch–Vermelles road. There was hard fighting on 1 and 2 October, as the Germans tried to extend their foothold and the British tried to hold them and force them back, but in the early hours of 3 October the Germans managed to recapture the Hohenzollern Redoubt, originally captured by the 7th Seaforth and the 5th Cameron Highlanders on 25 September.

The loss of the Hohenzollern Redoubt, coupled with the German possession of Fosse 8, The Dump and The Quarries, meant that it would now be impossible for the British to advance towards the German second line without coming under intense fire from their flank. General Haig was firmly of the view that all else must wait until those positions could be recaptured, and on the night of 4/5 October the newly constituted XI Corps was put back into the line, between IV Corps, holding the front from the Vermelles–Hulluch road south until linking up with the French IX Corps at Loos, and I Corps which would now hold a shorter sector from the Vermelles–Auchy road north to the La Bassée Canal. XI Corps would be responsible for restoring the British line, and to this end the Guards Division, back in the line after three days' recuperation in billets, would be responsible for capturing the Hohenzollern Redoubt and Fosse 8, while the newly arrived 12 Division would take on The Quarries. The attack would be supported by all of First Army's artillery and there would be gas and smoke. As the preparation of jump off lines and the installation of the gas cylinders would be a back breaking and time consuming operation, there would be yet more delay. The French were informed by the British Commander-in-Chief that the attack could not start until 9 October.

For the renewed British offensive XI Corps would remain under command First Army, and Sir Douglas Haig now reorganised that army's front. Instead of two corps in the line there would now be all three. In the south IV Corps would shift its left boundary south, and would now hold the line between the French Tenth Army and the Vermelles/Hulloch road, or a frontage of about 3,000 yards. The centre, from the Vermelles/Hulloch road north to just short of the Vermelles/Auchy road, opposite the Hohenzollern Redoubt, would be held by XI Corps. In the north I Corps would hold the rest of the of the First Army sector as far as the La Bassée Canal. This redeployment was carried out during the night of 4/5 October.

As the Hohenzollern Redoubt and Fosse 8 would have to be taken before very much else could be achieved, the first phase of the attack would see the Guards Division on the left attacking the Hohenzollern Redoubt and Fosse 8, while 12 Division would take on The Quarries. In support would be the whole of the First Army artillery, and as experience had shown that even that would be insufficient, there would be 120 gas cylinders in front of each attacking brigade. As each division would attack with two of its three brigades up, there would be a total of 480 cylinders to be laboriously manhandled up to the jump off line, and positioned and dug in, the whole effort to be carried out by night. As a preliminary to the main attack 12 Division was instructed to capture the German-occupied Gun Trench by a night attack on 8 October.

The news that there would be yet more delay before the British could resume the offensive was not received with unalloyed joy by Generals

Joffre and Foch, for they had intended to begin their renewed offensives in both Artois and Champagne in conjunction with the British effort at Loos, which they had assumed would be on 6 October. In Artois the state of the ground meant that the French could do nothing anyway, but in Champagne they did attack on 6 October, after a five-day preliminary bombardment, and achieved little before once again bringing the operation to a halt to await the British.

As it happened, the Germans got their blow in first, and on 8 October they launched a major attack on the Allied line. The first the British and French knew of impending action was on the morning of 8 October when French outposts on the slopes of Hill 70 reported that there were a number of breaches in their wire, mainly effected by artillery but some cut through by hand, presumably by German patrols during the night. The British had been relying on the Royal Flying Corps to give warning of any movement of fresh German troops into the area, but bad weather had restricted flying, and although an increase in the number of railway trains moving up to the front had been reported, no increase in road traffic had been detected.

All day the German artillery thundered, and at 1200 hours a deliberate bombardment of the whole sector from the La Bassée Canal to Lens began and went on until 1500, when it increased markedly in intensity. At 1700 hours eighteen battalions of German infantry – about eight thousand men – erupted from their trenches and advanced against the Double Crassier, Hill 70, Chalk Pit Wood and Loos. Once the German artillery lifted however – as it soon had to to avoid shelling its own men – the tables were turned and now it was the turn of the Allies to wreak havoc on attacking infantry. The twelve battalions on the left of the German attack were stopped by the French IX Corps, while on the right six battalions were faced by 3 Brigade of 1 Division with two regular battalions and a Territorial Force battalion in the line. Despite the considerable damage done to their trenches by the German bombardment, 1/9th Battalion the King's Regiment, 1st Battalion the Gloucestershire Regiment and the 2nd Battalion The Royal Munster Fusiliers[9] stood fast and with heavy and accurate rifle and machine gun fire stopped the attack forty yards from their own positions. Those Germans still able to retired to their starting points.

Simultaneous to their main attack the Germans also launched a subsidiary attack on Big Willie, the trench that ran south-east from the German-held Hohenzollern Redoubt back towards what had been the original German first line, which it joined at Quarry Trench. Big Willie and Quarry were still held by the British – by the Guards division now – and fighting was intense. The Germans attempted to bomb their way from The Quarries along St Elie Avenue, and initially it looked as if they might succeed. Fortunately, for once at this stage of the war, the British had a plentiful supply of bombs, and when the Guards were issued with nine thousand Mills Bombs[10] the Germans were beaten at their own game.

By now the Germans had formalised the art of bombing along trenches. A platoon normally formed a bombing group, which was led by two to four riflemen with bayonets fixed, to deal with any rush down the trench; they were followed by three bombers. The Number One would throw, the Number Two would prepare the bomb and hand it to the Number One while the Number Three was responsible for keeping the Number Two supplied with bombs. Behind the bombers came a carrying party of thirty men who passed bombs up from the rear and acted as reserves. Once the British were able to provide enough grenades to make bombing a regular and practical means of trench warfare, they too adopted a very similar system.

Despite the interruption to British planning and preparation caused by the German counter-attack, the preliminary attack on Gun Trench still went in, with 37 Brigade using bombing parties to support a conventional infantry attack at 1815 hours, by which time it was already dark. Despite 6 Royal West Kents (a New Army battalion) managing to get into Gun Trench, they soon ran out of bombs and could not be resupplied. The battalion pulled back, having lost an officer and forty-nine soldiers killed.

Although preparations for a renewed Allied attack on 10 October were temporarily disrupted by the German counter-attack on 8 October, they quickly resumed, the intention now being to attack on 13 October. The situation on the British front now was that in the north and opposite the Hohenzollern Redoubt the British were in the original British front line as far as the road running south-west through Le Rutoir. It then ran along Big Willie, just short of the original German first line, then south-east and skirting The Quarries, roughly south opposite Gun Trench and across the Vermelles/Hulloch road from where it ran parallel to, and about three hundred yards from, the German second line, until it joined with the French east of Loos.

The French, meanwhile, were having second thoughts. Once General Foch, commanding the group of armies, heard that the British could now do nothing before 13 October, he decided to go ahead independently with another attack on Vimy Ridge. This happened on 11 October and achieved very little; the French artillery had failed to cut the German wire, and their infantry was stopped dead (in some cases literally) by it. Foch thought (rightly) that this failure was due to inadequate artillery preparation, and wanted to attack again as soon as he could: the French Tenth Army was, as he put it 'within a bound of the crest' and unless the French could get there – and Foch was convinced that they could – they would have to pull off the hill altogether, dominated as they were by the Germans on the top.

Joffre, Foch's commander-in-chief, did not agree. Aware of the bigger picture he knew that the French artillery ammunition state was now parlous, and there was simply not enough to mount another major offensive, even if the weather had been suitable for the movement of guns, which it was not. Joffre's orders, therefore, were for the battle to be closed down, and for any further French participation to be limited to General d'Urbal's IX Corps to assist the British with an artillery demonstration only.

Notes

1. Other Ranks were not permitted to go abroad until they were 19, but officers could go from 18, provided that they had completed one year's service.
2. The whole matter of John Kipling's death and subsequent identification is dealt with in great detail by Toni and Valmai Holt in *My Boy Jack*, Leo Cooper, Barnsley, 1998. It is difficult to argue with the Holts' conclusions that the grave has not been positively identified as being that of Kipling.
3. Divisions, corps and armies had a Royal Artillery officer in charge of all that formation's artillery, usually, but not always, one rank below the formation commander. Thus a division, commanded by a major general, had a Brigadier General Royal Artillery (BGRA) and a corps, commanded by a lieutenant general, had a Major General Royal Artillery (MGRA).
4. Nickalls (63 Bde 21 Div) and Wormald (5 Cav Bde) were killed, Borradaile (26 Bde 12 Div), Pereira (85 Bde 28 Div) and Pollard (2 Bde 1 Div) were wounded, and Bruce (27 Bde 9 Div) was taken prisoner.
5. As few media managers have any experience of military service, and as some positively dislike the Armed Forces and all that they stand for, the situation today is a lot worse than it might have been in 1914–18. BBC staff reporting the recent Iraq campaign were instructed not to refer to British troops as 'ours' in case such nomenclature impaired the BBC's wish to be impartial. Thanks, BBC.
6. It was from these positions that the BEF, the Canadian Corps leading, were finally able to capture Vimy Ridge on 9 April 1917.
7. Scott, Sir Arthur and Brumwell, Revd P Middleton, *History of the 12th (Eastern) Division in the Great War*, London: Nisbet, 1923.
8. The author recalls (with, needless to say, disapproval) bored watchkeepers during the occasional quiet night in Northern Ireland telephoning public houses in the (vehemently anti British and pro IRA) Bogside region of Londonderry to make bookings for the annual dinner of the (Protestant militia) B Specials Old Comrades, or the (ferociously anti Roman Catholic) Orange Order. This was always fun, provided that the watchkeeper could imitate an Irish accent.
9. This was a reconstituted 2nd Battalion. The original, pre-war regular, battalion had been wiped out at Etreux, during the retreat from Mons, when they were acting as rearguard to I Corps. Surrounded, they fought on until their ammunition gave out. Nine officers and eighty-seven Other Ranks were killed, and only four officers and 240 men were alive and unwounded. While not a heavy butcher's bill by later standards, it was significant for the time, and the sacrifice of the battalion had bought time for I Corps to make a clean break. The survivors were fallen in and congratulated personally by the

German divisional commander. The battalion was rebuilt from drafts from the 1st Battalion, men recalled from extra-regimental appointments and recruits.

10. Later termed the 36 Grenade, it remained in British service until the 1980s. It had a three-second delay fuse for throwing and a seven-second fuse for use when the grenade was fired from a cup discharger fitted to the muzzle of the rifle.

CHAPTER VIII

The Final Round

On the evening of 12 October Field Marshal Sir John French issued fresh instructions to Commander First Army, General Haig. Up to this point the aim of the offensive and the objectives to be taken remained those laid down in Sir John's orders of 18 September. Now, said Sir John, the First Army was no longer required to reach the line of the Haute Deule Canal, but was only required, once it had secured its left flank (by taking the Hohenzollern Redoubt, Fosse 8, the Dump and The Quarries), to establish itself in such a position that it could resume the offensive when ordered. Reading between the lines, First Army was to tidy up what it had achieved so far, and straighten out the line where it could.

The 2nd Battalion Grenadier Guards were holding most of Big Willie, the trench that ran east from the Hohenzollern Redoubt. In the same trench, and separated from the Guards by a block made by hastily filling in part of the trench, were the Germans in the portion of Big Willie that ran into the redoubt, and they also held part of a communication trench running south from Big Willie, known as The Loop, which allowed the Germans to enfilade part of the Grenadiers' line. On the night of 10 October the Grenadiers attacked The Loop with bombers, captured it, and held it the next day, 11 October, against a determined German counter-attack. Shelling continued, and one German shell mortally wounded both the padre and the commanding officer of 1st Battalion Irish Guards. Command of the battalion was temporarily assumed by an officer of the 2nd Battalion, Major the Hon. H R Alexander, who after the next great struggle for Europe would be Field Marshal Lord Alexander of Tunis. On the afternoon of 12 December German artillery opened up a bombardment on Big Willie and the Loop that lasted two hours and preceded another attempt to re-capture The Loop. Despite the attack being beaten off by the Grenadiers, desultory German shelling and mortar fire continued for most of the day, and it was not until midnight on 12/13 October that the planned relief of the battalion by 7 Suffolk and 1/5 South Staffords could begin to take place. The period 8 to 12 October cost the Grenadiers thirty-six men killed.

Although relatively little had been happening on the British front as preparations for the resumption of the offensive on 13 October went on, the press still had the eyes of their reporters glued to Loos. With nothing very much that was new to report, a sort of short-term nostalgia began to creep into the reports. On 6 October *The Times* carried a Reuter report dated 1 October:

> … The story of the Battle of Loos is one glowing epic of the heroism of the British army … Throughout that first long day men fought as though possessed – thrusting, stabbing, shouting, swearing, laughing and crying. Battalions charged as one man, hacking their way through the thickest barbed wire, forcing a passage into the enemy's trench and then on, in one glorious rush, across the open into the next line …

The following day the same newspaper carried a series of 'Letters from the Front' containing 'stories of the "Big Push"'. With no indication of the individuals involved, or their units, or exactly where the various incidents described took place – all having been expunged by the censor – they could have been tales of anywhere on the Western Front. On 9 October the German counter-attack of 8 October was accurately described, alongside a somewhat optimistic account of French progress.

At last the necessary redeployment of troops on the British front in preparation for the renewal of the offensive, albeit a less ambitious renewal than originally contemplated, was complete, although problems in the Guards Division area, where German attempts to regain The Loop continued well into the night of 12/13 October, meant that their relief by 46 Division was not complete until 0600 hours on the morning of the attack.

The plan for the operation was relatively simple, and would be achieved in two phases. First, beginning at 1200 hours, there would be an artillery bombardment of the German positions by every gun that First Army could muster. Along the 6,000-yard front, and concentrating on the areas to be attacked, fifty-four heavy howitzers, eighty-six field howitzers and 286 eighteen pounder field guns would batter the German wire, trenches, machine gun posts and redoubts. At the same time another 114 guns would concentrate on counter-battery work, that is they would bombard German artillery positions – spotted by air reconnaissance by the Royal Flying Corps – in order to put their guns out of action and prevent them being used to break up the coming attack. In tandem with the British artillery bombardment, the artillery of the French IX Corps would batter Hill 70 and Bois Hugo. North of the canal the Indian Corps and III Corps would make feint attacks and bombard the German line opposite them, to prevent the transfer of reserves to the south.

After an hour of the artillery bombardment, gas and smoke would be released, the gas until 1350 hours, the smoke until 1400. If the wind was unfavourable for the use of gas then the attack would be postponed. Assuming the wind was in the right direction, Zero Hour would be at 1400 hours, when four divisions would leave their jump off trenches. For Phase One 2 Division (of I Corps) on the left (north) would make a bombing attack on Little Willie, that trench which ran from the Hohenzollern Redoubt north to the first German line; to their right (south) 46 Division (XI Corps) would assault the Hohenzollern Redoubt, The Dump and Fosse 8, while farther right again the same corps' 12 Division would take The Quarries. The southernmost corps, IV Corps, was to push 1 Division on up against 1,400 yards of the Lens/La Bassée road, along which the Germans had constructed a trench line. The division was to take the new German trench and then consolidate as far north as the crossroads with the Vermelles/Hulloch road. Phase Two was to be an attack on the German second line around Hulloch.

D Day, 13 October, was a bright, clear autumn day, a pleasant contrast to the windy and wet weather that had gone before. The wind was blowing from the south-west at five miles per hour, which was exactly as hoped except for the north of the front, where the gas would, if released, have simply travelled along the British line rather than over no-man's-land to the Germans. The artillery bombardment started on time, and, except for the north where a few cylinders were switched on and as quickly switched off again, the gas was released. At 1400 hours the whistles blew and the soldiers moved off towards their allotted objectives.

On the left 2 Division's bombing attack went up New Trench, which as its name implies, had been recently dug by the British and went due east towards Little Willie. The division's bombing party, led by a subaltern of the Oxfordshire and Buckingham Light Infantry, headed up New Trench supported by teams from the two battalions occupying the division's front-line trenches, 9 Highland Light Infantry on the left and 1 Queen's on the right. No sooner had the bombers left the shelter of New Trench, however, just short of Little Willie, than they came under intense flanking fire from German machine guns. Only one officer, Lieutenant Abercrombie, and one soldier got into Little Willie, and as they were completely on their own, Abercrombie sent the soldier back to ask for support. The soldier was hit and wounded, and the message never got back. Abercrombie, showing considerable determination, advanced up Little Willie alone, and put a German machine gun out of action before he ran out of bombs and had no option but to return to his battalion's front line and report. As the Germans were now thoroughly aroused and as the little gas that had been discharged had been ineffective, nothing more could be attempted that day, although the divisional commander hoped that something might yet be achieved by night.

46 Division, fresh from the Ypres Salient, and which was to take the Hohenzollern Redoubt, The Dump and Fosse 8, had relieved the Guards

Division during the night, but due to German activity had not been able to get all its units into position until the morning of 13 October. The men of the division were, of course, unfamiliar with the ground and, although as many officers and senior NCOs as possible had been sent up in groups during the morning in order to look out over the ground they would have to cross, the risk of German sniping and, later, the British artillery bombardment limited what they could actually see. The right-hand attacking brigade of the division, 137 Brigade, had been ordered to cross Big Willie where it was held by the British, and were then to pass south of The Dump and occupy Fosse Alley, a German trench that ran behind (east of) The Dump. This would, it was hoped, cut The Dump off from any possibility of German reinforcement and render it relatively easy to take. While this was happening the other attacking brigade, 138 Brigade, would attack straight through the Hohenzollern Redoubt and go into position north of The Dump. That was the theory, and a perfectly reasonable theory too, had things gone to plan.

As it happened, things did not go to plan. The gas had virtually no effect on the Germans, and indeed only served to warn them that something was up. As the German respirator was markedly inferior to the British smoke helmet, it can only have been the quantity of gas, rather than its quality or the direction of the wind, that was at fault. Very little gas actually reached the German lines; rather it seemed to settle down into shell holes and abandoned trenches. As the assaulting troops left their jump off trenches the British bombardment had perforce to stop firing at the forward German positions, and this allowed the German artillery, which had not all been put out of action by the British counter-battery programme, to begin their own bombardment, which caught many of the British troops in the open.

137 Brigade could make no progress; a few men did manage to get into the German portion of Big Willie and tried to bomb along it, but they could not hold. At the day's end the survivors of 137 Brigade were back where they started. 1/5 North Staffords, the left-hand battalion of the brigade lost 105 men killed, and the two companies of 1/5 South Staffords, on the right (the other two companies were already in the British occupied stretch of Big Willie) lost ninety-five.

At first the attack by the left-hand brigade, 138 Brigade, seemed to be going rather better. Their attackers were sheltered to an extent by the redoubt itself, and they had a shorter distance to go, but as the lead battalions – 1/4 Lincolns on the left and 1/4 Leicesters on the right – penetrated beyond the redoubt they came under heavy fire from Mad Point and the Corons. Nevertheless, Fosse Trench was reached, and some few men did get as far as the Corons themselves. This could not be maintained, however, as Fosse Trench could be enfiladed by the Germans in Mad Point, and there were numerous German machine guns in carefully concealed positions around the Corons. Confused fighting went on until after dark, as small groups of men under whatever officer or NCO happened to be in the vicinity tried to make some progress, but with both flanks of 46 Division exposed, it was simply impossible to survive beyond the Hohenzollern Redoubt – which was still in British hands and was now held by 1/1 Monmouthshires. Soon the survivors of the fighting in Fosse Trench and the Corons had withdrawn to the redoubt. The day cost the Lincolns 163 dead while the death toll for the Leicesters was even worse – 195 killed. When one considers that around three times as many were wounded, it will be appreciated that all four of those 46 Division battalions were effectively written off.

The task of 12 Division was to take The Quarries and the trench system running south-east from there. The division used two brigades in the initial assault, 35 Brigade on the left and 37 Brigade on the right. There had been no gas released on the 12 Division front, so the men used smoke candles and smoke grenades to provide some cover from view. In general this was of little help as the Germans simply fired through it. 35 Brigade attacked with 7 Suffolk on the left and 7 Norfolk on the right, followed at a distance of 500 yards by 9 Essex and 5 Royal Berkshire. Their task was to take The Quarries and then link up with 46 Division on their left, but intense German fire prevented them from doing more than establish a foothold in the south-west corner of The Quarries, which they achieved mainly by bombing, at one stage employing no fewer than 300 men to pass up bombs to those at the sharp end. Although they could get no farther, this lodgement was to prove useful later on.

On the right of the division 37 Brigade was to take Gun Trench and the trench linking it to The Quarries. On the left of the brigade 6 Buffs had about 500 yards of open ground to cross. They never made it; within minutes two officers and 180 men were dead, and the battalion could get no farther forward. To the Buff's right 7 East Surrey followed up by 6 Royal West Kent fared rather better. They only had 150 yards of no-man's-land to cross, and by rushing it they managed to take 250 yards of Gun Trench, capturing sixteen Germans who had been slow to pull out. Having taken the trench they then filled in fifty yards of the communication trench running from Gun Trench to Cité St Elie, which meant that when the inevitable German counter-attack came in it could only be above ground, and was beaten off, albeit not without cost to the East Surreys, who lost two officers and seventy-nine soldiers killed in the operation.

On the face of it, 1 Division, the southernmost division of the attack, had the simplest task. They were to advance straight ahead and take the newly dug German line which ran north to south along the Lens / La Bassée road. As the division had the longest sector to capture – around 1,400 yards – the division intended to attack with all five of 1 Brigade's battalions, supported by 2 Brigade behind them. This would give each of 1 Brigade's battalions just under 300 yards of German trench to capture, a not unreasonable requirement. A total of 310 cylinders of gas were released in front of 1 Division, and while this initially provoked very heavy fire into it, it soon died away, and when the battalions of 1 Brigade, from left to right 1 Cameron Highlanders (regular), 10 Gloucesters (New Army), 1 Black Watch (regular), 8 Royal Berkshire (New Army) and the London Scottish (territorial) advanced with bombing parties preceding them, there was virtually no fire directed at them until the smoke began to clear about fifty yards from the German trench.

Then the defenders did react, but not enough to prevent the British infantry from closing up to the German wire. It was at this point that things began to go badly wrong. The artillery had failed to cut the German wire, except in four places each about fifteen yards wide. It is probable that the failure to cut the wire was due to some of the guns firing at extreme range, it having proved impossible to get them any closer to the objective, and given that the German defenders were at no time backward at sniping and mortaring it would have been difficult for the artillery observation officers in the British firing line to see exactly what the results of the bombardment were. In any event the attackers were soon channelled into killing areas as they bunched together trying to get through the few existing gaps. Men attempted to cut through the wire with wire cutters but as the smoke and the gas cleared, and as supplies of bombs ran out, this became increasingly dangerous, and eventually impossible. As conflicting reports of what was happening came into brigade and divisional headquarters, supporting troops from 2 Brigade were sent up, but as the day wore on and it became apparent that no lodgement in the German trenches could be made, the British infantrymen took cover in the long grass of no-man's-land and waited for darkness. During the night those who could withdrew back to their own lines.

During the night reports came in and were analysed. It soon became clear that the day's operations had achieved little. Apart from small lodgements in the west face of the Hohenzollern Redoubt, in The Quarries and in Gun Trench, all the attacking troops were either back where they started from, or dead or wounded in no-man's-land. The five battalions of 1 Brigade lost 260 men killed between them.

The operations on 13 October had been very disappointing, but lessons were learned. One was that advances across open ground must, as far as possible, be avoided until such time as an overwhelming volume of artillery could be brought to bear. Until such time, considered General Haig, means must be found to allow assaulting troops to approach so close to the objective that they could take it in a sudden rush. Plans for further operations were now based on siege tactics that would have been instantly recognisable to the Duke of Wellington a hundred years before. All objectives that still had to be obtained to make the British line secure should be considered as single targets. Approaches (saps) should be dug under cover of bombing raids, and what Wellington would have called parallels, and we call jump off lines, would be constructed progressively closer to the objective. All work would be accompanied by diversionary operations north of the canal, and more and more the timing of the final assaults would depend on whether sufficient gas was available.

By evening on 13 October it had become apparent to Commander XI Corps, General Haking, that the casualties to 46 Division were such that it would have to be pulled out, and during the two nights 14/15 and 15/16 October the Guards Division were once more put into the line, taking over from 46 Division.

While Commander First Army was formulating the basic principles that would govern his future operations in the Loos sector, Sir John French discovered that the French had now abandoned the offensive. As a Loos campaign on its own made no sense at all (many thought it made little sense even as part of a French offensive), on 15 October the Commander-in-Chief of the BEF instructed First Army that in order to close the battle it should do no more than was absolutely necessary to secure its left flank from attack from the Auchy direction.

General Haig considered that the minimum needed to ensure that his new line was safe included the capture of The Dump, Fosse 8 and The Quarries. As he considered that it would take two weeks for the revised siege warfare tactics to obtain jump off lines sufficiently close to the objectives to enable them to be taken without exposing his men in the open, Haig provisionally fixed the date for the capture of these objectives as 7 November. In the meantime, divisions would begin to push their lines steadily forward.

Having taken over from 46 Division, the Guards were now ordered to take Dump and Fosse Trenches, which ran between the Hohenzollern Redoubt and The Dump, in order to provide a defensive flank for a subsequent attack on Fosse 8. Major General Lord Cavan, commanding the Guards, broke the divisional objective down into targets for his brigades, and brigade commanders then issued detailed orders for battalions. Cavan ordered 2 Guards Brigade, on the left, to capture Little Willie, the trench that ran north from the Hohenzollern Redoubt, while on the right 3 Guards Brigade would take the triangle formed by Slag Alley, Dump Trench and South Face. This would give the division a firm hold just to the south of The Dump and east of the Hohenzollern Redoubt (3 Guards Brigade), and also north of the redoubt, thus isolating the redoubt and creating favourable conditions for a further advance to Fosse 8 by another division.

The attack by the Guards division was planned to begin at 0500 hours on 17 October, and considering that the division had completed its take over from 46 Division only twenty-four hours previously, this says a lot for Lord Cavan's staff (who were, of course, almost all officers of Guards regiments and therefore knew each other and the officers of the battalions

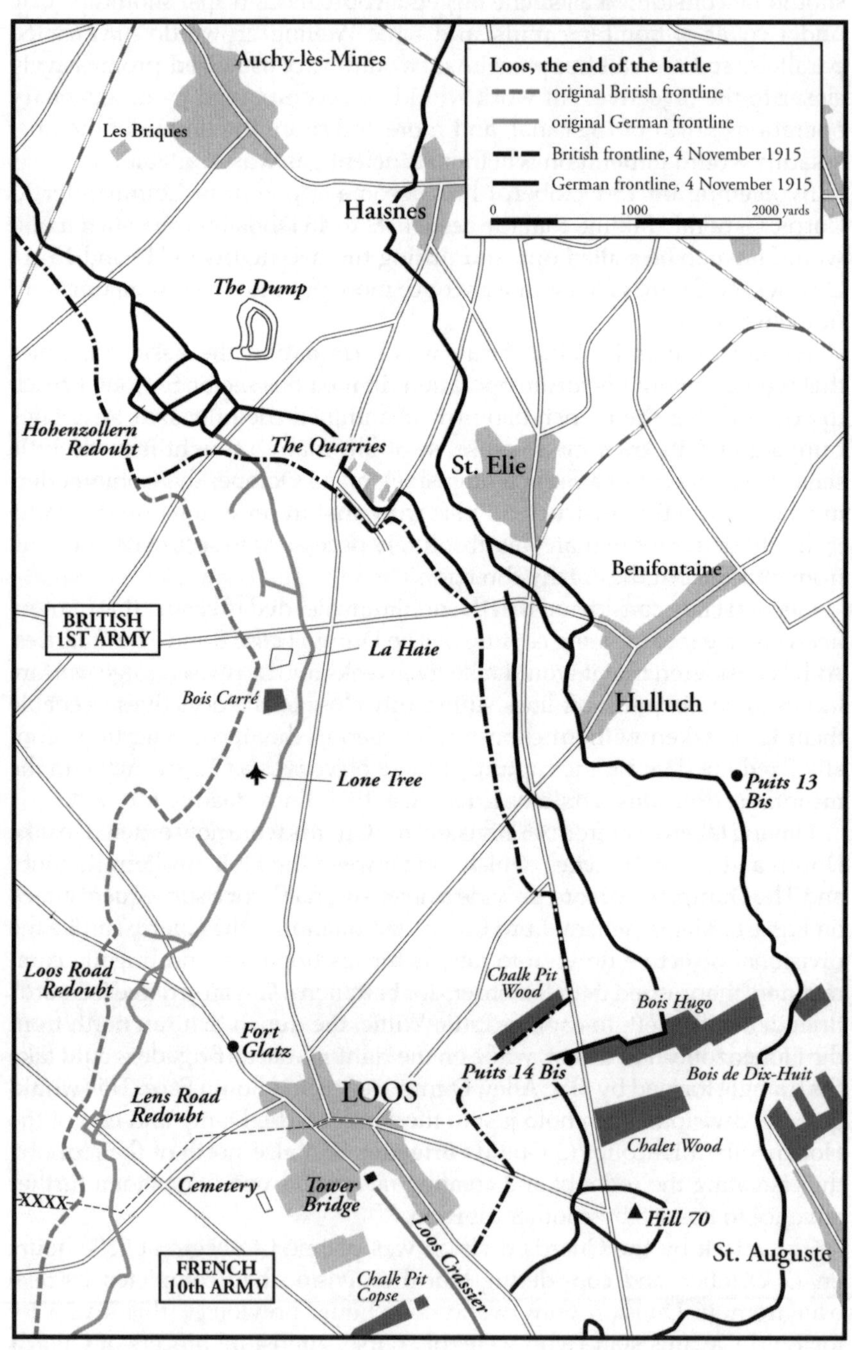
Loos, the end of the battle
original British frontline
original German frontline
British frontline, 4 November 1915
German frontline, 4 November 1915
0
1000
2000 yards
Auchy-lès-Mines
Les Briques
Haisnes
The Dump
Hohenzollern Redoubt
The Quarries
St. Elie
Benifontaine
BRITISH 1ST ARMY
La Haie
Bois Carré
Hulluch
Lone Tree
Puits 13 Bis
Loos Road Redoubt
Chalk Pit Wood
Bois Hugo
Fort Glatz
Puits 14 Bis
Bois de Dix-Huit
LOOS
Lens Road Redoubt
Chalet Wood
Cemetery
Tower Bridge
XXXX
Hill 70
Loos Crassier
St. Auguste
FRENCH 10th ARMY
Chalk Pit Copse

that would have to implement their plans). Although the soldiers would not have to advance a great distance – only around 250 yards – the condition of the ground was appalling. As the War Diary of 1 Coldstream Guards remarked:

> The state of the trenches was terrible, unburied bodies lying everywhere, and the parapets and communication trenches blown in on all sides. The trenches allotted to the battalion were knocked about and we found dead bodies, equipment and debris of all kinds mixed up together. Salvage parties worked all day. Just as much damage was done to the communication trenches as to the front line trenches.

The leading battalions duly left their trenches as planned, after a short bombardment by artillery and trench mortars. 2 Guards Brigade advanced with one battalion, 1 Coldstream, supported by 3 Grenadiers, while 3 Guards Brigade put two battalions, 1 Grenadiers and 2 Scots, in the van, supported by 4 Grenadiers. Surprise was impossible. The Germans could hardly be unaware that some form of offensive action was inevitable, and after their repulse of 46 Division morale was high. The men of the Guards found that saps and communication trenches in no-man's-land had been largely destroyed by German artillery, which would not have mattered in itself but now turned them into obstacles to movement and impossible to take cover in. This, and enfilade fire from German machine guns made it impossible for any Guards battalion to reach the allotted objectives, and at 0800 hours Lord Cavan very wisely called off the attack, which had already cost the attackers 101 dead.

General Haig still intended his new siege tactics to enable some offensive action to be taken, and on 21 October Sir John French formally approved his plans for local attacks to improve the First Army front. Factors now began to conspire against First Army however. The weather, generally wet during the summer with 13 October a welcome change, now reverted to type and by the end of October heavy rain was making the ground, already badly cut up by shelling, even more difficult to cross. Coupled with the regular downpours, German shelling was concentrating on British saps, dug to allow the proposed bombing parties to advance under cover, and on the communication trenches running back from the firing line. It soon became clear that preparations were taking much longer than anticipated, and that the target date of 7 November for a resumption of the offensive could not be met. This, and the approach of winter, led General Haig to conclude that it was now impossible to continue the offensive in 1915, and on 4 November he told Sir John French so. The Battle of Loos was over.

* * *

The fighting around Loos between 25 September and 18 October 1915 had advanced the British line not at all in the north, where between the canal and the Hohenzollern Redoubt only a precarious lodgement in the redoubt had been taken and held – although to be fair that did seriously disrupt the German defensive layout. South of the redoubt the line had moved east from between 800 yards opposite The Dump to 2,500 yards just north of Loos. Over a front of 6,000 yards the German first line had been completely overrun and a new British line established well beyond it, and west of Hulluch the new British line was not far short of what had been the German second line. The battle had not been utterly futile, in that some ground had been gained and the British positions after the battle were, in most places, better situated than they had been before it, but the cost was very heavy.

British official figures for the casualties sustained at the Battle of Loos show that the BEF had 50,000 all ranks killed, wounded, missing or taken prisoner.[1] Of these the staggering figure of 800 officers and 15,000 Other Ranks were killed in the three weeks and one day of the battle, or an average of 718 per day, or twenty percent of the total death toll for the entire BEF for the whole year! When this is compared with an average of 674 deaths per day on the Somme it becomes clear just how intense the fighting at Loos was.[2] While remembering Disraeli's maxim that reliance on statistics is the province of the mendacious, it is nevertheless worth noting that deaths on the Somme ran at an average of eighty-nine per division per week, while at Loos they were 279 per division per week. One should not push the comparison too far – on the Somme only in the north and only on the first day were British deaths anything like 'the bloodiest day in British military history' as has been claimed – but the death toll was considerable for much less tactical and strategic gain than that achieved on the Somme.[3]

German casualties at Loos can only be estimated – at the time the German army tended to understate casualties so as not to hand information to the Allies, and many detailed German records were destroyed by Allied bombing during the Second World War – but the British Official History suggests a German casualty figure of 26,000, of which eighty-three officers and 1,754 Other Ranks were killed. Even allowing for the fact that attackers take more casualties than defenders this seems a very low figure.

As for the larger picture, of which Loos was but a part, that too had little to show for the great expectations that had been aroused, and encouraged by General Joffre. There are many reasons for the overall failure of the campaign to achieve more, but one stands out. In purely land-based warfare the defender will always sustain fewer casualties than the attacker, who must expose his troops across open ground. War is in any case a constant jockeying for superiority between the defence and the offence.

As a breakthrough in offensive power is achieved, so a means to defend against it is developed. The tank is succeeded by the anti-tank gun, the mine, or another tank; the submarine by the depth charge; the bomber by radar controlled guns and so on. In 1915 it was the Allies' bad luck that the means of defence were in the ascendancy, and the machine gun, barbed wire, concrete and trench mortars were superior to men's bodies protected by little more than raw courage. Germany, having failed to win the war by the Schlieffen Plan in 1914, never went on the offensive again, save for Verdun in 1916 and the so-called Kaiser's Offensive of March 1918. Those occasions apart, the German army was more than happy to sit in well prepared defensive positions in someone else's territory and let the Allies throw men at them. The Allies, on the other hand, had an invader squatting on their property: they had to expel him and any French government that suggested going on the defensive and doing nothing would have fallen. It was the BEF's misfortune that in a coalition war, where it was by far the junior partner on land, there was no choice but to participate in French efforts to drive out the Germans despite British readiness or lack of it. Field Marshal Sir John French and his Commander First Army were very well aware that the British Army was not yet in any state to undertake a major offensive, and they were both adamant that even if it were, Loos was no place to be doing it. Their views were listened to by the British government, understood even, but greater issues of Allied solidarity and coalition politics made it imperative that the BEF played a part.

The First Army at Loos attacked with six divisions on 25 September, of which three were regular (1, 2 and 7). All three of these divisions had been out since August 1914, and after a year of intensive fighting on the Western Front they were considerably diluted with reservists and recruits. They did have more experience in their ranks than anyone else in the BEF but they were not the hard, canny professionals of 1914. The Territorial Force divisions were half trained and totally inexperienced with the exception of a very few battalions that had been at the front for a few months. The New Army divisions were not even half trained, with units lucky if they had two officers and six NCOs with any regular army experience – many battalions had nobody at all with any real understanding of what soldiering was about. French and Haig were, of course, well aware of these shortcomings – although French thought that in some ways the New Army divisions might be advantaged by not having any pre-conceived ideas – and the two New Army divisions that took part in the initial attack were sandwiched between divisions with greater experience, 9th Scottish with a regular division on each flank, and 15 Scottish with a regular division to its north and a Territorial Force division to its south. The inescapable fact is, however, that the use of the New Army divisions was a disaster. The men were excellent material – physically and educationally superior to most regular soldiers – and they showed quite remarkable bravery, but through no fault of their own they simply did not have the experience and the training to see them through when command and communications broke down and when their leaders were incapacitated. They suffered greater casualties than their regular counterparts because they were not capable of using sophisticated fire and movement tactics at platoon level.

In hindsight, the British army was militarily unwise to raise the New Armies as divisions. A better result would have been achieved had New Army battalions been put into regular brigades and the army increased by splitting regular divisions, forming two from one, and then splitting again, rather as the German army did in the 1930s. The same could be said about the Territorial Force, which might have been better employed as reinforcements and by being placed by battalions into regular divisions. The expansion of the British army was not, however, governed by purely military reasoning. This was the first time Britain had ever raised a citizen army, and there were all sorts of local interests that had to be placated. The pressure to use the Territorial Force in its own divisions was intense from county and local authorities, and the 'Join Together and Serve Together' promise would have made it very difficult to drip feed New Army units into regular formations.

At the tactical level the British decision to use gas was the right one. Both Sir John French and Sir Douglas Haig well knew that there were far too few guns and far too little ammunition to provide the sort of supporting fire that would carry the assaulting infantry forward through two formidable defensive systems, and allow them to keep what they might take. That being so then gas was the only possible compensation. The gas was by no means useless; while in the north the wind was in the wrong direction, in the south it made a real and definite contribution to the British local successes in that part of the front. It was not that the gas did not work, but rather that there was not enough of it to swamp the defending Germans and keep swamping them until their inferior protective measures gave out.

It might be thought that on a battlefield like Loos, with prominent Puits, Corons, Fosse and slag heaps, navigation in daylight would not be difficult, but this turned out to be a very real problem, with at least two divisions, 21 and 15, going off in quite the wrong direction on 25 September. At the micro level, once the cohesion of brigade and battalion was lost, as on more than a few occasions it was, platoons, often under junior NCOs, found themselves concentrating on survival – an understandable reaction – rather than on going to where they should be. Add to the damaged ground gas, smoke, enemy fire and shelling and the task of keeping direction becomes even more difficult, particularly as very few men have a natural sense of direction, but most believe that they have and will, particularly if inexperienced, tend to assume that it is the compass

– if they even consult it – that is wrong, rather than their own instinct.

A number of commanders – particularly, but not exclusively in the Guards Division – identified quite early on that bombing parties could achieve more than conventional infantry attacks across exposed ground. The problem was that there were not enough grenades, even if the numerous types on issue had been reliable. The Mills Bomb was an excellent grenade, and when there were enough of them then great things could be achieved, as the Guards had shown at Big Willie and The Quarries on 8 October, but far too many of the other types either did not work in wet or muddy conditions, or were far too complicated to ignite and use in the confines of a trench with the enemy bearing down.

The matter that split the army into opposing factions, then and later, was the question of the reserves. Sir John French never really had a BEF reserve of any consequence. As soon as the army expanded sufficiently for him to form one, he was ordered to take on yet more of the front from the French and this absorbed the erstwhile reserve. For Loos he held most of the cavalry and XI Corps as his own GHQ reserve, with the understanding that it would be deployed when needed. As the cavalry could only really be of use to influence the battle if there was a breakthrough that they could exploit, it was only XI Corps that could be available for the actual battle, and XI Corps had only one division in reserve that was any good – the Guards. The other two divisions were full of enthusiastic wartime volunteers, but like the other New Army battalions were completely inexperienced and under trained.

The disagreement between French – who insisted on keeping the reserves under his own command until he judged it necessary to release them to First Army – and Haig who would have liked them to be his from the start of the battle, stems from French's opposition to the whole concept of this offensive from the outset. The Commander-in-Chief never wanted to fight this battle, for sound military reasons, reasons that he had emphasised to Lord Kitchener, the Secretary of State for War, and to both Joffre and Foch. Given that he was ordered to fight it – for sound political reasons – he wanted to minimise losses, which he considered would in any case be great, and may have felt that by keeping the reserves under his own control, at least initially, he could keep those losses to a minimum. Haig was also very well aware of the risks inherent in the overall plan. He too advised against it and, like his commander-in-chief, would not have embarked upon the Loos offensive had he been given any choice in the matter. Having been told to get on with it, however, Haig was determined to fight the battle to the utmost. To embark on a half-hearted attack would be more, rather than less, costly in lives and would achieve nothing, whereas a full-blooded effort might at least achieve something. Haig wanted the reserves to be placed under him from the start, or if they could not be, to be positioned well forward and released to First Army as soon as they were asked for. In the event, French's insistence on placing himself in a tactical headquarters close to the battle but devoid of proper communications delayed his response to Haig's request for the reserves to be placed under his command; the lack of proper traffic management to get them to the battle area rapidly, and the impossibility of getting them fed and rested before deployment all meant that by the time they were ready for battle it was too late and the moment had gone. Haig was right and French was wrong.

Even if the reserves had been available when Haig needed them, it has to be a matter of doubt as to whether the result would have been very much different. The original plan was for the three corps of First Army to assault and penetrate as far as the Haute Deule Canal, crossing two complete German defence lines – each with their supporting trenches, redoubts and machine gun posts – to get there. Normally an attack like this would be broken down into three phases: Phase One would be the taking of the first line, and Phase Two would see fresh troops passing though and taking the second line. When that was secure Phase Three would involve yet more fresh troops (led by cavalry) securing the canal. On First Army's front this would mean having three corps available for each of the first two phases, and a cavalry division for the third, or attacking with half its troops in the first phase with the second half leapfrogging through for Phase Two. Unfortunately, three corps was all that First Army had available for the attack, and the frontage was such that each corps had to put the majority of its assets into the first assault. Had the gas been more effective than it was, and had the first assault captured the first German line 'on the bounce' (that is in a rush with few casualties) then they might have been able to go on and get through the second line too, but as it was by the time the first line had been crossed the attacking troops were in no condition to go on. Had fresh assault formations been close up behind them, then things might have been very different, but that second wave would have needed to be rather more than the three divisions of XI Corps, only two of which – 21 and 24 – were allocated to First Army initially, and were too far away to be of use when the *moment critique* arrived. It was claimed at the time that the three divisions of XI Corps were all that could be provided as a reserve, but 12, 28 and 46 Divisions were eventually provided for Loos, and had they been added to XI Corps and available at the outset, and properly positioned, things might have been different.

There was a time, around 0900 hours on 25 September, when a major and decisive breakthrough might have been achieved had the troops been available to carry the advance on beyond the second German line, but those troops were not available and once momentum was lost the Germans were given time to consolidate, reorganise and move up reserves. That moment would not occur again.

Notes

1. Edmonds, J E, *Military Operations France and Belgium 1915*, Vol. II, London: Macmillan, 1928.
2. The Somme offensive began on 1 July 1916 and ended on 18 November 1916. There were fifty-three British divisions engaged on the Somme compared with eighteen (including those involved in subsidiary attacks north of the canal) at Loos.
3. The first day of the Somme killed 19,000 British soldiers, in a British population of 45 million, so 0.04 percent of the population was killed on that day. At Towton, 29 March 1461, some historians think that as many as 10,000 may have been killed – a staggering total for a medieval battle – from a population of at most 3 million; but even if the actual figure was only half that, Towton was still five times as bloody a day as the first day of the Somme.

Epilogue

Loos was an unwanted battle. Nobody wanted to fight it except the French, and they saw the British contribution as providing only some minor distraction on the left flank of their own Tenth Army, and having the political advantage of forcing the British into taking part in an Allied offensive. The BEF was not ready for such an adventure; it had not the men nor the guns nor the ammunition, and everybody who mattered knew it. Whether or not the appalling butcher's bill and the destruction of what was left of the old regular army was worth the political advantage gained in the councils of the coalition is doubtful; to a soldier looking back from a distance of ninety years it was not, but one can only say that at the time the British government thought it was, and in modern Britain military considerations are subservient to political imperatives – and rightly so, even if this author sometimes wishes they weren't.

As the battle came to a close in October the hunt for scapegoats began. *The Times* of 2 November dissected Sir John French's dispatch of 15 October, which gave a summary of operations to that date, and asked:

> ... This dispatch does not allow us to ascertain why the first line of the attack remained unsupported throughout the day of September 25. Sir Douglas Haig had the 3rd Cavalry division less one brigade under his hand. The 21st and 24th Divisions of the New Armies, posted at Bouvoy and Noeux Les Mines, were placed under his orders at 0930 a.m. and were at once ordered up by him in support, but do not figure at all in the reports of the operations of this day ...

One has to wonder whether this report could really have been written by a journalist, or whether the detailed knowledge of military matters does not indicate the hand of an officer planting what he wants to be read. The implication here is that the reserves were given to Haig at 0930 hours on the morning of 25 September, but were not used. We, of course, know that while the order to release the two New Army divisions to First Army went out from GHQ at 0930 hours (having been asked for by Haig at

0700 hours), that order did not get to the two divisions until 1320 hours, at which time they were still seven miles from the battle area. There is no evidence whatsoever that French was behind the insinuations in this part of *The Times'* report, but he had already shown his readiness to use the press to advance his own cause when he used Charles a'Court Repington, disgraced lieutenant colonel turned journalist, to precipitate the 'Shells Scandal' earlier in the year.

Of course it may have been the reporter's honest opinion that persuaded him to close his report with:

> … If we have to regret anything it is that, as our Armies grow, the very great qualities of Sir John French as a leader of troops are no longer available in the fighting line, and that he is forced to delegate to others fighting duties of which no one else but he, since the death of Lord Roberts, is so great a master.

In other words – French did not fight the battle, Haig did and he is to blame. This is, of course, nonsense, and a disgraceful slur on the Commander First Army. The reality is that no one was to blame. Even if Sir John French had – as he should have – delegated control of the reserves to Haig from the outset, it has to be very unlikely indeed that the line of the Haute Deule Canal could have been reached and held; there were just not enough troops nor enough artillery to get forward across that ground against positions that the Germans had spent a year in preparing. The fact is, however, that by his failure to order that routes forward for the reserves were properly recced, marked and kept clear, and by his lack of understanding of the importance of the Commander-in-Chief being able to communicate properly, Sir John had shown that, very gallant officer though he undoubtedly was personally, he was just not up to the requirements of modern warfare.

Despite his blimpish appearance French was not a stupid man, and he had shown considerable ability as a commander in South Africa. He had been judged capable of promotion to Chief of the Imperial General Staff, the professional head of the army, and only had to relinquish that post because he had got himself involved in the politics of the Ulster question. He was the obvious man to command the BEF in August 1914 and had then found himself in the almost impossible position of having to support the French to his utmost on the one hand, and preserving the only army Britain had on the other. That said, he had begun the war in command of four infantry divisions, and by September 1915 he was in command of thirty-seven divisions. He was 62 years of age, tired and overweight. It was all getting a little too much for him, and he began to express serious doubts as to a successful outcome of the war.

At home, despite *The Times*, the government had been losing faith in Sir John. A succession of battles – minor in French terms but heavy in casualties by British standards – which did not seem to achieve very much, were leading to questions being asked about the competence of the commander-in-chief. Neuve Chapelle was a victory, but never recognised as such; Second Ypres was forced upon the Allies by a German attack, and Aubers Ridge and Festubert had been limited offensives for local reasons. Nobody else could have achieved much more, but French was the commander-in-chief and inevitably he had to take the blame. Now the government was faced with Loos, which it had forced French to fight but for which, in true politicians' style, it was not going to shoulder the blame.

It was not only the government that was losing faith in Sir John French but, much more seriously, the army too. French's relationship with Lord Kitchener, War Minister and a fellow field marshal, deteriorated steadily as the war went on, and French displayed a quite childish resentment of Kitchener's appearance in France in uniform. The constructive dismissal of Sir Horace Smith-Dorrien, Commander Second Army, by French in May 1915, and particularly the way in which it had been done, had left a nasty taste in the collective mouth of the senior echelons of the BEF. The other army commander, Haig, although previously a close friend of Sir John, had reluctantly come to the conclusion that French was not up to the job. In his dairy of 9 October Haig says:

> Lord Haldane[1] came to lunch … Afterwards Lord H came to my room and asked me to give him my views on the Reserves … He said feelings were so strong on the subject in England that he had come to France to help in arriving at the truth. I gave him all the facts. The main criticism to my mind is that the Reserves were not at hand when wanted … I also felt it my duty to tell Lord Haldane that arrangements for the supreme command during the battle were not satisfactory …[2]

Haig was a product of his background and upbringing, which included a reluctance to 'sneak', particularly to a politician, even one whom he knew well and with whom he had worked closely and harmoniously in the past. That he was prepared to be so open with Haldane is an indication of his concern for the future of the BEF. He went further, and his diary entry of 17 October noted:

> … As regards Sir J French, Robertson [Lieutenant General Sir William Robertson, 'Wullie', Chief of the General Staff (chief of staff) of the BEF] told me that when he was in London Lord Stamfordham [private secretary to the King] called him up on the telephone from Sandringham and asked him by the King's orders whether it was not time to remove Sir John French. Robertson did not answer. He saw the King in London and now he came to discuss the point with me. I told him that up to that date I had been more

> loyal to French and did my best to stop all criticism of him and his methods. Now at last, in view of what had happened in the recent battle over the reserves, and in view of the seriousness of the general military situation, I had come to the conclusion that it was not fair to the Empire to retain French in command in this the main battle front. Moreover none of my officers commanding corps had a high opinion of Sir J's military ability or military views, in fact they had no confidence in him. Robertson quite agreed and left me saying 'he knew now how to act and would report to Stamfordham'...[3]

With government, army and King now convinced that French should go, it was only a question of how the sacking should be effected. In the event, it was done in a gentlemanly manner; Lord Esher[4] arrived in mid-December 1915, as an emissary of the Prime Minister, and told French that he had to go, but that the initiative should come from him. As a sweetener, he would be granted a viscountcy and appointed Commander-in-Chief Home Forces. On Sunday 17 December Field Marshal Sir John French resigned as commander-in-chief of the BEF.

There were really only two possible candidates to succeed French as commander-in-chief: Commander First Army, Haig, and French's Chief of the General Staff, Robertson. Haig became commander-in-chief while Robertson, promoted to full general, went home to become CIGS, the professional head of the army, where for three long years he did his utmost to support the armies in the field, protect Haig from political flights of fancy, and prevent mischief-making by politicians affecting the army's ability to fight.

Historians should generally avoid speculation, but it was surely right to remove French. He had done little wrong, but he had not won the war in 1915, and a scapegoat was needed. That no one else could have won it in 1915 is irrelevant, and in that sense French was hard done by. Had French still been in command in 1916, however, it is difficult to imagine him having the stomach to persist in the Somme offensive, and had he not done so then the German attack at Verdun might well have had a different result, indeed it is not inconceivable that the war could have been lost. If Loos did nothing else, it propelled Sir Douglas Haig into the supreme command on the Western Front, and it was Sir Douglas Haig who took a tiny British army and expanded it, trained it, deployed it and fought it, until by 1918 it was the only army capable of defeating the German army in the field. And for that, we must be thankful.

Notes

1. Ex War Minister (who with Haig as his Director of Staff Duties and Director of Military Operations had created the general and imperial general staffs, and the expeditionary force), and ex Lord Chancellor but excluded from Asquith's coalition government in May 1915 on the ludicrous pretext that he was pro-German. He was nevertheless used by the government as a trouble-shooter.
2. Blake, Robert (ed.), *The Private Papers of Douglas Haig 1914–19*, London: Eyre & Spottiswoode, 1952.
3. Ibid.
4. An extraordinary character who wielded enormous influence without holding any official position. He was a member of numerous committees, including the Committee of Imperial Defence which he sat on throughout the war, and while he had never been a soldier his advice – generally sound – was listened to by royalty and politicians on matters of defence. As a homosexual he was, of course, a huge security risk, but he seems to have got away with it.

Appendices

APPENDIX I

Outline Order of Battle First Army Loos 1915[1]

Commander: General Sir Douglas Haig
Major General General Staff [chief of staff]: Major General R H K Butler
DA&QMG [chief logistics staff officer]: Major General P E F Hobbs
Major General Royal Artillery: Major General H F Mercer
Chief Engineer: Major General S R Rice

I Corps

Commander: Lieutenant General H de la P Gough
Brigadier General General Staff [chief of staff]: Brigadier General A S Cobbe
DA&QMG: Brigadier General H N Sargeant
Brigadier General Royal Artillery: Brigadier General J F N Birch
Chief Engineer: Brigadier General R P Lee

2 Division – Major General H S Horne

5 Brigade (Brig-Gen C E Corkran)

1 Queens
2 Ox & Bucks LI
2 Worcesters
2 HLI
1/7 King's(Territorial Force)
1/9 HLI (Territorial Force)

6 Brigade (Brig-Gen A C Daly)

1 King's
1 R Berks
2 S Staffs
1 KRRC
1/5 King's (Territorial Force)
1/1 Herts (Territorial Force)

19 Brigade (Brig-Gen P R Robertson)

2 RWF
1 Mx
1 SR

2 A&S Hldrs
1/5 SR (Territorial Force)

7 Division – Major General Sir Thompson Capper

20 Brigade (Brig-Gen Hon. J F Hepburn-Stuart-Forbes-Trefussis)

2 Border
2 Gordons
8 Devons
9 Devons
1/6 Gordons (Territorial Force)

21 Brigade (Brig-Gen H E Watts)

2 Bedfordshire
2 R Scots Fus
2 Green Howards
2 Wilts
1/4 Camerons (Territorial Force)

22 Brigade (Brig-Gen J McC Steele)

2 Queens
1 RWF
2 R Warwicks
1 S Staffs

*9 (Scottish) Division – Major General G H Thesiger

26 Brigade (Brig-Gen A B Ritchie)

8 Black Watch
7 Seaforths
8 Gordons
5 Camerons

27 Brigade (Brig-Gen C D Bruce)

11 R Scots
12 R Scots
6 R Scots Fus
10 A & S Hldrs

28 Brigade (Brig-Gen S W Scrase-Dickens)

6 KOSB
9 SR
10 HLI
11 HLI

28 Division – Major General E S Bulfin (joined I Corps 28 September)

83 Brigade (Brig-Gen H S L Ravenshaw)

2 King's Own
2 E Yorks

84 Brigade (Brig-Gen T H F Pearse)

2 RNF
1 Suffolk

1 KOYLI
1 York & Lancs
1/5 King's Own (Territorial Force)

2 Cheshire
1 Welsh
1/6 Welsh (Territorial Force)[2]

85 Brigade (Brig-Gen C E Pereira)

2 Buffs
3 R Fus
2 E Surrey
3 Mx

IV Corps

Commander: Lieutenant General Sir Henry Rawlinson Bart
Brigadier General General Staff [chief of staff]: Brigadier General A A Montgomery
DA&QMG: Brigadier General W L White
Brigadier General Royal Artillery: Brigadier General C E D Budworth
Chief Engineer: Brigadier General R U H Buckland[3]

1 Division – Major General A E A Holland

1 Brigade (Brig-Gen A J Reddie)

1 Black Watch
1 Camerons
10 Glosters
8 R Berks
1/14 London (Territorial Force)

2 Brigade (Brig-Gen J H W Pollard)

2 R Sussex
1 Northants
1 Loyal N Lancs
2 KRRC
1/9 King's (Territorial Force)

3 Brigade (Brig-Gen H R Davies)

1 SWB
1 Glosters
2 Welsh
2 R Munster Fus

15 (Scottish) Division – Major General F W N McCracken

44 Brigade (Brig-Gen M G Wilkinson)

9 Black Watch

45 Brigade (Brig-Gen F E Wallerston)

13 Royal Scots

8 Seaforths
10 Gordons
7 Camerons

7 RSF
6 Camerons
11 Argyll & Sutherlands

46 Brigade (Brig-Gen T G Matheson)

7 KOSB
8 KOSB
10 SR
12 HLI

47 (London) Division Territorial Force – Major General C StL Barter

140 Brigade (Brig-Gen CJ Cuthbert)

1/6 London (City of London)
1/7 London (City of London)
1/8 London (Post Office Rifles)
1/15 London (Civil Service Rifles)

141 Brigade (Brig-GenW Thwaites)

1/17 London (Poplar & Stepney Rifles)
1/18 London (London Irish)
1/19 London (St Pancras)
1/12 London (Woolwich Blackheath)

142 Brigade (Brig-Gen F G Lewis)

1/21 London (1st Surrey Rifles)
1/22 London (The Queen's)
1/23 London
1/24 London (The Queen's)

XI Corps

Commander: Lieutenant General R C B Haking
Brigadier General General Staff [chief of staff]: Brigadier General H M deF Montgomery
DA&QMG: Brigadier General R Ford
Brigadier General Royal Artillery: Brigadier General G G S Carey
Chief Engineer: Brigadier General L Jones

Guards Division – Major General The Earl of Cavan

1 Guards Brigade (Brig-Gen G P T Fielding)

2 Guards Brigade (Brig-Gen J Ponsonby)

2 Gren Gds
2 Coldm Gds
3 Coldm Gds
1 Irish Gds

3 Gren Gds
1 Coldm Gds
1 Scots Gds
2 Irish Gds

3 Guards Brigade (Brig-Gen F J Heyworth)

1 Gren Gds
4 Gren Gds
2 Scots Gds
1 Welsh Gds

12 (Eastern) Division – Major General F D V Wing (To Loos 29 September 1915)

35 Brigade
(Brig-Gen C H C van Straubenzee)

7 Norfolk
7 Suffolk
9 Essex
5 R Berkshire

36 Brigade (Brig-Gen H B Borradaile)

8 R Fus
9 R Fus
7 R Sussex
11 Middlesex

37 Brigade (Brig-Gen C A Fowler)

6 Queen's
6 Buffs
7 E Surrey
6 RWK

21 Division – Major General G T Forestier-Walker

62 Brigade (Brig-Gen E B Wilkinson)

12 Northumberland Fus
13 Northumberland Fus
8 E Yorks
10 Green Howards

63 Brigade
(Brig-Gen N T Nickalls)

8 Lincolns
8 Somerset LI
12 W Yorks
10 York & Lancs

64 Brigade (Brig-Gen G M Gloster)

9 KOYLI
10 KOYLI

14 Durham LI
15 Durham LI

<u>24 Division – Major General Sir John Ramsay</u>

71 Brigade (Brig-Gen M T Shewen)

9 Norfolk
9 Suffolk
8 Bedford
11 Essex

72 Brigade (Brig-Gen B R Mitford)

8 Queen's
8 Buffs
9 E Surrey
8 RWK

73 Brigade (Brig-Gen W A Oswald)

12 R Fus
9 R Sussex
7 Northampts
13 Middlesex

<u>46 (North Midland) Division Territorial Force</u>
<u>Major General Hon. E J Montagu-Stuart-Wortley (To Loos 3 October 1915)</u>

137 Brigade (Brig-Gen E Feetham)

1/5 S Staffords
1/6 S Staffords
1/5 N Staffords
1/6 N Staffords

138 Brigade (Brig-Gen G C Kemp)

1/4 Lincolns
1/5 Lincolns
1/4 Leicesters
1/5 Leicesters

139 Brigade (Brig-Gen C T Shipley)

1/5 Sherwood Foresters
1/6 Sherwood Foresters
1/7 Sherwood Foresters
1/8 Sherwood Foresters

ARMY RESERVE FROM BEGINNING OF BATTLE

3 Cavalry Division – Major General C J Briggs

6th Cavalry Brigade (Brig-Gen D G M Campbell)
7th Cavalry Brigade (Brig-Gen A A Kennedy)[4]

3rd Dragoon Gds	1st Life Gds
1st Royal Dragoons	2nd Life Gds
N Somerset Yeo	Leicestershire Yeo

8th Cavalry Brigade (Brig-Gen C B Bulkeley-Johnson)

Royal Horse Gds
10th Hussars
Essex Yeo

Notes

1. In this outline ORBAT I have shown only the infantry brigades. Each division also had eight field batteries and two howitzer batteries of the Royal Field Artillery, three field companies Royal Engineers, a squadron of horsed cavalry, a cyclist company and a pioneer battalion. Lack of space, rather than disregard for their importance, has persuaded me not to list these arms by name. Readers who wish to know the Artillery, Engineer, Cavalry and Pioneer units in each division are directed to Edmonds, *Military Operations France and Belgium, 1915*, Vol. II, Macmillan, London, 1928, Appendix III.
2. To pre-empt a flood of letters from those readers with a penchant for detail, The Welsh Regiment was redesignated The Welch Regiment in 1920. In the Official History it is shown as Welch, the OH having been published in 1928. The regiment was nevertheless Welsh in 1914–18 and so it shall be in this book.
3. Apart from the Corps Commander, many of the Corps HQ senior staff officers in some of the corps were one rank below that established for the post. In a rapidly expanding army it often happened that promotion lagged behind appointment.
4. 7 Cavalry Brigade was split up into detachments and allocated to divisions as increments to the divisional cavalry squadron before the battle began.

[illegible]

6th Cavalry Brigade [illegible]
7th Cavalry Brigade [illegible]

[illegible]

Notes

[illegible]

APPENDIX II

A British Infantry Division in 1915

Divisional Headquarters

(Major General commanding and staff)

1 Signals Company

Artillery

HQ Divisional Artillery

12 batteries of 18 pdr guns (total 48 guns)
4 batteries of 4.5″ howitzers (total 16 howitzers)
1 heavy battery (4 x 60 pdrs)
1 Divisional Ammunition Column

Engineers

HQ Divisional Engineers

3 Field Companies Royal Engineers

Infantry

3 brigades, each brigade 4 battalions, total 12 battalions. Each battalion 4 Vickers medium machine guns

Mounted Troops

1 cavalry squadron, 1 cyclist company

Pioneers

1 pioneer battalion

Service and Support

3 field ambulances
1 motor ambulance workshop
1 sanitary section
1 mobile veterinary section
Divisional train

Total all ranks: 19,614

APPENDIX III

Victoria Crosses Awarded for the Battle of Loos

The Victoria Cross was instituted in 1856, backdated to 1854 to cover the Crimean War. It is Britain's highest award for gallantry and by 1914 was open to all ranks of the British and Empire forces. It was and is an exceedingly difficult medal to earn, only awarded for outstanding personal heroism in the face of the enemy: the deed has to be witnessed and a recommendation has to survive scrutiny at every level including that of the monarch him or herself. To date (2005) only 1,355 have ever been awarded, of which 292 have been posthumous. During the Great War, 1914–18, 633 VCs were conferred, of which 187 were posthumous. As around 14,000,000 men and women were eligible during that period, the odds against winning one were over twenty-two thousand to one. Twenty-four VCs were awarded for Loos, of which seven were posthumous. Of these, eleven were awarded for actions in connection with an attack, one for defence, seven involved the rescue of wounded men under fire, and one was for both attacking and rescuing. Four VCs were for actions that, if not unique, were certainly unusual. These latter cases comprised a piper who piped the men forward when it looked as if they might not advance; a man who removed the fuse from a mortar bomb that landed in his trench and threw the bomb out; an Engineer who under enemy fire removed leaking gas cylinders affecting friendly troops, and a soldier who made repeated journeys under fire to replenish stocks of grenades.

The case of the mortar bomb is interesting. Usually an act which saved the man's own life, as well as those of his comrades, was unlikely to be eligible for the VC because of the element of self preservation, but in this case the various levels of scrutineers noted that the man could easily have taken cover in a nearby trench bay where he would have been quite safe.

It is a popular conception that deeds of great gallantry are performed either by officers and or by the very young and naïve, who have no conception of the risk they take. It is certainly true that proportionately more officers than Other Ranks receive a gallantry medal – which simply proves that the system that selected them to be officers probably got it right – but it is easier for officers to show bravery than it is for private soldiers. The officer is well aware that he is expected to show an example and that he is responsible for the lives and welfare of his men, as well as carrying the can if the operation does not go as it should. The expectation that an officer will behave as an officer should is a very powerful stimulant. The private soldier, on the other hand, is not expected to set an example to anybody; there is no expectation of leadership and provided he obeys orders no opprobrium will be directed at him should he not seize an opportunity to perform an act that could save a desperate situation, turn a promising one into a triumph, or save lives. For this reason, while all recommendations for VCs are scrutinised with the utmost care, those for officers are even less likely to be accepted, on the grounds that the officer may only be doing what he is expected to do in any case. Of the twenty-four Loos VCs nine were awarded to officers, ranging from one battalion commanding officer through major and captain company commanders to subaltern platoon commanders and including one lieutenant medical officer.

The theory that life-threatening deeds of great gallantry are more usually carried out by those who have no idea of what they are doing is not borne out by the battle of Loos. There the oldest recipient of the VC was aged 51 (posthumous, to a lieutenant colonel commanding an infantry battalion), and the second oldest was Piper Laidlaw who was 40. Of the remainder, six were aged between 30 and 40, eight between 25 and 30 and eight were under 25. The youngest was aged 18. Most could therefore be said to have been old enough to know exactly what they were doing. Thirteen of the twenty-four were regulars, men with plenty of experience and immune from the rush of patriotism that attracted the New Army recruits.

A list of Loos VCs is shown opposite. The best source for details of individual actions and the careers of those who carried them out is *The Western Front 1915*, in the excellent *VCs of The First World War* series by Peter F Batchelor and Christopher Matson, Sutton Publishing, Stroud, 1997, and subsequently re-published by Wren Park in 1999.

Name	Rank	Regiment	Type	Date of birth (Age)	Date of action	Place	Posthumous	Date of death and place of burial	Remarks
Laidlaw D	Piper (later Sgt)	7 KOSB	Regular reservist	26 Jul 1875 (40)	25 Sep 1915	Hill 70	No	2 Jun 1950. Norham, Northumberland	Originally 2 DLI from 1896, KOSB 1898–1912. Recalled from reserve 1914.
Peachment GS	Rfn	2 KRRC	Regular	5 May 1897 (18)	25 Sep 1915	Hulluch	Yes	Body never identified. Name on Memorial to Missing Dud Corner, Loos.	Only 18 when killed. As legal age to serve overseas 19, presumably gave false age on enlistment Apr 1915.
Read AM	Capt	1 Northants	Regular	27 Oct 1884 (31)	25 Sep 1915	Hulluch	Yes	Dud Corner CWGC Cemetery, Loos	Served Glosters, Indian Army, RFC and Northants
Vickers A	Pte (later LCpl)	2 R Warwicks	Regular reservist	2 Feb 1882 (33)	25 Sep 1915	Hulluch	No	27 July 1944. West Heath, Birmingham	
Wells H	Sgt	2 R Sussex	Regular reservist	19 Sep 1888 (27)	25 Sep 1915	Le Rutoire	Yes	Dud Corner CWGC Cemetery, Loos	
Kenny HE	Pte	1 Loyals	Regular reservist	27 Jul 1888 (27)	25 Sep 1915	Loos	No	6 May 1979. St Johns Cemetery, Woking	
Johnson EH	2/Lt (later Maj)	RE	New Army	15 Aug 1890 (25)	25 Sep 1915	Hill 70	No	Killed in Action 11 Dec 1917. Body never identified. Name on Memorial to the Missing, Cambrai.	
Kulbir Thapa	Rfn (later Sgt)	2/3 Gurkha Rifles	Regular	15 Dec 1888 (27)	25 Sep 1915	Fauquissart	No	3 Oct 1956. Nepal	Subsidiary attack
Maling GA	Lt (later Capt)	RAMC	New Army	6 Oct 1888 (27)	25 Sep 1915	Fauquissart	No	9 Jul 1929 Chislehurst Cemetery	Subsidiary attack
Kilby AFG	Capt	2 S Staffs	Regular	3 Feb 1885 (30)	25 Sep 1915	Cuinchy	Yes	Arras Rd CWGC Cemetery, Rollincourt France	Subsidiary Attack
Hallowes RP	2/Lt	4 Middlesex	Territorial Force	5 May 1881 (34)	25 Sep 1915	Hooge	Yes	Bedford House CWGC Cemetery, Zillebeeke Belgium	Subsidiary attack
Douglas-Hamilton AF	Lt Col	6 Cameron Hldrs	Regular reservist	20 Aug 1863 (51)	25/26 Sep 1914	Hill 70	Yes	Body never identified. Name on Memorial to the Missing, Dud Corner, Loos	
Dunsire R	Pte	13 Royal Scots	New Army	Not known	26 Sep 1914	Hill 70	No	Died of wounds 30 Jan 1916. Mazingarbe Communal Cemetery, France.	

Saunders AF	Sgt	9 Suffolk	New Army (but see remarks)	23 Apr 1878 (37)	26 Sep 1915	Loos	No	30 Jul 1947. Garden of Rest, Old Cemetery, Ipswich.	Served RN 15 years, retiring as a Petty Officer 1909. Joined army on outbreak of war, promoted Sgt within the month. Served as RQMS Home Guard WW2
Pollock JD	Cpl (later Capt)	5 Cameron Hldrs	New Army	3 Jun 1890 (25)	27 Sep 1915	Hohenzollern Redoubt	No	10 May 1958. Ballochmyle, Ayrshire.	
Burt AA	L Cpl (later Sgt)	1/1 Herts Regt	Territorial Force	3 Mar 1895 (20)	27 Sep 1915	Cuinchy	No	9 Jun 1962. Garston Cemetery Watford	Subsidiary attack
Turner AB	2/Lt	1 R Berks	New Army	22 May 1893 (22)	28 Sep 1915	Vermelles	Yes	Died of Wounds 1 Oct 1915. Choques CWGC Cemetery	
Fleming-Sandes AJT	2/Lt (later Lt)	2 E Surrey	New Army	24 Jun 1894 (21)	29 Sep 1915	Hohenzollern Redoubt	No	24 May 1961. Torquay Crematorium	
Harvey S	Pte	1 York & Lancs	Regular	17 Sep 1881 (34)	29 Sep 1915	Big Willie Trench	No	24 Sep 1960. Ipswich Old Cemetery	
Brooks O	L/Sgt (later Sgt)	3 Coldm Gds	Regular reservist	Mar 1888 (27)	8 Oct 1915	Loos	No	25 Oct 1940. Windsor Borough Cemetery	
Raynes JC	A/Sgt (later BSM)	A Bty 71 Bde RFA	Regular reservist	10 Apr 1886 (29)	11 Oct 1915	Fosse 7	No	12 Nov 1929. Harehills Cemetery, Leeds	
Dawson JL	Cpl (later Col)	187 Fd Coy RE	New Army	25 Dec 1891 (24)	13 Oct 1915	Hohenzollern Redoubt	No	15 Feb 1967 Eastbourne	Originally joined Inf. Compulsorily transferred to Special Bde as held chemistry degree. Cousin of Pollock VC(qv)
Vickers CG	Capt (later Col)	1/7 Sherwood Foresters	Territorial Force (OTC)	13 Oct 1894 (21)	14 Oct 1915	Hohenzollern Redoubt	No	16 Mar 1982. Goring Crematorium	
Christian H	Pte	2 King's (R Lancaster)	Regular	17 Jan 1892 (23)	18 Oct 1915	Cuinchy	No	2 Sep 1974. West Cumberland	

Select Bibliography

Atkinson, C T, *The Seventh Division*, London: Naval & Military Press, 1998 (reprint).

Autin, Jean, *Foch*, Paris: Perrin, 1998.

Barker, Ralph, *The Royal Flying Corps in France: From Mons to the Somme*, London: Constable, 1994.

Batchelor, Peter F and Matson, Christopher, *VCs of the First World War: The Western Front 1915*, Stroud: Wren's Park, 1999.

Becke, A F, *History of the Great War: Order of Battle* Parts 3a and 3b, London:HMSO, 1938.

_____ *History of the Great War: Order of Battle* Part 4, London, HMSO, 1945.

Beckett, Ian F W, *The Great War 1914–18*, Harlow: Pearson Education, 2001.

Blake, Robert (ed.), *The Private Papers of Douglas Haig*, London: Eyre & Spottiswoode, 1952.

Boraston, J H and Bax, E O, *The Eighth Division*, London: Naval & Military Press, 1999 (reprint).

Bourne, J M, *Who's Who in World War One*, London: Routledge, 2001.

Charteris, J, *Field Marshal Earl Haig*, London: Cassell, 1929.

Clayton, Anthony, *The French Army 1914–18*, London: Cassell, 2003.

Conte, Arthur, *Joffre*, Paris: Perrin, 1998.

Corrigan, Gordon, *Sepoys in the Trenches*, Staplehurst: Spellmount, 1999.

_____ *Mud, Blood and Poppycock*, London: Cassell, 2003.

Davies, Frank and Maddocks, Graham, *Bloody Red Tabs*, London: Leo Cooper, 1995.

Duroselle, Jean-Baptiste, *La Grande Guerre de Français 1914–18*, Paris: Perrin, 1998.

Edmonds, J E, *Military Operations France and Belgium 1914*, Vol. I, London: Macmillan, 1926.

_____ *Military Operations France and Belgium 1914*, Vol. II, London: Macmillan, 1925.

_____ *Military Operations France and Belgium 1915*, Vol. I, London: Macmillan, 1927.

_____ *Military Operations France and Belgium 1915*, Vol. II, London: Macmillan, 1928.

Ewing, John, *The History of the Ninth (Scottish) Division*, London: John Murray, 1921.

French, F M, Viscount, *The Despatches of Lord French*, London: Chapman & Hall, 1917.

General Staff HQ, France, *Order of Battle of British Armies in France*, 1918.

Hathornthwaite, Philip J, *The World War One Source Book*, London: Arms & Armour Press, 1992.

Headlam, Cuthbert, *The Guards Division in the Great War*, London: John Murray, 1924.

Hogg, Ian V, *Allied Artillery of World War One*, Ramsbury: Crowood, 1998.

Holt, Toni and Valmai, *My Boy Jack*, Barnsley: Leo Cooper, 1998.

IWM, *Trench Fortifications 1914–1918. A Reference Manual*, London & Nashville: Imperialwar Museum & Battery Press, 1998.

Maude, Alan H, *The History of the 47th (London) Division*, London: Amalgamated Press, 1922.

Merewether, J W B and Smith, Frederick, *The Indian Corps in France*, London: John Murray, 1919.

Palazzo, Albert, *Seeking Victory on the Western Front. The British Army and Chemical Warfare in World War I*, Nebraska Press, 2000.

Rawson, Andrew, *Loos – Hill 70*, Barnsley: Leo Cooper, 2002.

Sandilands, H R, *The 23rd Division 1914–1919*, London: Blackwood, 1925.

Serman, William and Bertraud, Jean-Paul, *Nouvelle Histoire Militaire de la France*, Paris: Fayard, 1998.

Stair, Gillon, *The Story of the 29th Division*, London: Nelson, 1925.

Stewart, J and Buchan, John, *The 15th Scottish Division 1914–1919*, London: Blackwood, 1926.

Terraine, John, *General Jack's Diary*, London: Eyre & Spottiswoode, 1964.

Warner, Philip, *The Battle of Loos*, London: William Kimber, 1976.

Wyrall, Everard, *The History of the Second Division*, London: Naval and Military Press, 2000 (reprint).

_____ *The History of the 19th Division 1914–18*, London: Edward Arnold, 1926.

Index

General Index

Index of Military Units:

British: